PRESCRIPTIONS FOR CHILDREN WITH LEARNING AND ADJUSTMENT PROBLEMS

PRESCRIPTIONS FOR CHILDREN WITH LEARNING AND ADJUSTMENT PROBLEMS

Second Edition

By

RALPH F. BLANCO, Ph.D.

Department of School Psychology
Temple University
Philadelphia, Pennsylvania

CHARLES C THOMAS • PUBLISHER

Springfield • Illinois • U.S.A.

Published and Distributed Throughout the World by
CHARLES C THOMAS • PUBLISHER
2600 South First Street
Springfield, Illinois, 62717, U.S.A.

© *1972, by* Temple University
©*1982 Second Edition by* CHARLES C THOMAS • PUBLISHER
ISBN 0-398-04511-9
Library of Congress Catalog Card Number: 81-5247

Library of Congress Cataloging in Publication Data

Blanco, Ralph F.
   Prescriptions for children with learning and adjustment problems.

   Bibliography: p.
   Includes index.
   1. Problem children. 2. Learning disabilities. 3. Problem children—Education.
I. Title. [DNLM: 1. Child behavior disorders. 2. Learning disorders.
WS 350.6 B641p]
R J499.B57   1981   618.92′89   81-5247
ISBN 0-398-04511-9   AACR2

Printed in the United States of America
PS-R-1

This book is dedicated to my outstanding colleagues in the Department of School Psychology at Temple University: Irwin A. Hyman, Roy P. Martin (now at the University of Georgia), Joel Meyers, Joseph G. Rosenfeld, and Trevor E. Sewell. Each is a remarkable, well-known and reputable psychologist with unique talents and style adding depth and breadth to our training program. It is a great privilege to share my professional life with them.

ACKNOWLEDGMENTS

The 146 psychologists who responded so competently in the survey research portion of the 1972 edition of this book are sincerely thanked as contributors. Many of their ideas are still embodied in the revision. The initial endeavor could not have been completed in this manner had I not received their valuable assistance. I have met and thanked many of my early contributors while conducting workshops around the country and attending conventions and I remain deeply grateful for their cooperation. I hope that the revised edition meets with their approval.

Special recognition is given to Joseph G. Rosenfeld, Project Consultant as well as friend, who offered excellent advice, encouragement and editorial skill. He is a uniquely talented psychologist and a pleasure to have as a co-supervisor in our Psychoeducational Clinic at Temple University and Chairman of our department. Further acknowledgement is given to the personnel in the Department of Research and Program Development at Temple University and for the splendid assistance offered by Richard W. Smith. Dr. Carl A. Silver and Jack Laveson of Drexel University provided expert assistance in regard to statistical concerns. Professor Silver helped me to pursue the necessary grants and also gave generous editorial assistance. Mrs. Anne Madden helped the production through her excellent typing skills and sustained interest in this book. Two personable and stimulating doctoral students gave me initial encouragement and a challenge to develop more fully my early interest in such research: Dr. Gerald Celebre and Dr. Paul Goode. Many other students have offered genuine encouragement for me to revise the book and have suggested where they needed help in particular: Prescriptions for preschool and young handicapped children. It is also fitting to thank HEW personnel from the Bureau of Education for the Handicapped who, although not permitted to be named personally, gave me the original grants sponsoring the research. HEW and Temple University have received one-half of the royalties for their initial contributions.

Grateful acknowledgement is given to the Group for Advancement of Psychiatry for permission to reproduce a portion of the Symptom List in *Psychopathological Disorders in Childhood: Theoretical Considerations and a Proposed Classification,* Report no. 62, 1966.

Finally, my wife, Lillian, and our children, Jeff, Janet, and Karen, added a final measure of support. Writing a book is truly a stressful experience for more than just the author. The family feels its impact heavily and derives but few of its benefits. I thank them for their patience, understanding, and love as I now turn my interest back to them.

A PROFESSIONAL RESPONSIBILITY

It is explicitly noted that the author does not guarantee the effectiveness of the prescriptions contained here in aiding troubled children. The professional person who uses these ideas bears the burden of responsibility for initiating, maintaining, and evaluating a treatment program derived from such concepts for his or her own clients. Supervisors of trainees must be especially alert in this regard. Any therapeutic suggestion should be judiciously selected only after a comprehensive study of the child's situation. Since the prescriptions are generally attuned to broad diagnostic entities and descriptive behavioral patterns rather than a particular child, it is an ethical imperative that the treatments be individualized for the specific child being assisted. Under no circumstances should the intervention strategies be used without adaptation or revision appropriate to the case in point. There should never be automatic translation of such prescriptions from this book into psychological reports, Individualized Educational Program (I.E.P.) summaries, or consultation guidelines without the careful scrutiny and necessary refinement by a competent psychologist or related professional.

PREFACE

The essential purpose of this book has not changed over the nine years since it was first written. It is still intended to be a resource or reference book for psychologists in school, clinical, or educational settings, in training, or in the field who focus on children with school-related problems. Conceivably it should prove helpful to professionals in closely related specialties: child psychiatry, social work, education, guidance, therapy, etc. For those who wish to expand their current repertoire of treatment strategies, such a book may be helpful. The author himself has sought ideas in the material many times when developing appropriate prescriptions on his own cases and consulting experiences as no one can mentally scan and retrieve such numerous ideas from a fragile memory bank. Such a book is written primarily for school and clinical psychologists with an academic background in psychopathology, exceptionality, and handicapping conditions which interfere with a productive life in school and home settings.

Previous to the passage of Public Law 94-142, Education for All Handicapped Children Act, 1975, the first edition of *Prescriptions for Children with Learning and Adjustment Problems* was offered in 1972 to suggest intervention strategies for handicapped children in school. These were to be regarded as "creative springboards" for field psychologists and related professionals as well as students in training in an attempt to provide practical systems to change the lives and environments of troubled children. The concept of supplying concrete ideas for experienced professionals and those in graduate school has met with some suspicion in the academic setting, but apparently an outright acceptance by most practitioners who appreciate such a resource when faced with the stark reality of children's problems. The early apprehension (Comtois, 1974; Lesiak, 1974) that such a "cookbook" reference might unstabilize the profession of school psychology has obviously not come to pass. Although some criticisms were professionally legitimate, others appeared to border on hysterical over-reaction (Reger, 1975). Other reviewers (Franks, 1973; Seiderman, 1979) saw the work in a "developmental" perspective and welcomed it as a long-needed contribution to those consulting in a psychological vein or debated the issues in such a compilation (Blanco, Bardon, Farling, Mann, and Nesvan, 1973; Todd, 1973).

Since its earlier publication, over 22,000 copies have been sold in six printings of the first edition. An investigation about the purchases of this reference revealed that they were used primarily in departments of school psychology, counseling, and special education with practicing psychologists a close second. Hundreds of letters sent to the author revealed the appreciation of readers and many have requested an expanded edition to include a greater array of handicapped conditions for children, curricular and remedial suggestions, and a focus on preschool and developmentally delayed children.

Obviously no reference book in applied psychology can equal the stature or scope of the *Merck Manual of Diagnosis and Therapy* (1977) for medical personnel, now in its thirteenth edition. The discipline of medicine, with its centuries-old, historical roots encompassing initial trial and error and, later, scientific experimentation, has developed an incredible and enviable knowledge base. Yet medicine does not approach the relative exactitude of physics and freely acknowledges that it has many, many areas of remaining ignorance. Scientific psychology, by comparison, even with its remarkable gains over the last fifty years, has the proverbial "long way to go" in contributing to the goals of science: understanding, prediction, and control.

In an embryonic attempt to organize, categorize, and make clear the various treatment options for field psychologists, the author has anticipated a lifelong effort to provide revisions. Recently three similar thrusts have appeared in the area of applying treatments to children's psychoeducational and social disorders: Catterall and Gazda, *Strategies for Helping Students* (1978), and the two books by Schaefer and Millman *Therapies for Children* (1977), and *Therapies for Psychosomatic Disorders in Children* (1979). These excellent books also approach the problems of treatments eclectically and feel no compunction, fortunately, about stating the remedial strategies created by others as well as some of their own. Such references cannot but add to the growing list of intervention strategies needed by treatment specialists.

Unfortunately, even with such worthwhile references available, some field practitioners still prefer to intervene with the same, nonspecific and generalized way with a dull, nonindividualized trio of prescriptions: (1) Place the child in some available special education program, (2) have the child and/or family seek therapy, and (3) review the case in two or three years. Does one have to be a psychologist to suggest these?

If school psychology is to become more effective and useful as well as receive the support of taxpayers and school personnel, it must continue to change in several dimensions. Some obvious suggestions are too radical or politically impractical to adopt, e.g. eliminate the "deadwood" of routinized, noncreative school psychologists, although this idea has obvious merit. Another possibility is to mandate retraining of school psychologists in quality programs in the universities and offer supervised field placements under high quality psychologists so that the trainees would become better problem-solvers. They should learn to be sensitive consultants, better listeners and learners, more expert at diagnostic work, and above all, more vigorous "trouble-shooters." Such changes require that the old guard of Binet and WISC-R testers be regulated to perhaps doing initial screenings, identifying the gifted, and executing the relatively monotonous tasks of psychometrists. Contemporary psychologists with more problem-solving approaches should be charged with handling the standard, complicated cases which always call for depth evaluation (Blanco & Rosenfeld, 1978) and dynamic consultation (Meyers, Parsons, & Martin, 1979). If nothing else, Public Law 94-142 clearly requires that each child thought to be exceptional be entitled to a comprehensive, relatively error-free psychological evaluation in the process of possible placement for the children with recognized and measured handicaps.

To this end, the current revision of this book has significant modifications along several dimensions. Each prescriptive strategy noted in the 1972 printing has been revised, updated and "retuned." It has been the author's practice to discard many of the generalized or less-incisive strategies previously noted and replace them with practical and hopefully more stimulating ideas.

Rather than undertake a second, and prohibitively expensive nation-wide survey, the author has instead consulted myriad texts and journals as noted in the reference section of the book. Some of the newer concepts are psychological in nature while others are derived from multidisciplinary practices. Some references deal with strategies derived from developmental optometry; occupational, speech, and physical therapies; clinical and counseling psychology; values clarification approaches; special education curricula; and behavior modification techniques. There is clearly a permanent place in psychological strategies for insight-oriented approaches providing that the child in question has higher than moderate mental retardation. However, fewer approaches in the revision will require long-term therapy which relatively few parents can either accept or afford. Obviously, those children with significant emotional disturbances may well profit from psychotherapy in the hands of talented professionals. The author posits a realistic belief that, although many problems of children can be minimized or extinguished, some problems will remain for a lifetime due to, say, their impervious nature (brain damage), degenerative dysfunction (muscular dystrophy), or the inability of the educational and social system to change sufficiently (prejudice and poverty). These also refer to chronic cerebral palsy conditions, intractible psychosis, and delimiting health problems that, as yet, have found no resolutions in medicine or other professional disciplines. Although there is much room for improvement for children through continued research, psychologists must also help parents and teachers accept the inevitable fact that some children will be permanently dyslexic, unable to walk, or retarded for a lifetime, no matter how much effort or money is expended in trying to change the basic condition. This still leaves, of course, a great majority of children who will find a better life through accurate and multidisciplinary, therapeutic interventions in schools, clinics, residential treatment homes, and the child's normal home. Our clients are legion.

Experienced psychologists know full well that even the greatest prescriptive strategies will be totally ineffective if the teacher, parent, or primary care person dealing with the handicapped child is resistant to change or too reluctant to help the child in specified ways. It is essential that an excellent relationship between the psychological consultant and the caregiving person be present (Meyers, Parsons, & Martin, 1979). This can often be accomplished by involving reasonable consulting approaches: expert listening, the manifestations of caring behavior, the reflection of feeling tone, the recognition of the complicated aspects of the case, and the regarding of the other professionals on a co-equal basis. Such consulting skills are not easy to learn and certainly do not minimize every possible case of resistance in the field.

Helping multi-handicapped children calls for a multidisciplinary effort wherein a school psychologist can make major contributions in the cognitive, academic, perceptual and emotional assessments of the child and give supplementary assistance to educators, physicians, speech therapists, occupational therapists, music therapists, etc., and help in the behavioral management of the child in the home, school, and treatment settings. And what of our efforts to assist the parents of the handicapped child? This is an area of great concern only partially tapped by Public Law 94-142 where psychologists have significant help to offer. It is a devastating, mortally wounding experience to be the parents of a handicapped child. Apparently very few professional persons are trained to assist parents in their protracted mourning reaction in aiding them to live constructively with the handicapped child who survives traumatic birth experience. Being such a parent often means a change in life-style, a downward modification of aspirations for the parents and the child, and even an unfortunate change in the marriage relationship. Who else is trained to help in interpreting the intellectual, academic and emotional areas if not school psychologists and reflecting the depth responses of disappointed parents? Although much educational work is being done for the child in question, an equal amount of counseling is often needed for the parents of such children to help them maximize their lives and find some relief and satisfaction in their new role as parents of the handicapped.

A new area of concern has appeared by law in regard to

"mainstreamed" children who are able to spend at least a portion of their day with "regular" and nonhandicapped children. Such mainstreamed children still have significant problems which they bring to the class and, as such, need to have responsive teachers who want to help them. Such teachers are frequently not trained in the special education, medicine, counseling, behavior modification strategies or even curricular adaptation. Teaching is emphatically a stamina-draining profession leaving little time and energy to conceptualize and write IEP strategies and develop systematic approaches for handling mainstreamed children. In addition, many teachers are uncertain of their writing skills and are thus reluctant to state their intended procedures to reach IEP goals. Should they wish to consult references, they will find them scattered among countless journal articles, monographs, and dimly recalled lectures on theory, curriculum, and educational psychology. Very few teachers refer to such references and would prefer to rely heavily upon school psychologists and consultants who have prescriptive ideas ready.

In earlier times, psychology has been long on diagnosis but short on treatment. With the auspicious developments in behavior modification and the refined thinking in special education curriculum plus the development of affective education and the widening of psychotherapeutic strategies, a large array of treatment strategies is now more available to teachers, parents, and interested professionals.

It is particularly important to note that, although Public Law 94-142 has mandated the writing of short- and long-term goals in the IEP, nowhere does it specify that professionals must know how to achieve these goals. This book is written, in part, to reduce the perceived, genuine, and understandable helplessness of professional people as they work to discover these strategies for children. It is one thing to list "increase the child's self-confidence" as a long-term goal, but yet another to know specifically many prescriptive approaches to achieve this mature condition. Having an array of approaches gives an added flexibility to the professional psychologist and a firmer basis for knowledgeable consultation with parents and other professional colleagues.

Licensed psychologists and certified school psychologists

ordinarily have an extensive background in graduate training, supervised clinics, and internships prior to accepting the awesome responsibility of changing human behavior. Such persons are knowledgeable about comprehensive diagnostic procedures (as summarized in Chapter Two), classification systems, relevant research and issues in the field, Public Law 94-142, theories of personality and learning, behavior modification approaches, and an array of counseling and therapeutic practices. No one will find a panacea here, but rather a large set of stimulating ideas for creating better strategies for their own clients in the field.

As a textbook for class, the material has been used extensively in graduate courses focusing on psychopathology and exceptionality, clinical diagnosis, writing psychological reports, and inventing remedial strategies. It fits comfortably as a reference for students in university clinics and internships, according to many past students at Temple University. Assuredly it has provoked discussion in class about viable treatment approaches.

The special educator, regular class teacher, or principal whose children reveal behavior and learning problems might best request consultation from a competent psychologist rather than rely on this reference alone. Although the ideas might be appropriate for a teacher, they depend heavily on how they are implemented. A consulting psychologist with broad training and experience will "sharpen" the delivery system and increase the probability for effective change.

However, no one profession should have possession of knowledge to parcel it out patronizingly at its own discretion. Thus it is impossible to state categorically who should or should not have access to the materials in this volume. It is repugnant in science to withhold ideas because someone may misinterpret them or view them from a different vantage point. In addition, how else can young psychologists develop if they do not have available the concepts and strategies of their seniors and then improve upon those efforts? The most basic criteria for use deal with the competency and maturity of the professional person seeking to aid a child in stress.

Ralph F. Blanco

CONTENTS

PRESCRIPTIONS FOR CHILDREN WITH LEARNING AND ADJUSTMENT PROBLEMS

Chapter I

PRESCRIPTIONS FOR CHILDREN

INTRODUCTION

SINCE THE ADVENT OF Public Law 94-142 (Education for all Handicapped Children Act, 1975), school psychologists have been mandated to perform comprehensive psychological evaluations on all referred children thought to be exceptional and in need of special education services. Although some school psychologists were justifiably upset to find the breadth of their work curtailed to include less consultation and more diagnostic testing, an unknown number of others were literally forced by this law to improve the quality of their mediocre appraisals of such children. Such superficial evaluations often consisted of one I.Q. test (regardless of the child's handicaps), a visual motor test (even if some children had cerebral palsy), a brief achievement test, and perhaps a drawing test to assess "personality." The errors in diagnosis and derived recommendations were horrendous (Rosenfeld and Blanco, 1974).

Reasonable parents, resentful of such brief and often erroneous evaluations, organized and obtained legal assistance to demand not only comprehensive and fair psychological studies, but also to obtain appropriate, public educational services to suit any variety of handicapping condition. In effect, no child was to be excluded from a full public school education by virtue of being handicapped. The Pennsylvania Association of Retarded Children decision made in Federal Court is now history (1971), but the impact remains with us. There is no doubt that P.L. 94-142 has its serious flaws and abuses, i.e. handicapped children "main-

3

streamed" into inferior educational programs, but its intention was to guarantee a higher quality of service for handicapped children and their respective parents.

Competent psychologists were not upset by these laws since they had always operated in high quality ways previously, carefully and openly. But the law made it possible for parents, through the Individualized Educational Program (IEP), to expect changes to occur for their children. Not only were short- and long-term goals to be established, but also there was the *implication* (not specified in law) that psychological and educational experts should know how to achieve these goals and by what methods they expected changes to occur.

As school psychology and related disciplines began, the educational and scientific world was essentially optimistic about what psychology could do for human behavior and school children in particular (White, 1969). Unfortunately, much of what was anticipated decades ago has never materialized. A question yet remains: Although many children have been diagnosed and classified, how many had been helped? Even now the many individual differences, needs and problems identified in children are rarely taken into full account in the IEP in spite of well-intentioned professional personnel. However, in the last decade or two, the desire to make significant impact on the lives of troubled school children has been gradually maturing into the fact of accomplishment (*Psychology in the Schools*, Vol. XVII, No. 1, 1980). These changes in professional thinking, both quantitative and qualitative, have been reflected not only in the practice in the field, but also revealed in relevant journals— *Journal of School Psychology* (1980) and in related texts, e.g. *School Psychology: Perspectives and Issues* (Phye and Reschly, 1979), and *School Psychology* (Bardon and Bennett, 1974).

The best school and clinical psychologists demonstrate their professional acumen and regard for children by being careful in practice and rigorous in their demands for accuracy. They devise an ever-expanding array of approaches to problems and professional endeavors aimed at the change in the lives of children. No longer are all clinicians content to sit in private offices to "solve problems from afar," but are meeting directly with principals, counselors, and teachers in the latter's domain in an effort to assist the child in his daily environment.

The competent psychologist today, in working with exceptional and handicapped children, now executes his or her skills in the areas of applied research, supervision, and administration of psychological services, in-service training of public school personnel, influence in the school's testing program, construction of better assessment devices, the execution of comprehensive psychoeducational diagnoses and prescriptions, the offering of psychotherapy and behavior modification programs and, especially, in the skilled consultation with teachers and parents. The psychologist is more frequently a consultant to administrators in agencies, residential treatment homes and schools, and thinking through the psychological aspects of problems which directly and indirectly affect the welfare of children.

Although it is true that the traditional diagnostic model or medical model is time consuming for psychologists who are unable to handle the demands for service, such depth assessment is critically necessary on the majority of cases. Since each case may be appealed by a parent or parental representative and is subject to review in a court of law, it is even more important that comprehensive and accurate work be done on the initial and follow-up evaluations of each child thought to be exceptional. What some psychologists may complain about is that the diagnostic model is difficult to comprehend and execute and that they are unwilling to invest such effort and time in its execution. It does, however, provide an incredible data base for making educational and clinical judgments that cannot be matched on any other dimension. From this wide base of information, the psychologist may understand the possible neurological deficits, the psychodynamic roots of a child's problems and also grasp the reinforcing conditions that have maintained the troublesome behavior. Even if the teacher is not particularly interested in the many causes of the child's problems, it is the parents of the child who care deeply about etiology as it may reflect their responsibility. Thus, they feel the effects keenly in the home with relatives and friends. The child, when reaching adulthood, may legally demand to see the psychological report which contains this important information. The psychological report affects more than just the teacher but rather a community of interested individuals. Since this is the case, the psychologist must serve more than the child's teacher, namely, all potential readers through this legal document, and must show what actions were recommended.

The author does not share the view which rejects the value of comprehensive evaluation and diagnosis, although he has participated in psychological consultation for decades. Having been a full-time school psychologist for ten years, a counseling psychologist for two years, a university teacher for fifteen years, and a consultant in many residential treatment homes for handicapped children, his view is presumably broad-based and representative of other experienced clinicians. Competent psychologists should select their areas of interest and then attempt to execute them at their highest level, whether these be in the area of diagnosis or the broader concerns of policy and system-wide intervention. There is so much work to be done at all levels of education and treatment that one professional or profession need not downgrade or overvalue the tasks of another, but rather focus on quality in respective, equal roles aimed at the enhancement of children's welfare.

Since psychology is now a mature, self-respecting discipline of the social sciences, its members must face up to the sensible expectations of its clients. Other professional groups less strongly grounded in science and its methodology would likely enjoy the prestige as well as the work obligations of psychology. They have attempted to exaggerate psychology's admitted short-comings but have little to replace its generally systematic effectiveness. Their twin themes have erroneously been, "Diagnosis is dead," and "The medical model cannot help the teacher with her class," while claiming effectiveness of dubious special education approaches. Methods that often "worked" quite well in special classes have often been the principles of *psychology*.

What psychology must do is to offer its services quietly and efficiently, making itself indispensable to thinking people.

Superintendents and school directors across the country want nothing better than to have competent, reliable, problem-solving psychologists on their administrative teams. They want them to operate successfully as accurate diagnosticians, sensitive consultants, and reliable professionals with both broad and specific ideas aimed at resolution of the myriad problems in the schools of America.

Psychologists cannot earn this valued reputation by boastful proclamations, but rather by demonstrating effective work at all levels of their assigned tasks. One grows in value by developing a hard-earned reputation through successful work with a minimum of errors. The goal of a capable clinician is to be error-free, no doubt the unrealizable aspiration of all service-minded professionals. Other closely related professionals, sometimes speaking outside of their areas of competence, are giving advice to parents, teachers, and administrators, often while psychologists stand aside waiting to be invited as participants. It is a contention of this author that psychologists sometimes behave in this self-defeating manner because some are (1) not trained in problem-solving, (2) unwilling to exert the effort to keep current with innovations and change, and (3) not consulting the available references aimed at developing solutions (Catterall and Gazda, 1978; Schaefer and Millman, 1977, 1979).

Particular dissatisfaction with school psychologists' reports was found in the small unpublished study undertaken at Temple University by the author some years ago. Here, the brief investigation sought the reactions of special education teachers in two graduate classes to the past reports they had read of school psychologists in the local school districts. In common with Mussman's (1964) study, the modal complaint (40.7% of 184 criticisms) dealt with the lack of specific educational recommendations to help teachers with referred children. The following list contains illustrative quotations from that study:

1. The school psychologist does not suggest methods of approach to individual problems and thus I get no real help.

2. Their reports are too sketchy for specific remediation. . . . Do not tell what to do to change the situation.

3. Should list specific weaknesses of the child with sugges-

tions on helping the child to develop.

4. I get only an "official label." . . . The psychologist only describes the problems; what about ideas to help the child?

5. Evaluations are not interpreted or translated into educational terms so we don't quite know what we should do or not do.

6. They do not give practical advice.

On the positive side, the same teachers added comments which balanced their initial reactions:

1. The psychologist is not given enough time to counsel the teacher since there are not enough psychologists to go around; they have too many cases and are overworked.

2. My school psychologist is really capable.

3. Some psychologists would like to spend time developing remedial programs.

If these complaints of experienced teachers are representative of educators, then school psychology as a profession is still in jeopardy (see Barclay, 1971).

The following quotations, accumulated by the author, are the actual and questionable prescriptions made by experienced, certified school psychologists and illustrate what should be avoided in practice:

1. This boy has a weak ego. He has not had adequate opportunity for growing pains. Give him opportunity for mistakes.

2. Time, patience, and a manifest faith in this girl would seem a good beginning in helping her to respond to her environment.

3. There is evidence of disorientation and disorganization. Give him library books to take home. This should help him a lot.

4. Mary may be a slow learner due to lack of intellect. Help her.

5. He needs experiences to regain a feeling of self-worth. There are either neurological, emotional, or family problems present; the parents should let him be independent.

Too often the beginning psychologist settles superficially for behavior described as "immature," "not motivated," or "upset" with little or no behavioral referents. Left with such vague concepts, the psychologist can only suggest vague or generalized treatment like, "Provide the child every opportunity for success," or "The teacher should use various methods of instruction to aid academic growth." By contrast, a necessary diagnostic goal is to be precise in the descriptions of symptoms and the deviant behavior, as well as the final recommendations for change. The day should be over when the school or clinical psychologist, after intensive evaluation of a child and the unique circumstances concludes only that "psychotherapy" and "special education placement" are recommended, *period.*

What about the dozens of other prescriptions from a multi-theoretical orientation that also may lend aid to the child, his teachers and parents? For example, from a behavioral viewpoint, where can *behavior modification techniques* reduce his impulsivity, lengthen his attention span, or perhaps double the motivation to learn? From a psychodynamic consideration, what *insights* should the child gain or *values* need clarification through counseling approaches concerning his low and incorrect self-concept and his contributions to his own self-defeating behavior? From a developmental vantage point, what can the parents change in their *attitudes* and *expectancies* about their child's developmental delay and how this might influence their own behavior? From a need-motivation theory, what *needs* are most neglected and can be met through specific environmental manipulation and social changes? From a special education perspective, what specific kinds of a *reading curriculum* should be started? The field psychologist of today is best armed with options from several theoretical bases.

But how precise should a psychologist become in consultation and in report writing? *Just as precise as the teacher and parents require for changes to occur!* Although a competent psychologist can operate comfortably from several theories of personality or theories of learning, it is difficult and often confusing to many teachers and parents. Since they are often the only direct change-agents in the case, it is they who must execute the specific plans, their own plans plus those developed in consultation with their psychologist. Such change-agents may be only as effective as their consultant.

The whole point of psychoeducational assessment and diagnostic appraisal is to develop remedial plans or prescriptions for the school and home setting of the exceptional child. Thus an exquisite grasp of diagnosis, dynamics, and etiology alone leaves the psychologist and his report readers with an excellent understanding of the development, intensity, and direction of the exceptionality, but with no clear-cut strategies for action. Sympathy may be elicited but not changes in the world of the child. School psychologists, in conjunction with other professionals and ongoing research, must help to answer the legitimate question of teachers and parents: "Now what do we do?"

The necessary prescriptions (behavioral, counseling, or otherwise) are generally scattered about the literature and found in, perhaps, fifteen related journals. To be aware of all this material is clearly an impossible job for both the young psychologist in training or the experienced practitioner in the field. Forness (1970) likewise emphasized that, "The school psychologist . . . appears unable to move from the analysis of the child's problem to the next logical step: Recommendations for remediation" (p. 96).

Three conditions are primarily responsible for this sparsity of written ideas for treatment, in the author's estimation. First, university training programs, in the correct concern for instilling a sound appreciation for theory and research, may not sufficiently stress the remedial aspects of school and clinical psychology. It is unfair, however, for the training faculty to take the brunt of blame when research about remediation is so often lacking.

Secondly, it may be that too many psychologists are attempting to solve too many cases and also using inefficient retrieval systems to select recommendations. All too often, psychologists attempt to retrieve from memory, recall old strategies, or consult disparate texts when selecting strategies for treatment. Under such pressures, the clinician may resort to unsatisfactory generalities.

The third and least popular reason why psychologists may be reluctant to state prescriptions, especially in writing, is that they may not know very many. To resolve this problem, one may deal in vague "Aunt Fanny" generalizations, as Tallent (1963) has cleverly expressed it, i.e. a psychologist may use such phrases as,

"Meet the child's needs," or "Let the child experience success," or hope that sheer "maturation will extinguish the problem." With such recommendations the psychologist cannot pointedly be called wrong, but what real changes could possibly result from such ideas?

It is obvious that there is not only a profession in need, but also that children are still in need of assistance. As long as the professions, the schools, and the children function at less than full potential, we will all be limited in our ability effectively to attack the larger problems of our society.

BACKGROUND AND RATIONALE

A deficiency in the profession of school and clinical psychology and related disciplines is the quantity and quality of psychoeducational recommendations available to help exceptional and handicapped children. Although psychologists often possess remarkable expertise in diagnosis, they frequently have difficulty in formulating treatment plans to alleviate the problems they have just diagnosed. Too often the prescriptions offered are stereotyped, nonindividualized and irrelevant.

Many of the educational approaches suggested in journals and texts have not been subjected to rigorous experimental investigation to test their validity. It is hoped that they will be and that the professional will learn of their precise application. While it is well to consider only quantitatively documented remediations, the immediate exigencies of the individual case and the presence of large groups of exceptional children currently in schools do not allow the psychologist the luxury of waiting for all research to be completed before action can be taken.

Other professions already have their "cookbooks" of the basic prescriptive interventions. Particular mention is made here to the *Merck Manual of Diagnosis and Therapy* (1977), now in its thirteenth revision, an ingenious compilation of medical symptoms and respective treatments organized by physicians for physicians, *The Pediatric Patient* (Gustafson and Coursin, 1964), and Conn's (1965) rehabilitation reference, *Current Therapy: Approved Methods of Treatment for the Practicing Physician*. These guides are available for the general purpose of treating medical problems. To suggest to a physician not to depend upon a desk reference is not only absurd, it is also unsafe. It is also unrealistic to expect any practitioner, physician or psychologist, to retrieve instantly all possible treatments from memory.

THE PROBLEM

Since no compilation was readily accessible which encompassed the broad spectrum of treatments for school-related problems, and since many psychologists were involved in such treatment endeavors, it was important to determine: What prescriptions were being offered by school psychologists for troubled and handicapped children in America?

PROCEDURES

The prescriptions for the first edition of this volume were gathered by the author by conducting survey research on all members (N= 1350) of Division 16, School Psychology, of the American Psychological Association. The survey was executed for the expressed purpose of obtaining psychoeducational prescriptions from potential contributors. This group was selected since it had a professed interest in school psychology and represented a sample of school psychologists operating at an experienced level in helping exceptional and handicapped children. Each member received a cover letter from the author, a letter of sponsorship from Division 16 officials, a set of Instructions, a Symptom List (Group for the Advancement of Psychiatry, 1966) to identify problem areas, and a Survey Sheet for their responses. Also included were a Personal Data Sheet to list their own qualifications and an article, "Fifty Recommendations to Aid Exceptional Children" (Blanco, 1970), the latter material to serve as models for the requested prescriptions.

To help guarantee a high response rate and to elicit ten to fifteen prescriptions, the psychologists were: (a) Sent another 100 recommendations (Blanco, 1969) upon the author's receipt of their own, (b) listed in the final report to HEW as contributors, and (c) notified when the results were published. All survey materials and their respective rationales, data tables, results of the statistical evaluations and conclusions are available to the reader through the ERIC System.* These data are too extensive to include in the revised edition.

ABBREVIATED RESULTS OF THE
SURVEY RESEARCH

One hundred forty-six contributors originally responded to the survey (10.8% of Division 16) and were less than a representative sample of the Division. Thus the statistical results can be generalized only to the survey contributors and not to any larger group of psychologists. Nonetheless, sixty-four (44%) had Doctorates (thirty-nine Ph.D.'s and twenty-five Ed.D.'s), the remaining eighty-two contributors had at least a Master's degree. (Several of the contributors are now Diplomates in School or Clinical Psychology, ABPP.) The contributors were trained, according to their submitted data, at many of the major universities of the country.

Seventy percent of them had majored in school, clinical, or educational psychology mainly through Departments of Psychology or Education. Some 57 percent had noncollege teaching experience. Actually, 145 of the contributors were or had been full-time or part-time school psychologists at the time of the study. They had a mean of eleven years of psychology experience, seven years as school psychologists.

About 48 percent were school psychologists at the time of the study; while 17 percent were university faculty; 13 percent were chief psychologists or directors of psychological services; 9 percent were directors of special education or pupil personnel services; with the remaining 13 percent being consulting psychologists, administrators, directors of training or research, or doctoral interns (4).

The highlight of the research was that approximately 3,700 psychoeducational prescriptions were received, resulting in a stack of 700 single-spaced, typed pages, probably the largest

---

*Blanco, R.F.: *A Study of Treatment Plans from School Psychologists for Exceptional Children*. Final Report, Project No. 482192, Grants No. OEG-0-70-0010 (607), H.E.W., Bureau of Education for the Handicapped, 1971, pp. 1-384.

collection of such strategies ever collected to date. Each concept was edited at least four times by the author and his Project Consultant according to criteria regarding: (1) Precision or succinctness, (2) identifiable theoretical root, (3) independence from other concepts, and (4) clinical appropriateness to the symptom or diagnostic category. (Other data relating to the prescriptions' appropriateness to teachers or parents and to a subjective weighting for the presumed "effectiveness" of the submitted prescription have not been included in this revised edition.) The great majority of suggestions were related to elementary school children and most of these focused on treatment strategies operational in the school rather than in the home.

A statistical evaluation assessed various between-group comparisons of the contributors and the differential effects of the backgrounds and experiences of the contributors and their treatment selections. Very few clear trends were apparent after statistical analysis of the efficacy ratings, hypothesized to be due primarily to the small N's in certain cells. There were no overall significant differences in ratings between males and females, or between less experienced and more experienced psychologists. Ed.D. and Master's personnel gave significantly higher (0.5 level) efficacy ratings to their recommendations compared to the Ph.D. group, for which the author could not give a reasonable explanation.

The most important aspect of the survey research was that thousands of prescriptions, specific to certain diagnostic categories, were now available for inspection, editing, and distribution to a profession in need.

CHANGES AND ADDITIONS IN THE
SECOND EDITION

In view of the impossibility of obtaining new research monies from funding agencies for an identical, follow-up survey of school psychologists' prescriptions, the author tapped other resources for additional intervention techniques. Although it would have been interesting to compare the data obtained in the first survey research published in 1972 with those potentially available from a second investigation, the likelihood of such funding was extremely small. The Bureau of Education for the Handicapped in the late 1970s tended to fund experimental rather than survey research or projects focusing upon basic research or efforts applicable to current social issues, e.g. culture-fair assessment of minorities, implementation effects of P.L. 94-142, etc. A privately sponsored survey by the author of psychologists in the American Psychological Association or the National Association of School Psychologists would have been prohibitively expensive.

An alternative approach to obtain similar information was deemed appropriate for the second edition by the author's consulting myriad journals and texts in clinical, counseling, and school psychology as well as closely related references in special education and educational psychology. These materials are listed in the reference section of this volume. Special effort was made to abstract innovative strategies, curricular modifications, adaptive techniques for the exceptional child, and prescriptive interventions for the handicapped at, primarily, the preschool and elementary school-age level. Some of these approaches had been experimentally verified, as purported in their respective journals, and others, frankly, appeared to their creators and to this author as "worthwhile ideas," without statistical validation, a disquieting remark to some readers.

It would have been immeasurably more scientific and respectable to have organized and presented lists of experimentally validated strategies previously demonstrated to have been effective on certain groups or individuals with particular diagnostic problems. Such is the eventual goal of psychologists in the future, but this cannot be done in this area at the present time, although scientists would unanimously and correctly applaud such contributions. The fact that practitioners work with individual cases or small groups of children with fictitiously homogeneous disturbances precludes rigorous follow-up studies with matched controls and large groups. Practitioners are rarely researchers. The former do not have the time (or take the time) to develop scientific contributions; they are hired and are interested mainly in applying what is currently known to relieve their clients' problems.

Fortunately not all psychologists practice in the applied areas as many are deeply invested in making contributions to theory through their strenuous research efforts.

What exists in this volume, then, are the severely edited contributions from the first edition plus prescriptive interventions deemed appropriate by the author after his review of current clinical and educational references. Each concept is to be considered by the potential user as experimental in nature for the particular client he or she is intending to aid. Just as each surgeon is responsible for particular surgical interventions, and each physician for each drug administered, so is each psychologist equally responsible for selecting, administering, and monitoring a prescription deemed appropriate for a client. The decisions of a practitioner are, in essence, an art form or clinical judgment made after weighing the known variables in the case and applying the procedures responsibly and ethically for the welfare of the client.

Chapter II

USING THIS REFERENCE PROFESSIONALLY

A. PROCEDURAL GUIDELINES FOR A DIAGNOSTIC EVALUATION

It is believed that a general adherence to the following diagnostic procedures and practices will increase the value of the prescriptions contained in this volume. The sequence of the procedures may be varied as circumstances require.

Comprehensive diagnostic assessment is mainly reserved for complicated and critical problems rather than minor ones. It is also true that expert consultation without psychometric assessment and case work-up may well resolve problems and change behaviors which were earlier believed to require nothing less than full evaluation and major therapeutic intervention. When diagnostic work is necessary, however, such a step-by-step listing may be helpful to psychologists-in-training in structuring their own plans for assessment and may guide clinicians generally to use the prescriptions for greatest advantage.

A comprehensive evaluation requires that the clinician:

1. Obtain extensive information and data about the problems of the referred child via the referring agent or a comprehensive referral form but reserve special consideration about the motives and bias of the referring agent. Determine the problem behaviors as precisely as possible and obtain baseline measures when appropriate.

2. Gather relevant school data about the child through a personal study of longitudinal and cross-sectional information

in cumulative folders, as well as from past and present teachers, administrators, or counselors. Learn much from the teacher through her observations and attitudes. This review of observations and "facts" ordinarily includes reports and quantitative and qualitative information about learning strengths and disabilities, social and personal characteristics, special problems, family concerns, and test scores of intelligence and achievement to help create diagnostic hypotheses.

3. Secure written permission of the parents to begin a comprehensive psychoeducational assessment of their child, should such an evaluation be deemed necessary. Obtain parent signatures on Release of Information Forms so that an exchange of information may begin with the child's physician and any social agencies assisting the family. Investigate sensory and physical contributions to the child's problems.

4. Observe the child in his classroom. At the elementary level determine the teacher's expectations through interview, her specific approaches to the child and the class, the social roles operating, and the general learning atmosphere of the class, school, and community. Record normal as well as atypical behavior of the referred child. Do not focus on the pathology alone. At the secondary level consult with guidance and administrative personnel about the scope and intensity of the problems as revealed to them.

5. Interview both parents, if at all possible, to determine their perceptions of the child, aspirations for him, plans and problems concerning him and his adjustment. Obtain an extensive social, educational, and occupational history on both parents and, of course, a developmental history that is both medically, psychologically, and educationally relevant. Determine how the parents have helped and hindered the child. Communicate to them that the examiner is their advocate as well as their child's. Grasp their respective value systems as this will be extremely important in recommending certain prescriptive interventions that must be congruent with their styles.

6. Begin the first contact with the child being respectfully sensitive to his initial apprehensions, values, and concerns. Complete the appropriate testing, if any is necessary, suited to

the essential problems earlier stated, especially if these relate to intelligence, achievement, perception, personality, development; and one should also conduct an in-depth clinical interview. Verify, refute, or retune the original diagnostic hypotheses.

7. Integrate the data to determine the most comprehensive and specific psychoeducational diagnoses with a grasp of etiological conditions and with reference to both quantitative and qualitative information. Recognize that most cases not only have multiple problems, they also have multiple diagnoses.

8. The primary purpose of the diagnostic evaluation is to create unique recommendations to minimize, modify, or extinguish the problems and contributing factors, thus enhancing the probability of changing ineffective or maladaptive behavior or learning. These first prescriptions should arise from the clinicians own resources: experience, theory, practice, and relevant texts and journals suitable to the child's problems.

B. THE SELECTION OF PRESCRIPTIONS FROM THIS REFERENCE

9. The most important next step is to isolate the correct chapter and sub-headings in this reference relevant to the child's multiple problems or diagnosis. From these, the precise symptoms or behaviors in question, select the section relating to treatment for that difficulty from the Index or Contents. Become familiar with the general chapter in terms of strategies attempting to fit the suggestions to the specific problems and adjusting them to the particular case, e.g. age, sex, ability, family value system, achievement, etc. Disregard recommendations which may be administratively convenient but inappropriate for the child. Omit those which are not reasonably congruent with the values of the home and school personnel. Should these be used in consulting or in the psychological report, they will inevitably be sabotaged.

10. Discuss the recommendations selected and their educational implications with school personnel; encourage understanding of the child's problems and contributing factors while developing additional prescriptions in the continuing relationship with the teacher and administrator.

11. While meeting with both parents, discuss the original problems, contributing factors, test scores generally, and a meaningful interpretation of the diagnosis in *their* language. Do not attempt to teach them scientific terminology at the feed-back session. Explain the unique recommendations appropriate to the child and to them in an effort to develop their acceptance and future implementation. Listen to their objections and reject those recommendations which are unsuitable from their point of view.

12. Write a comprehensive psychological report noting baseline behaviors, a summary of the highlights noted in the previous steps, the diagnostic impressions and the prescriptions determined to be acceptable in the school and the home. Recognize that this report is a legal document which can be read by the parents, subpoenaed in court, and possibly seen by the child in later years. Follow up the case extensively.

In the abbreviated summary of the clinical procedures for a psychoeducational evaluation, justice is not done to the subtleties of such a complicated and professional endeavor. Additional references (Buktenica, 1964; Gardon, 1965; Palmer, 1970; Simmons, 1969) are available which elaborate upon various aspects of these procedures. A previously noted reference (Blanco and Rosenfeld, 1978) has provided illustrative psychological reports which reflect comprehensive assessment practices and the appropriate use of prescriptions.

Chapter III

PRESCHOOL AND YOUNG HANDICAPPED CHILDREN

R EFERENCES (GEARHEART & WEISHAHN, 1980; Hare and Hare, 1978; Hartlage and Lucas, 1973) dealing with the preschool child with varieties of impairments stress the need for early intervention. There is no quarrel with this emphasis as long as the child's limitations have been assessed by a multitude of disciplines. The main professional persons called upon to assist preschool and young handicapped children with suspected limitations are the child's physician, speech and language specialist, school psychologist, teacher, physical and occupational therapist, pediatric neurologist, and educational personnel. It has been the author's crystalized belief, after working many years as a psychologist with multiply-handicapped youngsters in residential and public school settings, that coordinated, interdisciplinary teams are essential to the fuller development of each handicapped child. Although this principle may seem self-evident, many facilities assign vital and related professional roles (physical therapist, speech therapist) to relative insignificance in the child's school schedule, e.g. two weekly sessions per case with the mistaken belief that this is "appropriate," resting on a dubious legal definition of this term.

Obviously, where there are unlimited funds and professional expertise available, more children would receive the optimum quantity and perhaps quality of services needed to minimize their impairments. Depending on the circumstances of the case, certain disciplines should develop a significantly greater involvement with particular children: Physical and occupational therapy for spina bifida children, psychological services for the behaviorally disturbed, and concrete education for the mentally retarded, developmental optometry and special education for those with visual perception limitations, etc. How these decisions are made varies according to the leadership styles of the school or agency administration as well as the sensitivity and capability of the staff.

A depth analysis of such issues is not within the scope of this book, however, since its focus is on the imaginative concepts and scientific principles to be implemented rather than on the personal skills and styles needed to implement them. Whatever the case, willing staff members and parents need to know what strategies and prescriptive interventions are appropriate to the particular child within his or her unique combination of strengths and limitations. No longer will parents, teachers, or other professionals settle for vague generalities like "offer infant stimulation," "develop language skills," or "teach the child to become more independent." No one can argue with such overall suggestions or long-range goals, but other professionals noting such generalities will not offer support and cooperation unless the treatment plans are made with greater clarity. Thus, if the newly specified ideas are truly appropriate for the child, the parents, most often reasonable people, will not need to initiate legal objections through implementing Public Law 94-142 to contest questionable programming. Fortunately, relatively few handicapped children need the intensive, full-time, multitherapy programs of an institutional setting since many can function in a local school program well adapted to their habilitative needs while in the care of normal parents. Almost no one objects to the basic principle of normalization and "mainstreaming," as long as quality programs are offered to minimize the child's limitations. The objections surface when the parent, or a representative, perceives that inadequate services are present or no gains are apparent in the child beyond those evolving through maturation.

Further normalization can occur, not necessarily by shifting the child to a new classroom, but by executing the therapeutic strategies that the child actually needs, within the generally appropriate setting. What would have been considered a "failure" in a mainstreaming effort might not be if the staff in the regular setting could have executed appropriate and selected strategies to help the child adapt. Thus the burden of proof for normalization need not be on the setting or its physical facilities but on the content of the IEP and the execution of its predetermined prescriptions. Nor must the school or residential setting be the only one obligated to produce change, since parents with time, ability, and knowledge may supplement the child's program while he or she is at home or on vacation.

This chapter addresses itself to one particular belief: Some preschool professionals and interested parents of handicapped children have the prerequisite time and ability but lack the knowledge of what to do or how to do it. A basic assumption, of course, is evident in that the child is not so severely impaired that he or she cannot profit from early stimulation and growth experiences.

It is also evident that many well-meaning parents and professionals who start assisting the child may discover that the habilitation efforts are much more difficult than anticipated and that their own motivations may eventually wane. In this case, the prescriptive strategies are not at fault even though the persons involved cannot help but project their own limitations on these inanimate concepts. Of course, sometimes the ideas themselves are poorly conceived, nonsequenced, inappropriately advocated, or simply unworkable. In this circumstance, have naive professionals done the preliminary assessment? Have there been faulty or nonexistent links between evaluation, causes, and treatments? Is it not true that in the current state of art and sciences, we simply cannot manage or minimize every problem of every child with every possible combination of handicap? Thus our knowledge is sometimes feeble and as a consequence a professional can and will make errors of judgment. On other cases, ideal prescriptive strategies cannot be offered due to political, funding, administrative, or staff considerations or practical inconvenience. This is often a surprising and disturbing reality to beginning professionals and parents alike.

But from where are intervention strategies derived? Basically, out of the experience of others who have preceded us and from the even fewer people who have written them down. A prescriptive idea is a creative "brainchild" with natural roots in observation and theory, the data-based springboards of science itself. They have also developed from practical trial-and-error attempts to influence behavior and have been communicated by word-of-mouth from professional trainer to novice, the latter, in turn, communicating newly discovered strategies to a newer generation of practitioners a decade or two later.

Each professional specialty has its own values, theories, data, and goals and each tends to covet the treatment strategies it has found useful. To be effective as a profession in the modern schools of America, however, each group must now share its ideas with all other groups, including the parents, so that a unified, multifaceted effort is made for the child's benefit. Such an effort does not develop quickly even if legally mandated; yet it must and will come since the handicapped or potentially handicapped child is the prime focus of collective professional goals.

Although each young child is an infinite array of behaviors too scattered to be accounted for in all dimensions, a pattern eventually does emerge and a term, diagnosis, or label is attached to these behaviors. It does not mean that all children with such a pattern are alike, but such a diagnosis does integrate a commonality of observations. Children are therefore classified by the behavior they execute; some are gifted, others are language-delayed, have cerebral palsy or are emotionally disturbed. Such terms are a short-hand method for professionals to communicate quickly the observed behaviors so that action can be taken. Diagnoses are nothing more than a commonly agreed-upon verbal basis for action. Without such patterns, human behavior would be chaotic and unfathomable. When such diagnostic labels are noted, they give rise to programs, curricula, staff contributions, further research, the generation of theory, and the development of intervention strategies. Surely designating a child as having muscular dystrophy or learning disability does not connote all variations or attributes of the child nor does it, by itself, spell out a perfect set of treatment approaches. On the other hand, a diagnosis notes the major pattern of problems and often gives a hint about its multiple causes, as in the Down Syndrome. Attributing other negative characteristics to such a child is a problem in the perceiver and not in the diagnosis itself, i.e. if he has cerebral palsy, he must be retarded; if she is psychotic, the parents are to blame. Such generalizations are nonsense. Finally, if professional people do not diagnose cases by professional terminology, then the lay public will immediately invent even more repugnant words: "Stupid" for retarded, "weirdo" for behaviorally disturbed, and "queer" for homosexual. From such negative terms from the layman come powerful self-fulfilling prophesies. Thus the professional diagnosis has less stigma than its vulgar counterpart and offers greater objectivity in a non-condemnatory perspective. Yet, language and terminology do change. When better and more specific words are offered, science will use them and, hopefully, the public may soon follow.

In this chapter, several terms or diagnostic labels will be used to focus on certain common patterns of behavior or handicaps which limit normal functioning of young children. These problems deal with: (A) cognition, (B) speech and language, (C) gross and fine-motor coordination, (D) visual perception, (E) auditory perception, (F) self care and independence, and (G) a special section on adaptations for the physically handicapped. Impairment or delays in any of the above functions can portend mild, moderate, or severe problems for the preschool child and the young handicapped person. What is particularly regrettable is that so frequently the child in question has two or more handicapped conditions and, not infrequently, if only one problem is initially present, as in a motor defect, it often (1) precipitates delay in social acceptance, (2) restricts independence, and (3) triggers secondary problems in self-concept. Such a chain reaction of impairments is to be anticipated and not ignored in handicapped children. Their consequences appear geometric rather than arithmetic in impact. To prevent the traumatic effects of such handicaps is one goal of child-oriented professionals. The author and his colleague have tried to illustrate this viewpoint in fifteen such cases in the recent book, *Case Studies in Clinical and School Psychology* (Blanco and Rosenfeld, 1978). Many children are not referred to child psychologists or related professionals until the handicapping condition, e.g. severe reading problem, retardation, reaches crisis proportions. It is logically contended that if referral and therapeutic intervention were offered during the preschool years, then preventive work might forstall some serious handicaps later.

The prescriptions noted in this chapter are deemed to be appropriate, first, to preschool children thought to be impaired or delayed in development in any one of the six general areas noted previously. This age range would encompass from one year to five years, assuming approximately normal intelligence. A second group for whom these ideas are listed are the mentally retarded, brain damaged, or developmentally delayed of unknown potential who, from all observations, appear to function at a lower mental age or lower operational level than their chronological age. Thus cognitive and social delay suggests that they will likely require major educational and therapeutic intervention. Thus, an eight-year-old trainable retarded child when functioning as a three and one-half-year-old can be considered as a suitable subject for this "preschool" chapter.

A. COGNITION

1. "Bombard" the child with auditory, visual, tactile, kinesthetic, and proprioceptive stimulation from infancy in the hope that some stimuli may penetrate into the (assumed) damaged sensory pathways and receptive-central processing areas of the brain. The stimuli must be within the tolerable threshold, otherwise it may be painful to the child and withdrawal from noxious stimuli will result. Attempt to present the stimuli with a pleasant event or experience, e.g. being held, sung to, fed, gently rocked, etc.

2. Attempt to offer a cause and effect explanation to the developmentally delayed preschool child of perhaps three, four, or five years so that the fundamentals of reasoning may begin. For a child who does not comprehend the connections between events, the world is confusing and irritating, an anxiety producer which stimulates further withdrawal behavior.

3. Activate the child in visual and auditory channels simultaneously when engaged in any activity. When reading a

story, point to the pictures and name the main characters, objects, colors, actions, and the general process of how the pictures relate to the verbal production. Ask the child to help in the pointing and naming process and later require the child to do this without assistance.

4. In auditory areas, help the child identify sounds of the city, town, neighborhood by attaching words to the sounds and telling of their origins, frequency of occurrence, predictability, etc. Listen to music together, read aloud simple poems asking the child to tell which sounds are alike and which sounds are different. Repeat these experiences many times so that the child can feel increasing success identifying sounds and seeing the parents and teachers reaction to such obvious success.

5. Read two or three of the child's favorite stories many times even though this is dull for the reader. Children rarely seem to tire of hearing such stories as they are so meaningful and familiar to them. Later the child will request variations but will occasionally call for a repeat performance.

6. Ask for explanations of noises, sights, events, stories, circumstances, food preferences, performances of toys, T.V. episodes, etc., so that the child is required to think and develop relationships in a logical sequence. Merely requesting the child's explanation is insufficient, however, as the adult must then interpret reality which attempts to weave in the correct portions of the child's view. If the child claims, for example, that a "canary sings because its yellow," the teacher or parents should help the interpretation with realistic detail and accuracy.

7. Problem solving at the child's level is one of the best activities to develop cognitive abilities and, in fact, is often a first choice for many gifted children. Yet problem solving is difficult for the developmentally delayed who are easily frustrated, may have had nonstimulating experiences and may confuse the language they hear and the language they produce. Their problems are to be simple and appropriate to the approximate *mental age* or *operational age* of the child, not necessarily his or her chronological age. If the child generally operates at a three-year-old level socially, regardless of his older chronological age, then provide games, puzzles, pictures, stories, and activities for a

three-year-old. Such problem solving and fun activities do not keep him too long at the three-year-old level; they provide a basis for him to become successful and comfortable at a three-year-old level, permitting him to move gradually to a three and one-half- and then four-year-old level. The point is not to "speed him up" to relieve parental or teacher anxiety, but to give some pleasant and successful experiences at the "easy level" so that he will develop confidence to try some more complex problems and events at a four-year-old level. This does not mean "babying" the child but recognizing his delay as genuine and real and contending with it with sensible remedial approaches.

8. Behavior modification is a legitimate and often powerful technique for developing cognitive abilities when the child is rewarded by primary, token, or social means for executing approved behavior. Assuming that the reward-for-accomplishment system does not go contrary to the value system of the parent, teacher, or therapist, proceed to give specific rewards for the behaviors expected. First, one must reward occasionally in ways which the child finds rewarding; explain to him what are the nonrewarding aspects of his behavior so that he is at least cognitively aware, although this is not imperative for certain habit problems. In general, aversive therapy is not considered appropriate for developmentally delayed children, although in self-abuse cases, special planning may be necessary in residential facilities. If the child is expected, say, to identify certain colors or animals in his repertoire, he is to receive a small award for perhaps three of five or perhaps five of five identifications with accuracy. Incorrect identifications receive silence rather than criticism. Not all successes are rewarded because intermittent reward has been determined to be more effective than continuous reward. Behavior modification techniques can be used to reward improved walking, speech, self-feeding skills, sharing, taking turns, reasonable assertiveness, cooperativeness in play, localization, singing, the introduction of social amenities, the reduction of annoying habit patterns, etc. Behavior modification, under the assistance of a competent psychological consultant, has also minimized or extinguished head-banging, elective mutism, incessant crying, unwillingness to walk or eat, excessive

masturbation, inappropriate "hanging on," bowel and bladder problems, swearing and interrupting of others, etc. Ordinarily a psychologist with such specialized training is equipped to develop, explain, and monitor efficient behavioral approaches. It is highly recommended that other therapists, teachers, and parents not devise their own systems without direct consultation from a specially trained psychologist. Even those persons who have taken a course in behavior modification or read a book or two in this area very frequently should ask for appropriate consultation from an experienced clinician or school psychologist.

9. Teaching the child the next highest level of operation in a task or skill is a prime consideration for cognitive development. If the child recognizes three sight words, then add a fourth; if the child can self-feed with a spoon, then attempt to train him with a fork and later a knife, etc. Accompanying these tasks is the explanation of the parent or teacher so that gradually the child learns that words represent ideas, tasks, actions, feelings, objects, etc. Intellectual development in such training may be the end result of such efforts.

10. Children with problems of cognitive delay need not only a number of stimulating activities, they also need the presence of interested adults on a continuous and daily basis. It is important that the child be attended to by the parents, have playmates quite often, and if at all possible attend a preschool or a nursery program so that interaction with others and problem-solving may be a daily occurrence. If possible, all the children in the family should be informed about the delays of the younger child and requested to help him or her develop through play activities, conservation, taking him around, and offering a share of their own lives in helping him develop.

11. Have the child imitate the teacher or parent in stacking blocks or boxes. These may vary in size, color or texture. Associate the stacking with verbal encouragement and a description of what the child was doing so that he begins to comprehend action with words.

12. Permit the child to scribble and finger-paint but do not expect artistic productions. Sandboxes also permit tactile exper-

iences and a foundation of creative play with toys. The child should have a number of his own play objects in his room and be assigned, in general, a certain play area where he can be disruptive.

13. Starting with a large ball, roll it to the child while telling what the ball does. Ask the child to roll it back in a game-like imitation. Later advance to a smaller ball and finally initiate throwing the ball to the child. Always associate language with the actions and give the verbal approval for effort and increased skills.

14. Teach the child his name, age, address, etc., and as many social amenities as he can absorb. Teach the shaking of hands, saying "thank you," "please," etc. The parents and staff should make as many efforts to normalize the child as possible so that he will be more easily accepted into the mainstream activities of normal children without such handicaps.

15. Explain various kitchen utensils to the child while letting him explore them. Show their use, the dangers of the stove and hot water, how the refrigerator is used, where items are stored, etc., so that this world becomes more comprehensible.

16. To achieve approximately a twelve-month functioning, the developmentally delayed child may be assisted in building a two-block tower, releasing a cube upon request, dropping items into a cup and giving up a toy upon request. Other developmental items at one year include placing objects into a jar, playing with colored and noisy toys, walking with assistance or while holding furniture, and expressing a few nouns or names.

17. At the eighteen-month level the delayed child may be encouraged to walk alone, use small furniture for sitting, turn a few pages of a book, and build a tower of three blocks unassisted. Other tasks may involve filling bowls and boxes with cubes and small toys, scribbling, calling, picture naming, throwing a ball toward an adult, and following a few simple commands. Such tasks may require considerable repetition and some tangible reward on occasion.

18. At the twenty-four-month functioning a child ordinarily can handle the turning of a single page in a picture book, make towers using several blocks, offer objects to an adult upon

request, identify animals in picture books by name, kick a ball, hold a spoon correctly, and play in an animated fashion with dolls, toys, etc. Vocabulary is now at the twenty- or thirty-word level and three-word sentences might appear with the correct usage of most pronouns.

19. At three years, some children build a tower of eight to ten blocks, copy a three-block bridge when demonstrated by an adult, draw a recognizable circle with a preferred hand, and follow more complicated motor demands. Children can fetch and carry around the house and do small chores under supervision. Tricycle riding is accomplished through coordinated peddling; the child feeds himself and is capable of dressing except for tying and small buttoning. Stairs may be climbed with alternate stepping and small jumping is noted. The child can name something copied and can use plurals for objects and discriminate one sex from another. A few rhymes are available and a rudimentary grasp of taking turns now appears. Washing oneself is in vogue at three, and cooperative play begins to replace parallel play of the earlier year.

20. Cut out pictures with the child for magazines that present similarities in animals, colors, clothing, automobiles, play activities, food, babies, numbers, simple words, flowers, birds, fish, household pets, farm animals, circus action, cartoon characters, seasonal changes, cars, objects, etc. Paste these and review often the similarities and differences requesting that the child identify verbally how they are alike and how they are different. Help him discriminate these by adult explanations and illustrations.

B. SPEECH AND LANGUAGE

1. Provide opportunities to play with a variety of other young children so that language interaction is necessary and stimulating. Have the children participate together in parties, trips, lunches, and game time. Limit the amount of time for watching T.V., essentially a passive experience, although highly educational at times.

2. Request that the child use verbal language rather than use body language and gestures to communicate his or her needs.

Anticipating a child's needs will reduce his dependence on language; responding to his verbal requests will tend to reinforce his appropriate language skills.

3. Encourage description and elaboration about the child's experiences. Request other persons in his life to ask about his play, visits, trips, feelings, play objects, etc.

4. Ignore undesirable speech patterns (lisps, slurring, stuttering, etc.) while the child is concentrating on communicating his excitement and ideas in words. It is better that the child speak with speech impediments than not to speak at all or be reluctant to communicate for fear of ridicule or constant correction. A speech therapist rather than a parent may be available for help with articulation problems.

5. When the child uses language correctly, communicates a new concept, or tries a new vocabulary word, praise him so that the small increments of reinforcement encourage futher language development. Relate to the child's "growing up," being "big," and increasingly capable.

6. The teacher and parents should model acceptable speech and language. Omit rapid speech as this is often indecipherable to young children.

7. When speaking to a child, use a number of examples and familiar adjectives so that the child may enlarge his association in his native language.

8. By consulting an audiologist and otologist and by obtaining a screening test for hearing acuity, the family may rule out or discover hearing problems. Brief screenings are often routinely done at certain grade levels in public schools or if problems are suspected by the teacher. The parent need not wait, however, until the school initiates the screening. Occasionally, obstructions in the ear canal impede hearing, or the loss is transient and due to respiratory infections.

9. If the child continues to reveal confusion about the speech and language of others and is believed to be of (1) normal intelligence and (2) normal hearing acuity, the possiblity of a language specialist (audiologist, language pathologist) should be consulted to enable this complex problem to be evaluated. Such children have aphasic-like symptoms and cannot produce

speech and language any better than the way they understand it. If language is confusing at reception, then the child will consequently produce confused speech since his ideas are "garbied," misassociated, and semantically imperfect. Most large universities or major hospitals have clinical staff capable of evaluating such cases and providing remedial techniques.

    10. Commercial programs to enhance language development are:

        a. Distar Language Kit: I, II, III, Science Research Associates.

        b. Peabody Early Experience Kit, American Guidance Service.

        c. Early Childhood Enrichment Series, Milton Bradley.

        d. Peabody Language Kits, American Guidance Service.

        e. Learning to Develop Language Skills, Milton Bradley, Inc.

    11. Other commercial programs to be considered are listed below:

        a. Addison-Wesley with the Electric Company Phonics Kit and Electric Company Sentence Comprehension Kit.

        b. The Allied Educational Council with the Fitzhugh Plus Program, Galien, Michigan.

        c. Craig Education, The Craig Primary Language Arts System for Kindergarten through Third Grade, Compton, California.

        d. The Economy Company with the Early Approaches to Reading Skills and Space Talk and Word World of Oklahoma City, Oklahoma.

        e. Educational Activities in the Ready-Go Alphabet Program for the Kindergarten Level of Freeport, New York.

        f. Follett Publishing Company with their Language and Thinking Program for Preschool Children in Chicago, Illinois.

        g. Learning Concepts with the Developmental Syntax Program and Vocabulary Comprehension Scale for Preschoolers and Elementary Level located in Irvine,

California.

h. The Charles E. Merrill Company with the Merrill
   Linguistic Readiness Program, the Phonic Reading
   and Spelling Programs from Columbus, Ohio.

12. When there is some kind of language delay or confusion
about words, it is extremely reasonable to employ a speech and
language therapist in the public school agency, residential
treatment setting, or privately in the home. Such specialists can
often enhance the child's language skills remarkably far beyond
that which can be done in the group training programs in school.
Often children with developmental delays need highly individualized programs which can be provided by such specialists.

C. GROSS AND FINE MOTOR COORDINATION

1. In a developmental sequence, the general gross motor
areas that need attention are: crawling, creeping, walking
assisted, walking alone, walking on a board, swinging arms in a
coordinated fashion, running, hopping, throwing a ball, catch-
ing a ball, skipping (five or six years), climbing a ladder, jumping
rope, and engaging in formalized games and sports. Therapeutic attention is to be focused on not only the emerging or
target activity, but also on activities already manifested. To
reinforce these, each child should be rated on a developmental
scale and evaluated by a physical therapist or physical education
specialist experienced with children having orthopedic problems. An impaired child will need an individualized program
written out, executed, and monitored.

2. Use games which capitalize upon many muscles to aid in
general coordination: leap frog, see-saw, rolling and tumbling,
follow the leader, imitation of animals, and general running
games.

3. Have the child pick up large blocks and toys for
replacement in specific places and gradually introduce smaller
objects for grasping. These could be beads, buttons, marbles,
small blocks, lotto cards, miniature animals, toy soldiers, small
cars, etc., to provide many experiences with finger coordination,
wrist turning, and eye-hand coordination. Since the young child
may become bored easily after a few minutes, he will need

companionship of a parent, teacher, or playmate. Occasionally the parent or teacher may offer a tangible reward or a bit of food for sustained effort, as well as verbal approval for the child's persistence.

4. Although it is much easier to feed a developmentally delayed child or one with some degree of cerebral palsy with involvement in the upper extremities, in the long run the child and the parent will be immeasurably better off to train as many fine motor skills as the child can develop. This literally means a great deal of practice in teaching the child to feed himself, to grasp a spoon (later a fork), and to help him execute the intended movements with assistance. At first the parent may have to place the spoon in the child's hand and hold his hand, leading him to scoop some subjects from a bowl and move them directly into his mouth. Later, after months or years of patient training and gradual maturational development, the child may be able to execute these tasks himself and feel more confident in his own self-care. Each meal is a practice session with the expectation of occasional successes and frequent failures. The same motor skills need to be developed for writing, self-care, dressing, etc.

5. It may be necessary to consult a pediatric occupational therapist to obtain adaptive equipment for self-feeding: special wrist or hand bands in which to insert a spoon, a flexible handle to a cup, or a special straw for sucking. Few of these products are mass produced for easy purchase, since each child's handicaps are so unique. Thus an occupational therapist is often needed to observe the child's particular muscle coordination problem before devising equipment for use.

6. Tracing and coloring activities are excellent experiences for developing better eye-hand coordination. (Many such activities are suggested in the Learning Disabilities chapter of this book.) A child can be encouraged to start with large crayons and later large pencils for scribbling and coloring. As visual perception skills increase and cognitive development occurs, then pictures can be used to provide a format for the colors and tracings.

7. The child, starting at about a mental age of over three and one-half, may trace or copy letters, numbers, and large geometric

designs. Remember that a child of normal intelligence cannot draw a circle by himself until about a mental age of three and that the copying of a square requires about a five mental age while a diamond necessitates the mental age of about 6 and one-half years of age.

8. Pegs and holes games or hammer the pegs games are suitable for young children with fine motor difficulties.

9. Some preschoolers and kindergarten children can handle scissors for cutting out patterns and pictures. Such skills can be transferred later to cutting out pictures in magazines and pasting them in scrapbooks according to the child's interests.

10. Connecting-the-dots drawings are good experiences in this general area.

11. Have the child evaluated by a developmental optometrist to see if problems with binocularity or visual perception are fundamental to the eye-hand coordination problems. This doctor may recommend visual training experiences which should be used in the home and school.

12. Introduce the child to painting activities using rather small brushes to paint toys, objects, or in paint books.

13. Offer practice in buttoning or in unbuttoning jackets, coats, and other clothing.

14. Have the child place colored pegs in the same colored boxes or use paper clips or toothpicks for coins. For two or more children this can be made into a competitive game with each person winning a prize for completion of the task.

15. Practice turning one page at a time in a book or magazine.

16. Play finger games with the child.

17. Use soft clay or Play-Doh™ to permit exercises in finger manipulation. Children love to keep their hands occupied and this inventive device is most useful to strengthen fingers.

D. VISUAL PERCEPTION

1. Rule out visual acuity problems by initial referral to a developmental optometrist and opthalmologist.

2. Permit the child to match simple geometric shapes involving circles of different sizes, vertical and horizontal lines,

diagonal lines, triangles, squares, and crosses. Reinforce concrete responses by approval.

3. Have the developmentally delayed child point out which shape is different from others in a row, but be sure that one is distinctly different in the series. Have the child touch the dissimilar cards and try to tell how it differs from the others.

4. Request the child to express the differences in appearance and use between:

    a. A spoon and a fork
    b. A radio and television
    c. A coat and a hat
    d. Sled and skis
    e. A cat and a kitten
    f. A ball and a bat
    g. A pencil and crayon
    h. A toaster and oven
    i. A car and an airplane

5. Present printed larger letters to help the child become familiar with the alphabet. Ask the child to copy some by tracing over onion paper that is taped down.

6. If the child has a mental age estimate of at least four years, have him place all circles in one pile, all squares in another, all crosses together, etc. Do the same for letters and then numbers when he is older and understands their meaning.

7. Cut out pictures in magazines, comic books, and old picture books of similar things and help the child sort them by similarities and differences.

8. Offer similar two- and three-piece puzzles to put together.

9. Ask the pupils to look around the room and touch all the chairs, the tables, the boys, the girls, the pictures, the blackboard, etc.

10. Request identification of the largest and smallest items in the classroom or nursery school.

11. Have the child finish many incomplete letters, numbers and simple geometric designs, and dot-by-dot pictures.

12. Looking at a picture or scene, the child will turn away and recall as many items or people as possible from visual memory.

13. Assemble a small group of toys letting the child view them. Ask him to close his eyes, then remove one toy from him, and let him attempt to recall the missing item.

14. Reproduce a simple geometric design, letter, or number after it has been viewed by the child and then hidden.

15. Teach language acquisition to visual choice selection by holding an object or pointing to an item in the picture by saying, "Is this a _____, _____, or _____?"

16. Find an object or toy hidden in a pile of similar items.

17. Find all the circles or squares in a picture.

18. Locate by circling all the letter *a's* (or any letter or number) in a page of reading material or a newspaper with large print.

19. Color well-outlined letters and numbers.

20. Play visual memory games by having the child initiate a larger and longer list of motor behaviors of an adult: walking backwards, then hopping, then clapping, etc.

21. Practice memorizing sequences of stories, then parts of the alphabet or number series as in the telephone or address.

22. Practice visual tracking of a flashlight or a blinking light moved around the peripheral field of vision.

23. Sort color samples rapidly. Match sequences of a color wheel.

E. AUDITORY PERCEPTION

1. Rule out hearing defects through referral to an audiologist and an otologist.

2. Require the child to face the speaker so as to encourage full attention to sounds and words by engaging eye contact.

3. Seat the child near the teacher in small or large group activities. Avoid seating the child near a hallway or a noisy section of the room.

4. Speak at a moderate rate of speed using short sentences and brief instructions.

5. Permit exercises in sound localization of bells, snaps, whistles, etc. with the child's eyes shut.

6. If in a noisy place or on a shopping trip or a visit to a city, ask the child to identify various sounds in the environment. Help

the child with adult explanations.

7. Provide records of different animal and bird sounds and require identification and possible imitation.

8. Identify classmates by their voice alone while the listening child's eyes are shut.

9. Change one word in each sentence of a common poem, song, or rhyme and let the student identify what was incorrect.

10. Have the child listen to pairs of rhyming words with some that do not rhyme and ask for identification and explanation.

11. Encourage the child to describe differences in musical instruments on records, radio, tapes, or T.V.

12. Teach the child to depend more heavily upon the auditory channels by providing a blindfold and letting him "follow the leader" slowly around the nursery or playroom by verbal signals alone.

13. Make a list of "danger sounds" in the neighborhood.

14. Identify the many sounds in a normal household in terms of appliances, T.V., radio, footsteps, steam, air conditioning, the washing machine, etc.

15. Take a trip to a concert and teach the class what to listen for in the various instruments of the orchestra.

16. Ask children to supply rhymes for the teacher's words, "house-mouse," "plate-late."

17. Ask for a production of different voices and attempt to imitate them.

18. One of the best prescriptions is to have the child follow a series of brief verbal commands within his language comprehension level and offer a small reward if "all three commands" are carried out perfectly. These may naturally be extended to include a longer series. Other children may be the "command leader" rather than the teacher or parent. Such actions can involve even setting a table, picking up scraps, or putting away toys. It is obvious that other skills may be taught through such experiences.

19. Have the child pick out a "silly" word in a sentence that does not make sense and then substitute a more appropriate word. "All the three kittens played on the *water*."

20. Identify the sounds of a variety of zoo, household, and

farm animals.

21. Practice whispering, speaking slowly, and speaking quickly.

22. Sing meaningful songs in groups and also encourage solos.

23. Send the child to music therapy class to widen his interest in the larger world of sound and to provide successful sound experiences with other children.

24. Play cassette tapes of children's voices and different kinds of marching music.

25. Expect children to depend upon language and not just use of their body language for expressing their needs.

F. SELF-CARE AND SOCIALIZATION

1. Have the child evaluated by an occupational therapist who has had the experience with developmentally delayed and young handicapped children. Such personnel are often astute observers of precisely where a child is operating in several self-care, motor and perceptual areas, often using rating scales and knowledge of developmental levels to aid in the child's assessment. If suggested by the occupational therapist, take the child for regular occupational therapy sessions and observe the various activities used to help latent development emerge. Duplicate these activities at school or home.

2. Practice having the child help with dressing and un-dressing starting with the simpler tasks of his holding out an arm or leg on request while the adult pulls the clothing on. Later this can be done without verbal instruction as the child learns the sequence. Praise, a hug, and an occasional food reward may help to reinforce this emerging self-care behavior.

3. Occupational therapists have found that some children discover more initial success in self-care if the child learns to take off his clothing, piece by piece, as putting it on is a more complicated task involving higher developmental skills. For example, it is easier for a child to unbutton a shirt than to button it; the same is true for zippers and bows.

4. For some children with delayed motor development, clothing snaps rather than buttons can be used to aid in removal.

5. Motivation is a necessary ingredient in the development of self-care; thus, the intensely involved parent or child care worker must be certain not to indulge the child by performing his actions or solving his problems that are well within his scope of ability. The child must sense the need to change or some degree of discomfort in order to progress. Otherwise he sits and cries until "rescued" by a caring person. Offer encouragement to solve his own problems and expect him to care for himself where he is physically and mentally able.

6. Small increments of reward in the form of tiny pieces of candy or pretzel or a sip of tasty beverage paired with the social approval of an adult may help accelerate learning of a given task. Naturally the child must be slightly hungry or thirsty and not have a particular diet upset by, say, too much candy. Later, as the child matures, the need for edible reward will fade and the child's need for parental approval will be sufficient, providing that the parent-child relationship has been good.

7. Purchase and use the Minnesota Child Development Inventory as a means of assessing where the child is functioning developmentally in self-care (and several other areas). Wherever the child is just emerging into a more mature behavior on the scale is where training may begin.

8. Children with special problems need a chance to talk things over with a responsive and reflective adult who can be nonjudgmental and supportive of their feelings. Yet many such children cannot speak or relate such feelings because of speech impediments, and obvious developmental delays. What can be done in this case? One approach is to offer a form of play therapy and art therapy wherein the child can act out his frustration or angers on toys and dolls while under the guidance of a special adult. This person does not interpret the child's behavior to him in regard to the toys or dolls, but rather describes to the child what he is doing with them without interpretation and while stating the emotion behind the actions, i.e. "You are angry now," "Now you will feel better," etc. Professional play therapists might be ideal but few are available and even those are difficult to include in a public school or on a clinical budget.

9. If the child needs to develop self-feeding skills, the adult

encourages this by putting the child's hand over a spoon, clamping her hand over his, dipping the spoon for food, and aiming it into his mouth. Later the adult uses a lesser amount of hand contact and guidance and tries to substitute verbal instructions.

10. Give group lessons to young children in grooming and self-care. This could include the basic tasks of face-washing, drying, teeth-brushing, hair grooming, etc. Within a group and when children make progress or accomplishments these should be noted on a chart for all to see. More motivation is achieved usually when children have their peer group respond to them. Different levels of behavior are to be noted for different children as some may not be motorically or intellectually ready to acquire certain skills.

11. For the four- or five-year old child who is not seriously delayed in development, yet is untrained for bladder at night, purchase the Wee-Alert™ system or similar system from a major department store. The instructions are simple and soundly based in psychological learning theory. When the child wets, a bell and buzzer wakes him up (and the parents) to turn off the buzzer, change the sheet, void in the bathroom, and then return to bed. Gradually the amount of voiding is lessened as the child begins to awake earlier to bladder tensions and relieves himself at the toilet once he is awakened by himself. Ordinarily, five to eight weeks of training are sufficient for full bladder control, assuming that no urinary tract infections are present.

12. Provide some age models for the child to play with as he may then develop the desire to be as competent as his playmates in self-help skills and socialization.

13. Offer a checklist by pictures in the child's bathroom where he can see the steps needed to prepare himself for the day.

14. Teach the child the basic amenities of social interactions starting with forms of greeting; telling his age, name, and address; and the experiences of sharing cooperatively with playmates.

15. Enroll the child in a nursery or preschool setting so that socializing experiences with young children may begin on a regular basis. A full week enrollment may evolve if the child can tolerate the experience.

G. SPECIAL ADAPTATIONS FOR THE PHYSICALLY HANDICAPPED

1. Although no single physical arrangement of furniture, ramps, chairs, rails, etc., can serve all ages and all kinds of impairments of children, the basic adjustment should encourage a free flow of activities be they academic, physical, or social.

2. Several accessible learning areas should exist in each classroom for children when room allows: a play and exploratory area, music and art corner, academic center, building area, etc.

3. The furniture should be appropriate to the size of the children and to their specific handicaps: rails on steps, toilet facilities with grasping bars for lifting, carpets for floor playing and learning, desk sizes to suit individual heights and, finally, low shelves, doorknobs, and sinks for wheelchair children.

4. Standing boxes, highly purposeful for children with physical impairments, are essential in the classroom if recommended by a physical therapist and surgeon. Obviously, different size standing boxes will be required as the child grows. If the boxes have wheels, they can be pushed rather easily from room to room as activities demand. The amount of recorded time spent daily in a standing box is obtained from the physical therapist and might involve anywhere from a half hour to an entire morning. Such a device aids circulation, increases muscle tone, assists bone development and care, and provides an upright view of the world for the child from a less submissive stance. If a table top is attached, the academic program can continue in addition to the attachment of a language board.

5. Spina bifida children may require catheterization or diapering during the school day by school personnel until they are old enough and sufficiently trained to undertake these tasks. (Some school personnel are interested in "mainstreaming" such physically handicapped children, until the personnel recognize the unexpected duties involved with the children's daily care during the school day.)

6. Language boards may be provided for language or speech-impaired children under certain conditions to be decided upon by a team conference with a special input from a language specialist. First, the board can be fitted to the arms of a wheelchair

through special construction. Second, only children without the development of speech should obtain a language board; otherwise, speech itself may be delayed if the child depends only on pointing to a word or symbol. Third, only those with sufficient intelligence should have language boards since the symbols themselves may vary from signs for "yes and no" to highly complex forms of efficient communication like the Bliss symbols. The youngest mental age for a language board should be about two and one-half to three years of age. Obviously, printed words themselves require reading skill (six and one-half years mental age) and are preceded by pictures or agreed-upon symbols. Tailored refinements on the use of language boards may be discussed with the child's speech and language therapist.

7. It is important that the faculty and the teacher as well as the speech and language therapist learn to depend on the language board; otherwise, hard-earned skills in communication may extinguish through disuse.

8. Each physically handicapped child should have his or her own cubby holes in the classroom for easy access to his winter clothes, boots, raincoats, etc.

9. Occupational therapists trained to work with impaired children are often ingenious and indispensable consultants on adaptive physical equipment: special spoons or straws for cerebral palsy children, cups, arm aids for a fuller range of motion, helmets for children with grand mal epilepsy, eyeglass straps, special snaps or straps for clothing to replace buttons, inclined seats, etc. Other training adaptations may involve lessons in teeth-brushing for the physically or developmentally impaired, shoe-tying, grooming instruction, utensil training, and an array of visual motor training activities aimed at remediating related problems.

Since the physically handicapped child does not find the work generally accessible, the world should be made as assessible to him as possible.

10. If the child has only minor physical or strength restrictions, permit daily opportunities for vigorous play activity both indoors and out of doors, weather permitting; offer him the room to run, tumble, roll, jump, etc. It would be helpful if the home

offered a rug in the play area, a mattress, or a group of pillows.

11. Games can be organized for a child and his friend which involve races (wheel chair races), fast walking, tag, team tag, balance activities, general calisthenics and exercises, ball throwing, climbing on monkey bars, etc.

12. A balance beam made of a 2 × 4 on concrete blocks can be an exciting task for the youngsters at play and provides practice and balance in gross motor coordination.

13. A circle game with youngsters sitting while pushing a basketball or a beachball to each other may assist in timing and coordination.

14. "Simon Says" activities led by an adult or older child can be done for one or more children if the instructions are slow and well-modeled for the child. The leader should not attempt to eliminate the "contestants" early, but provide easy cues to follow and be liberal in ignoring errors of the preschoolers. The activities can involve rolling, lifting a leg, waving a hand, standing on tiptoes, etc., all of which give the child experience in using his body to match commands and control his body space.

15. Follow-the-leader with one or more young children can offer an array of gross motor activities which are exciting and in high demand. The activities should be within the physical capabilities of the children. Wheelchair children in school can pursue the leader around a room or hall, strength permitting, and can practice more complicated turns while developing arm strength and coordination.

16. An obstacle course on the school grounds with tunnels, steps, tires, jumping areas, and so on, could be constructed by interested parents for their mobile children.

17. The development of upper-arm strength is particularly important to spina bifida children who will require crutches and/or wheelchairs in the future. A physical therapist may wish to supplement the regular physical therapy activities with ones at home and school. These may include exercises in rolling, sit-ups, push-ups, pulling with weights, range of motion (R.O.M.), shoulder or torso twists, bean-bag throwing, etc. The physical therapist may wish to reserve new instruction on crutches, wheel-walkers, or Canadian canes for regular physical therapy sessions

rather than use parents or teachers, since the orthopedic surgeon may have suggested specific exercises for development.

18. The physically handicapped child should have a physical therapist list of prescribed exercises recorded in the medical records, subject to review and revision depending on the child's condition, age, development, and I.E.P. review.

19. Not only is exercise beneficial for the physical development of children, it also provides them with opportunities to meet new playmates and gives a basis for social relations and further companionship, a series of accomplishments, and the knowledge that they are all gaining in areas of development.

20. Gross motor exercises help in wheelchair-bound children to sit straighter, to develop neck and stomach muscles for erect posture, and to increase physical endurance for school and leisure activities. It is vital for optimum health to "keep the bones and muscles moving."

21. Adaptive physical education for the physically handicapped is mandated in school by Public Law 94-142 and indicates the vital contribution which such activities might play in the education and training of preschool children and those with handicaps.

22. A motor skills checklist can give the parent or preschool teacher a rough estimate about the child's gross and fine muscle skills according to age levels and provides a suggested list of goals for future development at the place where the child "fails" an item.

23. Time for gross motor development should be scheduled daily with cooperating family members to aid the child in activities specified by the physical therapist or teacher. Such a schedule also guarantees time for social interaction with siblings during the experiences and many opportunities for social reinforcement.

24. If leg muscles and coordination need development, perhaps a "big wheel" or tricycle can be used by the child. Kicking a large ball can develop timing and strengthen coordination as well.

Chapter IV

AGGRESSIVE BEHAVIOR

A GGRESSION IN CHILDHOOD relates to a behavioral style of attack, a disposition to operate beyond assertiveness, and a willingness to dominate a circumstance often at the expense of others. The aggressive child is often seen as willful, strong, frightening, self-centered, and angry. The aggressive adolescent is sometimes viewed as destructive, not only in social relations, but to property as well. When the manifestations of agression are extreme, they are terrifying to the observer and to the child himself. Continuance of aggression is intolerable in a stable society.

Although aggression is not unexpected in infants who are upset or thwarted, an inability to control aggressive impulses suggests social immaturity in older children. The child meets his environment head-on and sometimes aggravates adults with his displays of power and boldness.

Severe aggressive behaviors, especially those which influence others directly or threaten their welfare and status, are among the most common complaints of not only teachers and parents, but also of siblings and classmates of the child in question. Although an initial reaction is often a strike back in retaliatory fashion, adults who live with and teach aggressive children eventually recognize the limitations of such measures mainly because they were only temporarily effective and are poor models to mimic. They also have a "backlash effect" that is unpredicted. Professional personnel should seek instead the sources of the aggressive behaviors to redirect it more harmlessly as well as discover a variety of controls to contain and diminish the impact.

Aggression is apparently expected, indeed encouraged in our society generally, for certain forms of accomplishment including high grades and social mobility. In mild form it is considered "normal." When a child's aggression is manifested beyond the cultural, ethnic, and class norms, effective ways are sought to limit its force and effect. Behavior bordering on violence is antithetical to our general democratic process and is abhorrent to many persons even though it is condoned in subtle ways. In schools it is officially forbidden or tolerated only to a degree, although violence in sports is heavily encouraged by school personnel, boards of education, and the taxpayers. Apparently aggression is deeply imbedded in the mores of American culture. Aggression, whether externally or internally directed, tends to disrupt learning, confuse classmates, thwart teachers, and so befuddles administrators that specialists are called to change the behavior before expulsion from school is invoked. Juvenile courts are crammed in their dockets with problems dealing with aggressive behaviors in children.

The sources of aggressive behavior are much too numerous to categorize extensively, but the reader is urged to direct attention to clinical psychology and psychiatric texts. Depending upon one's theoretical orientation, aggressive behavior may arise from (1) repressed hostilities, (2) indulgent behavior of parents, (3) defective management in the home and school, (4) current reinforcement of aggressive behaviors, (5) a compensation for poor learning, (6) organic damage, (7) a defense against psychosis, (8) a responsiveness to expectations, or (9) a cry telling of unmet needs, among others. Sometimes several sources combine in one unit to provide impetus to the aggressive behaviors.

Internally directed aggression can be destructive to the individual if not society. It is often viewed by clinicians as behavior over which the person has little control or even awareness, at least prior to treatment.

This chapter contains some conceptual overlap with the diagnostic problems noted in Chapters V and VI to follow in that the material reflects social maladjustment. Such prescriptive interventions were separated mainly on the basis of editorial rather than theoretical considerations. The basic rationale for the symptom and diagnostic classification scheme throughout this volume is succinctly stated in the reference, Group for the Advancement of Psychiatry (1966), and was edited by the author to incorporate certain special education categories as mentioned in an earlier reference (Blanco, 1971a).

SECTION A: AGGRESSIVE BEHAVIOR— EXTERNALLY DIRECTED

1. Being knowledgeable about when aggression often occurs in class, the teacher can make a list of "trouble spots" and then prepare:
   a. Have the events, activities, or projects well managed in advance by thinking out procedures and assignments for children.
   b. Use a teacher aide or parent to assist.
   c. Give simple direct instructions.
   d. Place troublesome children close by the teacher.
   e. Ask the class for special cooperation and offer a class reward for excellence, e.g. a film strip, treat, five-minute "vacation" in class, etc.

2. Use a time-out procedure so that an aggressive child will have fewer opportunities to direct aggression toward peers. Place the child in a time-out room after an episode. Be certain not to reward him with a pleasurable time-out experience if he has been aggressive. If anything, it must be an isolating, nonrewarding condition in the room or classroom cubicle so that aggression is not positively reinforced. Any kind of attention the child gets during a time-out procedure is, unfortunately, reinforcing and may evoke the same aggression later. Sending the child out into the hallway may be convenient for the teacher, but it has too many reinforcing qualities from passers-by who talk to the child or otherwise give him attention.

3. The amount of time spent in the time-out room should be adjusted to the individual child, e.g. perhaps 5 minutes for a youngster and 15 or 20 for an older one. In general, it should be used for children who enjoy social activities, fun and excitement, and who have friends whom they will miss. They will be annoyed at themselves for missing these social contacts while in the time-

out room and this may help them learn to control themselves better.

4. Children who are very timid, apprehensive, fearful or who are particularly withdrawn are not good candidates for a time-out room as they can become frightened when alone or perhaps lost in the pleasure of being isolated. For example, schizophrenic and autistic children will generally not profit from time-out rooms. In other examples, children who masturbate, who enjoy singing to themselves, or making up a private mental game, will not profit from a time-out room to reduce aggression.

5. Another variation in the time-out room is that the child may signal when he "has had enough" and is ready to control himself better or apologize for the misbehavior. Naturally, the time-out procedure begins again if misconduct reoccurs.

6. Some residential homes have a policy of letting an adult sit in the same time-out room with the child but not speak or attend to him for a prescribed period of time. The attendant or child-care worker may read, perhaps, but will not permit the child self-mutilation or a sense of total isolation that is very upsetting to psychotic children. In this case of mild deprivation, the worker may decide when the child is calm enough to return to the classroom or activity.

7. Separate children who are seen to be fighting. A teacher's neutrality might be interpreted by parents as irresponsibility or approval of the aggression. If one or both children are hurt, the school personnel might be held responsible.

8. Redl's Life Space Interview might be used by a trained classroom teacher or a crisis counselor, if one is available. This person needs special training in crisis intervention, the acceptance of other school personnel, especially the administrator, and a private facility in which to counsel children who can trust him or her. Most children need an individual to whom they can complain and hear "my side of the story," and a crisis counselor can offer this cathartic experience. Only after anger subsides can the child become more reasonable and constructive and then perhaps see his or her own contribution to the difficulty that preceded the crisis.

9. To calm down two aggressive children in conflict in the

classroom, the two fighters are each given a damp rag to wash the opposite sides of a pane of glass on a classroom door. The children must face each other and be in view of the teacher. The teacher's instructions are, "Please wash the same window pane. The loser of the fight is the one who laughs, smiles, or giggles first. Please keep looking at the other fellow to be sure that he doesn't laugh first." Laughter follows as well as renewed friendship.

10. Allow the child to displace hostility onto neutral objects by channeling aggression through the use of punching bags, tetherballs, clay, gym mats, or perhaps drawing. Others may respond well to boxing or self-defense lessons at the "Y" or local Boy's Club.

11. In-school suspension might be used rather than suspending the child for a number of days by having regular work and school assignments in another school room alone. This requires parental understanding and approval. If necessary, employ a school monitor at the parents' expense to supervise the child's isolation in the work room at school. The child brings his lunch and does not interact with any other students or teachers; then he has his daily accomplishments checked by his teachers before afternoon dismissal. One teenager testified, "I learned more schoolwork in those five days than I did all semester long. I studied instead of just sitting around."

12. Include the child in a well-supervised, small play group. In this arrangement, it is easier to communicate more appropriate ways of relating to peers than by releasing aggression, grabbing, fighting, cursing, etc. In this circumstance the teacher, teacher aide, or counselor may actually teach the child how to cooperate, share, take turns, and be helpful as these rudimentary kindly behaviors may not be firmly in the repertoire of the child due to his impoverished social background or related circumstances.

13. Do not require or insist the child do an academic task at which he is very poor. This makes him feel inadequate and frustrated and is very likely to produce aggression. The academic lesson must then be offered at a lower level where he can feel successful. When a child is "over his head," tension is created and

it is often released by crying, withdrawing, or some antisocial act.

14. An aggressive child probably needs a firm but caring teacher and preferably a highly structured program where limits are clear and expectations are well understood by the child. Ordinarily the teacher and the children have set up a clear set of rules and regulations and the teacher is also ready to respond behaviorally with a set of appropriate rewards for self-control, work accomplished, acts of kindliness between students, etc.

15. The teacher must reward particular children for acceptable, nonaggressive behavior for a set period of time, such as 5 or 10 minutes, and later for longer periods using specific and perhaps tangible rewards which are desirable to the child. Most school psychologists can organize a reinforcement menu varying from social approval to a point system to primary reinforcements dealing with candy or special treats. In all cases, the child should have some options wherein he may elect certain rewards on certain days for appropriate behavior.

16. If at all possible the teacher should be very consistent in ignoring mildly aggressive behavior, otherwise it may become inadvertently reinforced. Much of the work on behavior modification has found that simple attention to destructive and aggressive children is highly reinforcing and tends to prolong the inappropriate behavior when a continuous ignoring of this response tends to minimize if not extinguish it.

17. The aggressive child usually has a low frustration tolerance and finds it difficult to change set quickly. He will need more time and preparation before shifting to a new activity. In this case, the teacher should give plenty of warning prior to changing to a new project, subject, or activity.

18. Avoid punishment in controlling aggression: Spanking, hitting, shaking, and strong reprimands are included here. The problem with physical punishment is that it produces more anger in the child (although it terrifies some) and the child is then even more likely to discharge this anger elsewhere especially since it has been modeled for him by the teacher. Spanking children in school provokes counter-aggression, as can be seen by vandalism around the schools, breaking of equipment, and the creation of chaos for children who have been physically abused by teachers or

administrators. Obviously the teacher must intervene if the child is striking the teacher or some other child or liable to injure himself in a emotional outburst.

19. As a derivative of Maslow's Need-Motivation theory, teaching personnel will try to satisfy in the classroom setting the basic psychological needs of aggressive children. In particular, is the child striving for attention, approval, recognition, or a sense of accomplishment? The teacher must create classroom conditions to satisfy the unmet needs as much as possible before aggression will diminish. She herself is the primary source of psychological satisfaction during the school hours for the child's need for attention and approval. It is relatively easy to be approving of the excellent students, but it must be recalled that inefficient and aggressive students also need recognition and attention when they are well-controlled and achieving, even if only during part of the day. Each child will require different levels of satisfaction for the psychological needs, but those with emotional problems or special limitations will need a more concentrated effort. A rule-of-thumb is to offer twice as much attention and approval, when earned, to these handicapped students as to a regular student who is achieving successfully.

20. In the classroom allow an extra free-play or recess for the purpose of releasing tensions and pent-up energy, especially if previous lessons have been difficult or demanding. The mere presence of a calm adult often has a quieting or controlling effect upon a child who is upset or potentially disturbing. Occasionally it helps just to touch a child to let him know that the teacher is still interested as long as he is nonaggressive.

21. Try to find out whom the child strongly identifies with at a national or world level in sports, the media, etc. This can be capitalized upon if the child should act out or become aggressive. A question then to him could be, "So and so wouldn't do that, would he?" Pointing out the strong points of this adult whom the child admires and is trying to emulate would also be important. This tries to use constructively the value system of the child to help him control his own behavior.

22. For violently aggressive, disruptive children who have a pattern of increasing difficulty, refer for psychological and

psychiatric evaluation prior to possible institutionalization, court commitment, or residential placement. Some children need commitment, either to avoid a psychotic break or to provide an all-encompassing treatment program. For a great variety of therapeutic programs, some are extremely effective over a relatively brief period of time, namely a month or two. In other circumstances, a sensible behavior modification treatment, using modeling and behavioral systems may be essential to change an inappropriate behavior. Children with extremely deviant behavior frequently cannot be contained full-time in the public schools. The children under the care of a therapist or social agency, the teacher may request a visit from this therapist to obtain a broader perspective of the child's problems or obtain ideas on managing him in the class. Parental consent is essential here and if the therapist cannot be free to travel, then school personnel may visit the agency or therapist.

23. Occasionally an aggressive episode will result because one child inadvertently bumps, gets in the way of another child, or upsets a project. When this does happen in school, it often helps for the teacher to reinterpret the situation to the children involved. The teacher should separate the angered children and calmly explain the realities of the situation, usually indicating that no one specifically can be blamed. This amounts to reinterpreting what actually led up to the aggressive discharge and keeps everyone reality-oriented.

24. It is well known that children who have aggressive outbursts will be less inclined to do so if they have an especially good relationship with the teacher or counselor in the school setting. It seems reasonable to suggest that the teacher should actively try to build a very good relationship with the aggressive child and use this as a lever to control his aggression. Eventually the teacher's approval or disapproval will be important to the child and he can be controlled better with statements like, "It would make me very proud of you if you would not hit so and so," rather than yell at the child and punish him.

25. In extreme cases of severely disruptive and aggressive behavior, the school administrator may shorten the length of the school day for the offending child or consider having him attend

on alternate days or possibly for only a part of a morning. Naturally the parents' cooperation is essential and there has to be approval by the clinical staff for this informal measure. In order not to violate school law, the child may have to be tutored for say one hour at home in the afternoon if he only attends morning classes, but the end result is that he may seek to control his own behavior so that he can return later.

26. For an aggressive intolerable child who swears at or strikes the teacher or disregards her reasonable rules in instructions, it seems reasonable to have the administrator place him with another teacher who perhaps has more patience, better controls, or the chance of a better relationship. This is not necessarily "passing the buck," as it is well known that certain teachers are excellent with some children and not others.

27. In other emergencies the school personnel may have to file a charge of school incorrigibility on the child in Juvenile Court requesting assistance if the child is unable to control aggression. Naturally many other procedures and steps have preceded this drastic event, but occasionally it is necessary. Usually it indicates the child is extremely resistant and stubborn and this may be a symptom of an impending psychological breakdown of the child.

28. It is not unusual to find that the child's aggression may stem partly from defensiveness about academic inferiority. Since this is likely true in most cases, school staff will want to offer remedial reading, special instruction in math, individual sessions with the school social worker to express difficulties in feelings and perhaps consider resource-room tutoring, home tutoring, a buddy system, and any other method for helping the child gain academic and personal confidence.

29. Provide for periodic release of tension or the need for physical movement through "helper" activities: Book or paper distribution, window shade adjustment, errands, helping others, picking up floor scraps, etc.

30. Use regular, private conferences in school to discuss the child's need for self-control and give full recognition when this appears from time to time. This opportunity can be used to discuss academic progress, homework, etc., and can be an integrating experience for the child to let him know of his

development and the places that continue to need work.

31. The teacher may construct a small badge to be earned for excellent behavior in cooperation. Perhaps it can read "King for a Day" or "Queen for a Day" or some special recognition displaying the child's unique qualities on that day. Other variations that are behaviorally oriented include various point systems, checks, tokens, or other systematic ways of recording appropriate behavior for specific periods of time and then allowing the children to "cash in" on their points for specific rewards.

32. Let the child sit next to someone who is larger and more mature than he and who will encourage his friendship and self-control.

33. Where clashes of groups are involved, hold small-group discussions with these students led by a school psychologist, counselor, or social worker. The goals of these sessions should include mutual recognition of problems, self-awareness, and possible solutions to difficulties within the school framework. Difficulties in the neighborhood and gang problems might be aided better by trained workers from the community and local agencies. In order to reduce the intensity or frequency of a child's attacks upon smaller children, require him to play with older and less vulnerable children on the playground.

Considerations for Parents

34. Counseling or family therapy is recommended for parents regarding child-management practices through the aid of the social work agencies, local medical facilities, or private therapists noted in the telephone yellow pages.

35. For relatively mild management problems at home, behavioral approaches are frequently quite useful. These can be obtained through a relatively brief number of sessions with a behavior therapist or in consultation with the local school psychologist, if appropriately trained. Such rebellious behavior almost inevitably is displayed in the school circumstance. It is legitimate for the school psychologist to monitor the child's behavior at home and offer direct consultation to the family members.

36. In conjunction with teaching personnel, the parents may also use a nonrewarding time-out room at home where, after aggressive behavior reappears with consistency, the child should be sent until he decides to control himself well enough to return in a cooperative demeanor. As with the previous limitations, this isolation should not exceed perhaps fifteen or twenty minutes for an older child and when that time is up and the child is calm, he may discuss his feelings and attitudes with the parent and offer some constructive suggestions for better self-control in the future. If the child is still angry after the initial twenty minutes, he is to return back and to stay in the isolating room again. This room should not have a television, set of games, or be enjoyable but might perhaps best be arranged with a seat in the corner without any kind of distracting activities during the isolating period. If the child refuses to enter the isolation room, he can be assured that further deprivations regarding weekend activities may be available if he does not cooperate.

37. If the child is impulsive and aggressive, let the parents refer him to his pediatrician to be evaluated for other medical disorders and to rule out if medication is a possibility.

38. Should aggressive behavior be obviously destructive for a considerable period of time, the parents are recommended to have the child receive a complete psychoeducational evaluation in addition to a medical evaluation. There are a great number of causes of aggression, and in certain cases, each one must be ruled out. These may encompass problems in visual perception, biological dysfunctions, endocrine malfunctions, hearing disorders, sibling rivalry, undue expectations from parents, forms of passive-aggressive behavior, reactions against childhood depression, etc. Only after a comprehensive study can a general pattern of causes be understood, thereby promoting specific therapeutic interventions at the source of those difficulties. Conceivably, behavioral approaches may equally be effective even though contributing causes may remain unknown.

39. For an extremely aggressive child, sports requiring greater passivity may be encouraged: Fishing, archery, golf, etc., which are self-competitive in the main.

40. Occasionally, at an unconscious level, parents may have

directly or indirectly rewarded their child for his aggressive behavior. Parents may have unwittingly telegraphed their approval of aggressive activities or at least acted in a neutral fashion. Sometimes children act out the controlled aggressive wishes of parents toward disliked neighbors' children, children of different nationalities, races or religions, which reflects back to their own unhealthy value systems. Sometimes this insight on the part of the parents gets them into action to help retrain their child in these areas, but the problems are usually more fundamental and difficult to change.

41. The parents should be made aware of the student's aggressive behaviors and indiscretions by way of the school authorities. In such a conference both the parents and student and school personnel should be present and likely include the school psychologist and counselor. It may be recommended that a "therapeutic expulsion" be attempted providing that this is within the guidelines of the state law. In this case, the child is expelled from school for perhaps three days, but he must keep the same hours at home in academic work as if he were in school. The parents are given his school schedule and assignments and the student works on these at home and gets the same time as his class does. Understandably, he gets the same lunch break and cannot play outside until the usual time that school ends. No television allowed and it is regarded essentially a "work experience." After three days of this at home, monitored by a parent or older sibling, the child is usually eager to return to school with some better internal controls and some desire to avoid a repetition of the strenuous event.

Antagonisms to Peers, Parents, Authority, and Siblings

42. Refer the child and parents for psychological evaluation.

43. Reinforce positively all nonantagonistic behavior with concrete reinforcements, while gradually pairing these with abstract social reinforcers like praise and recognition.

44. Place the child in play therapy or group therapy according to age.

45. Use sociometric devices to place the child in seating arrangements near his friends rather than those to whom he is

antagonistic.

46. If the child's home situation is not conducive to the development of a healthy self-esteem, then by default the school will have to take over the function of enhancing the child's belief in himself. The teacher should give approval for as many of the child's desirable acts as possible. A child's positive self-image can develop only out of the knowledge that he can behave in a socially acceptable way which others, particularly adults, regard as worthwhile and valuable. Unfortunately, desirable behavior is undramatic by comparison with hostile, acting-out behavior. As a consequence, desirable behavior may go unnoticed: coming in on time, sitting quietly, opening a book promptly, standing in line quietly, answering a question. All such undramatic but desirable acts deserve approval. All too often the overburdened teacher has little time for congratulating the child for doing what polite children do without a second thought. The attentive teacher can always find some desirable behavior to reinforce.

47. Keep rivalrous siblings at home separated as much as possible at the dinner table, during T.V. watching or homework, and offer them different play areas and possibly different bedrooms. Help them draw up rules that afford privacy at times and stress the fact that possessions must not be touched except by permission of the owner.

48. Parents can be taught to ignore certain aggressive behaviors and to reward positive behavior. Whenever the youngster involves himself in satisfactory play, the parents may then provide a social reinforcer such as praise, touching the youngster, or just talking with him. A point system with specific, much-desired objects as incentives might also be initiated.

49. A reward system might include monetary reward for approved social conduct. For example, a child might be given, say, $3.00 at the start of a new schedule. He is told that he will earn money for each day without fighting or abusive behavior, but that he will have subtracted $.25 for each fight. The child should work toward some specific gift or object.

50. Provide the child with pleasurable experiences with his peer group: going with them to the circus, roller coaster rides, carnivals, movies and parties, so that pleasure and thrills may

become associated with friends.

51. If antagonism is due to feelings of inferiority or fear of competition, then permit the child to play with less threatening and younger neighborhood children, but in and around homes where parents may intervene if child becomes too dominating or aggressive.

52. The parents should hold limits on only major issues, not countless minor ones. Avoid direct confrontation with the child when possible. If the child may be emulating one parent who is, in fact, antagonistic and aggressive, the parent should be so informed. The parents may reinforce their child's antagonistic and aggressive behavior because they feel that way toward people even though they are adults and "should know better."

53. If antagonism results from a behavioral pattern that was effectively reinforced by indulgent parents, teach the parents how to extinguish this by nonreinforcing the unacceptable behavior on their part and the child's. Tell them that the child will learn to control himself only as well as they require him to become self-controlled. They must serve as consistent models.

54. The parents should make a clear effort to show the antagnostic child a considerable amount of love, interest, and attention to reduce sibling rivalry. The antagonistic child sometimes feels cheated in his love relationships. Convince the child by acts of kindness and care that he is mistaken.

Cruelty to Peers and Animals

55. Teachers should closely supervise the child who is thought to be cruel and should intervene without getting upset at the child's acts. Always inform the parents and the local school psychologist or guidance staff when a pattern of cruelty is noted. Be specific to the child about the acceptable behavior you expect. Often such cruelty is displaced aggression which might have been given toward a sibling whom the child feels is more favored than he.

56. Remove the child from the object of cruelty. Substitute a doll, toy soldiers or toy objects for the real objects. Accept the expressions of cruelty toward these inanimate things. The cruelty, at least for the moment, will not be extinguished, but its

consequences will be far less dramatic.

57. Cruelty is often symptomatic of a more severe behavior disturbance and may be associated with other acts of destruction. Refer the child for complete diagnostic evaluation.

58. If a boy's cruelty may stem from a desire to show he is masculine, provide him with many approved masculine activities, especially through his father: vigorous games, body-contact sports, riding, scouting, and so on. The boy's maladapted behavior may be a way of "acting tough" and trying to emulate male behavior in his family. Both parents should show clearly their disapproval of his cruelty, but show their affection and regard for him in many other ways that parents often take for granted.

59. Cruelty to animals may be a sign of deep emotional dissatisfaction with the child himself or with certain love relationships. Psychotherapy may be necessary especially in late adolescence where cruelty may well be based on a sexual maladjustment. The choice of psychotherapeutic treatment will depend upon age, parental support, etc.

Destructiveness to Property, Games, and Toys

60. The teacher should remove the child from the class for a 10-minute "vacation" when she perceives an emotional explosion coming on. Perhaps the child can go on an errand, be sent to the washroom, or check on some supplies, so that emotional outbursts are deterred.

61. When destruction of property involves more than trivia, the local juvenile court authorities should be notified, especially if there is an obvious and continuing pattern. Giving the child a sentimental "one more chance" after a serious incident may well provide him with more reinforcement to be destructive again. The authorities may have extensive facilities to provide comprehensive evaluation of the entire situation, and their intervention may prevent more problems.

Fighting Excessively in School and Neighborhood

62. For excessive fighting the psychological staff at the school

should attempt to discover the particular reason for the child's fighting and obviously try to reduce that direct cause. The teacher or counselor may ask the student to talk about his feelings and try to discover other ways to solve the problem. Discuss with the child the consequences of future fighting: detentions, the rejection of classmates, or the withdrawal of certain privileges important for the child. Follow through emphatically on the next episode.

63. The teacher should set a rule such as, "No hitting in the classroom," and every time a child attempts to hit another, she should ask, "What's the rule?," and have the child repeat the rule verbally. If the teacher is absolutely consistent in this approach, hitting may gradually decrease because the child has been given a mental reminder to control himself.

64. A "cooling-off" period following blowups is often highly desirable. This time may be spent in some isolated spot such as the school clinic or at home. Following the episode, the teacher should not cast blame upon the child, but permit him to continue in the classroom activities so long as he can behave appropriately and not disturb others.

65. For an aggressive, emotionally explosive child, be certain that he gets only one clear instruction at a time. Such children may need reassurance by the teacher often after the completion of each instruction until they are calm enough to extend their activities for more than one instruction.

66. For some children their violent, aggressive behavior is an alternative to blatant psychotic adjustment. In this sense, the child has "decided" to be "bad rather than mad." Depending on the circumstances:

    a. Some such children should be discharged from school, via proper legal procedures, since they are disruptive beyond reasonable control and are a danger to themselves and others. They are then recommended for clinical evaluation for possible residential treatment.

    b. Others can be handled in school by assigning them to a Big Brother in the school program or a guidance counselor, a positive identification figure who cares and gives of himself. The counselor, conceivably, can be an ombudsman of the child in school to explain his circumstances to authority figures and teachers. Understandably, the school can only tolerate a certain degree of this kind of misbehavior.

c. Group therapy in the school might be instituted to help the child feel more secure. Here at least he is accepted at his level, primitive though it may be. This presumes that the professional staff have training in group therapy and take the responsibility for the sensitive procedures involved.

d. Family counseling by the school psychologist, social worker, etc., is recommended because it may coax the problem back where it originally belonged—to the family conflict and remove it from the school stage upon which it has been displaced.

67. Refer the child for a neurological and psychological evaluation to determine that his aggressive behavior is due in part to neurological dysfunction, emotional pressures, or both. The teacher with a child like this in her class for the first time should discuss his behavior with previous teachers to obtain some historical prospective of the problems' duration and intensity. Under what past conditions did the child become aggressive; and what were the more favorable conditions for change, including what strategies may have been effective previously? She may also observe the child's behavior by keeping short anecdotal records of incentives to aggressive behavior and noting what stimuli triggered the reaction. She will certainly wish to revise the academic program to suit the child's current level of functioning and reward him for academic progress and self-control.

68. Assign antagonistic children to different recess and lunch periods if at all possible.

69. Inform the parents that continued fighting will not be tolerated at school and that they should consider deprivation of certain privileges if the child persists. The teacher will wish to inform the parents by telephone at recurring events. If one parent is obviously deriving pleasure from the child's success in fighting and may be tacitly reinforcing an approval of this behavior, then

referral to the school psychologist should be acted upon and possibly an agency referral for parent counseling as well.

70. Often a child like this is struggling to make some identification for himself, perhaps to adapt to some real or imagined inferiority. Can he be encouraged to join organizations like the Scouts, the YMCA, a boxing club, active church groups, or competitive sports? Perhaps there he will have an opportunity to develop a sense of pride and identity and earn a more positive reputation. Could he be placed on the safety patrol or as an escort to school visitors?

71. Execute a sociogram in the classroom so that the aggressive child is seated with and surrounded by his friends. Another possiblity is to have the child seated directly in front of the teachers so that supervision is immediate and within arm's reach. A behavioral variation with a sociometric basis is that the child may "earn" some time in class to sit next to his friends if he is better controlled for a period of time. The child is permitted to whisper quietly when he is with his friends; but if he gets out of hand, this privilege is taken away for the rest of the day.

72. The teacher may ask some of her most mature pupils to make friends with the child who fights a great deal. Sometimes children who are lonely will actually welcome the responsiveness of other children and will diminish their fighting activity in direct relationship to the number of friendships that they can make.

73. The parents must both make it very clear to the child that neither parent condones fighting. They must certainly listen to the child's excuses for fighting and be sure the child is not being picked upon by older children, fighting in self-defense, or is involved in some sort of gang retaliation. The parents should try to understand why the child is fighting and be certain they ask him about it and what situations lead up to it. They might begin to suggest a series of alternatives when the boy starts to find himself getting very angry and provoked at others. In this sense, they might teach him to return home when he feels extremely angry or to offer him a reward every time they observe that he has controlled his temper and not fought.

74. If it is a girl who is fighting excessively, perhaps she is

manifesting "tomboy" symptoms and for rather subtle reasons is trying to identify with the male sex, perhaps to attract the attention of her father. Sometimes this occurs if she is the oldest of the daughters in the family where there are no sons. In this case, the crucial relationship is the one between the father and the daughter. He must begin to respond to her by accepting her femininity rather than overvaluing the masculine value system which she should not attempt to emulate. This man must become quite involved with his daughter's activities and must demonstrate that there are two relatively different but overlapping sets of behaviors for males and females in our culture and that both are equal and worthwhile. Most likely she needs a good deal of his attention for her nonfighting behavior, although he will want to approve of her desire generally to compete and achieve but channel it in more constructive areas. The clinician might also investigate if the mother is militant and modeling this behavior for her daughter. Each case obviously must be handled individually.

Homicidal Behavior, Violence Prone, Uses Weapons

75. In situations where a child is homicidal, this calls for immediate referral to a child guidance clinic. It should also come to the attention of the juvenile authorities because there are some complicated legal procedures and definitions of deliquency that must be considered. If school authorities observe homicidal tendencies, their function is to report this to the diagnostic staff immediately and, of course, to inform the parents of the precise details.

76. If the potentially homicidal child uses or possesses weapons in school, such as a gun, rifle, or knife, the school authorities must attempt to remove these from him. If the child refuses to relinquish a weapon, then the police should be called. The parents must be informed of this event and an extensive diagnostic evaluation should be made to determine why the child feels this type of weapon is necessary even for his defense or his aggression. Sometimes such out-of-control behavior may be a symptom of a deeper psychosis, while at other times it may have

started out to be a harmless and thoughtless prank that had no vicious intent.

Verbally Aggressive, Ridicules Others

77. If the child is annoying in class, send him to a time-out room or a private cubicle in the classroom where others cannot observe him. When he thinks he can control his annoying behavior, laughter, etc., he may rejoin the group. However, if he soon forgets and is again annoying, send him once more from the group, but this time he must wait until the teacher says he may join. He will not take many such sessions before he can exercise self-control by a look from the teacher as a reminder.

78. If the child has a sense of inferiority, ridicules and abuses others, the teacher should develop ego-building activities for him such as: special privileges, special errands, the choice of desired activities, release time for play, etc., that will enhance the teacher-child relationship as well as make school a more pleasant place to be. The teacher, in addition to being friendly, must make it very clear she will not tolerate repeated incidences of this kind and may have to deprive him of these granted privileges if he is unwilling to control himself in the future. Offenses after this may lead to temporary loss of a favorite seat in the classroom, an opportunity to deliver messages for the teacher, the deprivation of certain playtime activities, until the child realizes very clearly that the teacher is firm and earnest. Reinstate privileges for approved behavior.

79. The teacher may suggest role-playing activities for the child who is overly aggressive or who ridicules and abuses others. Such a child may have to play the role of a recipient of abuse so that he may perceive the feelings of others. The child may thereby learn something about his own aggressive behavior as being damaging to the self-concepts of others. Then the teacher may change places in role-playing and he may become the ridiculing child so that the teacher can express her feelings of defeat and inferiority. This may be done on numerous occasions generally with the class as well as the child so that all of them begin to learn how it is to feel badly when someone else ridicules, makes fun, or name-calls.

80. Record on tape for therapeutic purposes the youngster's aggressive, abusive speech when he is not aware of the fact of being so monitored. Play it back to him privately where his teacher or counselor can discuss his actions with him. Oftentimes the children are not aware of how they sound, and on occasion they even deny their own voices, comments, etc., when recorded only moments ago. Some aggressive children reject seeing the videotapes of their own behavior. Hearing themselves in action, however, can be a positive learning experience for them.

81. Although it may be a long-standing practice approved by the layman, the decision to let two boys "fight it out" in a boxing match even under supervision is actually very unwise. In the first place one of the children may become seriously injured and a lawsuit may follow. In the second place, the practice does not channel aggression, it enhances it, provokes more, and escalates later into, possibly, gang reprisals. Thirdly, the boys may learn, T.V. style, that problems are solved by physical aggression rather than by verbal reasoning, and that "might makes right," a totally erroneous conclusion except in the jungle. Lastly, it is often impossible to match with approximate equality the strength and skill of the boys involved. Naturally further divisions of friendship occur among the boys' respective friends and parents.

82. Parents who find their child to be verbally aggressive must first of all recognize that they themselves may unwittingly have contributed to the problem if they are verbally aggressive. Parents may need to communicate with social workers, psychologists, guidance counselors, etc., in order to understand their own children or people they themselves dislike. Children learn the techniques of the parents. The parents must basically offer excellent models for the child to follow.

SECTION B: AGGRESSIVE BEHAVIOR— INTERNALLY DIRECTED

Accident Prone

83. Children who have been diagnosed as accident-prone may have two relatively separate causes for this. On one hand, the

accident-prone child may (a) actually be a child with some type of vertigo resulting from an injury to the balance mechanisms in the inner ear or relating to minor brain injury, or (b) be psychologically maladjusted so that he seeks to injure himself. If the child has poor coordination and balance, as verified by a neurologist, then he may need to be restricted in his physical activities, recess, and travel in and out of the classroom if a physician so recommends. If the accident-proneness stems from some petit mal epileptic condition, where medication has been required, the parents would be informed by the teacher of these continuing "spells" or minor seizures so that the physician may be alerted. On the other hand, if there is a psychological difficulty involved without an organic basis, very likely the teacher and clinical staff would wish to encourage the child and parents to enter a treatment program to determine the causes of the child's difficulty.

84. The child's play activity must be supervised especially in physical education and recess in school. This might include eliminating him from trampoline activities, climbing up the monkey bars, and being involved in "dare" activities with other children. Tell the child and the parents of those restrictive plans.

85. Give cautions to the child in a positive rather than a negative manner: "Hold on to that carefully," rather than, "Don't drop it."

86. For the parents of an accident-prone child, the diagnostic staff should investigate etiological and contributory factors. This may also require psychotherapy dealing with the child's self-concept and his apparent need to injure himself. Often, this is a highly guilt-ridden child who feels the need to be punished for some real or imagined "crime or sin" in the past. It is not at all unusual for this motivation to be unconscious, and may only reveal itself in symptomatic behavior, the dream life, or projective testing. The parents, nonetheless, should recognize their responsibilities to remove dangers and risk circumstances from the life of the child. There are many kinds of sports and activities, of course, in which the child can participate that involve little or no danger.

87. If the child who is suspected as accident-prone is sixteen years or over (depending on state law), it is highly recommended

that the child not be permitted to obtain a driver's license. Adolescents with this difficulty should not be required or asked to do home repairs that are risky, especially on ladders. They should have continuous supervision at home. Often these children unconsciously hate themselves and as such continue to inflict bodily injury as a way of reducing guilt feelings. The child does not "grow out of it" by himself, but must receive the intervening help of a professional therapist. This is especially true if there have been dramatic events in the child's life where he feels somehow responsible for the death of a parent, sibling, or pet. Sometimes these children feel excessively guilty about relatively normal thoughts of aggression.

Masochistic, Inflicts Self-Injury, Self-Mutilating

88. If the medical diagnosis in self-mutilation is the Lesch-Nyham Syndrome, the prognosis is extremely poor and the biting behavior is apparently genetically set as irresistible and sex-linked for males only (females are carriers). Uremic poisoning is involved with the kidneys and needs constant medical treatment throughout life. Mental retardation, frequent spasticity, and clear developmental delay in all areas of functioning are also present in practically all cases as a result of brain damage that is irreversible. Since the self-mutilation frequently involves biting off of skin from the hands, the ends of the fingers, and skin off forearms, then splint-sleeves can be placed around the child's arms above the wrist and a few inches from the shoulder to prevent these body portions from reaching the teeth. Some flexibility in the arms permits hand activity for school work and play. Sometimes when the children are upset they will request that the sleeves be put on. Some children have had to have their teeth removed to prevent continual biting off of lips and tongue. Helmets are also used and padded wheel-chairs are required, as part of the child's behavior involves severe head-banging and injury. Adolescents with this condition are very anxious about biting themselves and sometimes sit on their own hands. Few live beyond early adult life due to kidney failure. Some behavior modification programs including extinction plus reinforcement-for-quiet-behavior have been helpful in reducing the destructive

behavior.

89. Head-banging and similar masochistic behavior is best approached through behavior modification principles and the results frequently involve some combination of the three possibilities noted below:

    a. Although it is virtually impossible for a staff or parent to tolerate head-banging behavior, it has been experimentally demonstrated that head-banging will extinguish itself if the child is completely permitted to execute this by himself with padded circumstances around a wheelchair, crib, mat, etc. It is very difficult for adults or other children not to interfere and try to stop the child. This does result in bruises to the forehead and sometimes bleeding; but in a period of time, perhaps weeks or a couple of months, this finally does extinguish, possibly forever. There are indications of spontaneous recovery, unfortunately, and this reoccurrence is much less severe and extinguishes even more rapidly as predicted by behavioral theoretical considerations. A second approach deals with rewarding the child in a variety of ways when he is not head-banging. This clearly means that the child must be rewarded usually in very primary ways in addition to touching and words of encouragement when the child is not banging. This means that the individual adult must look away and be noninterfering when the child starts banging his head again. The last approach deals with mild shock, which usually is only done in certain residential treatment programs and only with the full understanding and agreement of the parents and the approval under state law for therapeutic intervention.

    b. For infants and very young children who head-bang in the crib, sometimes this is merely self-stimulating behavior involved with rocking and movement, which is a substitute for the mother's physical presence. Some of these children have been neglected by their mothers due to the adult's illness or temporary separation and the child stimulates himself in a substitution behavior for the mother. The return of the mother and considerable affection often minimizes the bed-rocking behavior.

90. In a residential treatment setting, the teachers and house parents or child-care workers should execute, under the supervision of a psychologist, an operant conditioning program where non-masochistic behavior is rewarded, while masochistic or mutilating behavior is punished by withdrawal of prized privileges.

91. The self-destructive, mutilating individual generally is guilt-ridden and has a negative self-image. This person needs to feel good about himself and needs to hear that others respect him and admire him for the positive traits he possesses. The person is often blind to his own strong points or is unwilling to value them. He must be told often what they are and repeat them himself.

92. As in the circumstances dealing with masochism and suicidal tendencies, children manifesting self-destructive behavior usually require psychotherapeutic intervention and residential placement for twenty-four hour supervision. These children usually cannot be helped sufficiently in the public schools and there is no point in placing such a child in a class for mostly disturbed pupils in the schools because it is far too superficial a treatment. Children who mutilate themselves of course must receive medical attention for their injuries and must have their rooms at home inspected to remove potentially mutilating instruments. Of course all guns, kitchen knives, and the like should be made totally unavailable to these children. Since these adjustments are so difficult, it is obvious why residential treatment is recommended rather than mere parental supervision.

Suicide, Attempted or Suspected

93. A suicidal threat or statement by a child should never be taken lightly, laughed at, or dismissed because it seems preposterous or too frightening to consider. If the child discusses suicide as an "attention getting device," then it is extremely wise to give this clinical attention if the child is so desperate to use this ploy.

Contact clinic personnel. Suicide prevention services may be telephoned.

94. Establish a relationship with the individual that allows a telephone call or visitation by the teacher at the time of crisis or despondent condition.

95. A frequent cause of suicidal feelings is suppressed anger toward self. If a student comes to a teacher feeling very depressed and possibly somewhat inarticulate about what has affected him, try to get him to tell everything that happened in the last twenty-four hours. Maybe he can recall the incident that made him angry and what triggered off his suicidal feelings.

96. Always tell the parents when dealing with a potential suicidal child even if he wishes his private thoughts and plans to be confidential. Urge them to face the problem without panic, not to get angry with the child, or make him feel more stupid or guilty. Make every attempt to obtain the child's permission for this sharing of information. Obtain clinical evaluation.

97. Many of these children have extremely poor self-concepts, are in states of deep depression, and in some cases, view the environment as hostile and nonrewarding. These are children who often feel that the world has nothing to offer them except pain, agony, and possible desertion. They are oftentimes children who have extremely poor relationships with one or more parents to whom they would like to feel very close. Children who are suicidal cannot be "talked out of it" permanently by parents or teachers, since few of these people have had the training to comprehend the depth of depression and great feelings of foreboding and anxiety that prevail within the child. If the child like this stays at home, he should be receiving frequent psycho-therapy locally with continual supervision all hours of the day.

98. The child who is depressed is frequently undergoing a normal reaction to the loss of a loved object; this is frequently the death of a parent, girlfriend or boyfriend, or some close relative. Depression is expected to occur in our society and, in fact, if the individual does not become despondent and tries to deny this, then the period of mourning becomes even more lengthened. The individual child is encouraged to cry, talk about the terrible loss involved, and be permitted to stay an unhappy person until the

mourning period is over. The effect of the loss of a loved parent may of course last a lifetime but in diminishing degrees. Often within several months the depressed child who has contemplated suicide begins to focus on the present and future circumstances and begins to put the dreadful loss behind him. Sometimes children who consider suicide do so in a mystical way to "rejoin" the loved parent. Sometimes children who are suicidal do so to force the parents into some show of affection because they have felt desperately rejected. Cases regarding potential suicide always require therapeutic intervention.

Chapter V

ANTISOCIAL AND OPPOSITIONAL BEHAVIOR

S UCH BEHAVIORS ARE found at all age-levels and reflect a destruction and malfunction in social relationships of a rather visible variety. Particular references to antisocial behavior are characterized by force, nonconformity, and the destruction of property, in addition to devious and evasive actions which are more covert and less easily observed. Oppositional behavior, by some contrast, is characterized generally by passive-aggressive styles, resistance, stubbornness, rebelliousness, and disobedience in school and home. Although many children overtly resist rules and structure as well as ignore external controls, others are more subtle in their rebellion and are often unaware of their self-defeating and unproductive styles, thereby infuriating adults.

The causes of these behaviors sometimes stem from confused or destructive relationships between parents and children or teachers and children in the series of nonreinforcing contacts. Resistant behaviors in the child may diminish to the degree that these relationships change in a constructive and compatible direction, among other considerations.

A multitude of complaints lodged about children settle in this general problem area since it is here where the symptoms of conflict appear so readily. Schoolwork and social relationships, two main areas of potential confrontation, reveal where children often manifest serious problems which simply cannot be ignored. Although adults may be worried about underachievement in a global sense, their specific concerns may also be about the child's resistance to learn, his social ineffectiveness, the lack of motivation to achieve academically, and his strained relationships with those closest to him. For detailed case histories and their treatment regarding these behaviors, the reader is referred to *Case Studies in Clinical and School Psychology* (Blanco and Rosenfeld, 1978).

The following prescriptions pertinent to these aggressive behaviors compromise a gamut of ideas which may be effective only to the extent that they are appropriate to the unique child and his circumstance. The concepts refer to children who need assistance but who frequently are too hurt or angry either to. request or accept such help. A theme within the treatment considerations hint broadly that society and school personel inadvertently induce and foster some of the child's problems, whereas in other circumstances, the sources and reinforcement of such behaviors clearly arise from the home conditions, deprivation, anger, and conflict. Such treatments require not only careful thought and diagnostic appraisal, but very careful implementation, since they often deal simultaneously with modifying the overt behavior of adults as well as the children in question.

SECTION A: ANTISOCIAL BEHAVIOR

1. Before recommending that the child and parents consider counseling services, first obtain some grasp of their value system, social class problems, ethnic or minority status, etc. Perhaps the child is acting in a way compatible with his family or neighborhood system.

2. Confront the child in every situation where he is clearly violating school rules. Do not let him believe that the rules are for everyone but him.

3. A child who shows no empathy for others and lacks awareness that social rules apply to him may have learned such behavior from parental example or be overreacting against their pressures for perfect behavior beyond his years. Thus parental involvement in family therapy seems necessary to bring about lasting changes in a child's attitude and conduct.

4. For a child whose basic cause for antisocial behavior is strong parental rejection, it would appear that the best hope for

relief of the problems might be his placement outside of the home. This is often a very superficial solution that is almost impossible to execute unless there is flagrant child abuse. Although one might seek placement out of the home, it is very difficult to actualize inasmuch as friends and neighbors are often busy with their own difficulties and cannot be helpful even in a crisis.

Cheating in School and Games

5. Remove the pressures for cheating: grades, perfectionistic demands, social humiliation, excessive teacher aspirations. Tests in school should be used diagnostically to determine where more instruction is needed, not how worthwhile a child is. Cheating is often bred from fear which in itself is a poor motivation for learning. At test time, reduce the temptation to cheat by separating the seats of buddies known to "cooperate." Provide many adult monitors in large group testing.

6. If there is absolute proof of dishonesty, confront the child privately with the act and the proof in a simple calm statement. Never ask him to indict himself. Ask how he might control himself better the next time: change seats, be retaught, study better, etc. Never force a "confession."

7. If study and observation show lying to be an attempt to impress peers or adults or to gain status, interpret this to the child and create social conditions which help the child gain status, perhaps through recognition in his special talents or hobbies, achievements in club work, pleasant manners or appearance, helpfulness to others, etc.

8. Emphasize values of competition with self. Deemphasize such statements as, "Let's see who can run fastest," or "How many get it perfectly," etc. Instead, suggest how people can keep track of their own scores to see if they can achieve over themselves. The work should be checked by the teacher, and small rewards can be offered for continued improvement in knowledge over a previous score.

9. Review the child's academic progress and intelligence scores in relation to work assigned to ascertain if unreasonable demands have led to cheating. If the expectations are reasonable,

discuss the behavior with the child in private. Included in the discussion should be the reasons why he should not cheat, why he might feel it necessary to cheat, and what prevents him from doing the work. Offers for help in learning the material should be generously included and, finally, a statement about future punishment if the cheating persists. Recognize that the largest single reason for cheating is lack of knowledge and that remediation here pays off instantly.

10. Hold a conference with the parents in order to determine if their expectations have been excessive. Help them avoid becoming furious with the child in their own embarrassment. If the child becomes frightened, he may cheat even more to gain approval at any price.

11. Interpret to the parents the environmental reasons for the child's need for status perhaps dealing with sibling rivalry, family expectations, affiliation need with a peer group.

Firesetting

12. Besides closely supervising this child and making sure that he is educated regarding the nature and destructiveness of fire according to his age, he should have a comprehensive diagnostic evaluation and likely engage in extensive therapy for this destructive and frightening symptom. Often the repeater is a subconsciously angry and retaliatory child. The parents may permit the child to burn materials under their supervision.

Forging Parent's Name on Checks, Reports, Letters

13. Have parent-teacher contacts and personal interviews only; do not rely on the child to hand-carry letters or reports that require signatures. Use the telephone where face-to-face contacts are impossible even if it means evening phone calls. Allow him to demonstrate his trustworthiness. The teacher or clinical staff should inquire of the parents why the child might resort to this behavior. For example, is there excessive pressure for him to achieve? Is he buying friends, paying off a threat, or using drugs? Determine the motivations so that the remediations might fit these and therefore be helpful.

14. Psychotherapy or family therapy is recommended to understand and help the child overcome this behavior. If the forging is a function of abusive parents or fear of bringing home reports, then work with the parents toward making a less threatening environment and help them adjust their demands to the child's capabilities.

Lying to Authority and Parents

15. If there is a personality clash with the child's teacher that seems to create opportunities for lying, change the child's class.

16. The teacher should view such dishonest behavior as symptomatic of feelings of inferiority and rejection, and sometimes real deprivation. Emphasize the danger inherent in openly accusing a youngster of dishonesty or "forcing" the truth from him. Recognize that what generally is considered dishonest in school may not be for the individual's peer group based on the value system of the neighborhood gang.

17. Psychotherapy may aid in keeping the child within the limits of acceptable behavior in the school building. Consistent discipline and more positive but firm controls from both parents will be necessary. Assuming that sociopathic behavior is not under consideration, lying may be minimized by guidance sessions, reeducation, and example by adults.

18. The parents must hold similar and reasonable expectations for the child. If one parent is quite strict and the other markedly lenient, these contradictory standards will only serve to confuse the child further. The child rather inevitably will move toward the more tolerant parent for understanding. The parents likely will need professional counseling to learn how to present a united front.

19. Suggest that the parents unwittingly may be contributing to dishonesty by requiring too high standards. Advise the parents to be more tolerant, to look for favorable qualities in the child, and not to overreact to those forms of behavior which may be displeasing. It is possible that the parents, without realizing it, may value the child only for what he does academically. Most reasonable parents will appreciate getting a second look at their own style and how it influences their child.

20. Request permission from the parents for the trained school psychologist to offer psychotherapy or counseling for the child in the school setting. Once the child recognizes that he need not defend himself in this novel and nonthreatening relationship, he can be helped to explore the many causes of lying and defensiveness and adopt new and acceptable modes of behavior.

21. Alleviate by (a) substituting frequent praise for criticism, (b) improving his sense of individual worth by an appreciation of his personal assets, (c) assigning responsibilities of consequence, (d) building a feeling of mutual respect, and (e) giving opportunities for the child to give oral expression to his negative feelings.

22. In a small child, where there appear to be no serious physical or emotional problems, lying may simply be age-appropriate and merely a matter of learning and maturation.

Stealing Beyond Expectations of Subcultural Group

23. If the child has stolen an object from a store, the parent should take the child back and have him pay for it from his allowance or return it undamaged. He should not have to make a verbal apology to the store manager since most children at this moment are speechless with embarrassment. The parent can explain the circumstances. Do not let the manager reward the child by giving the stolen item to the child.

24. It is important to avoid sermons, dramatics, or namecalling when a young child brings home articles not his own. Tell the child calmly and firmly that the object does not belong to him and to take it back at once. Go with the child to give moral support.

25. Determine the causes of the stealing by privately interviewing the child. He may be stealing for food, to keep up social appearances by taking clothes, as revenge upon others who have stolen from him, as an incontrollable urge, as a dare, etc. The prescription must fit the presumed motives.

26. In general, the child must be informed that he is suspected or known to have stolen and he should face loss of school or home privileges in clear cases if the problems continue. The parents should be informed if the evidence is clear and the

incidences continue.

27. Often, small children steal desk items in school for the secret thrill of being mischievous and as a passive-aggressive behavior against too-strict parents or teachers. If the teacher does not overreact, then so much the better. The child is often one who is quiet and gets no special attention from the teacher and this surely makes him special when he steals; thus, she must provide this recognition regularly, in an indirect way to prevent theft. Normally children should be warned to safeguard their possessions and not to bring valuables to school.

Persistent Truancy from School

28. Make school and the school curriculum as interesting as possible. When the weather is good, take the class and the child on field trips through the town or city to get acquainted with locations of public buildings, factories, and parks. This helps the child look forward to school to some degree and perhaps he will not want to be absent, but it may be necessary to change his curriculum radically to keep hin in school at all. Truancy is frequently a symptom of high anxiety that needs therapeutic desensitization. When children feel failure, they become frightened and tense to the extent that they cannot tolerate the school day.

29. Contact the school attendance officer for a home visit and follow-up. Send a registered letter to parents regarding weekly school absences.

30. Contact the home personally and solicit support for getting the child to school. Determine if proper clothing, lunch money, etc., is available and if the child is not staying home because of shame. Determine if the home is knowledgeable of any reasons for truancy, e.g. health problems.

31. Offer help in remediating the causes since they are often real and severe. Remind the child of the legal aspects of truancy but not in a threatening manner. If persistent truancy results in pleasure-seeking activity, then make the penalty significant. The truancy should result in an uncomfortable experience for the parents if they have been the ones ignoring its consequences.

32. Try to redirect the child's interests into constructive

athletic or club activities where others depend upon his presence.

33. Make concessions in the child's daily schedule so that some portion of it consists of the child's activity of his own choosing. If other children complain, tell them honestly that he needs this special help and they do not or that they, too, may earn special privileges through work.

34. File a charge in juvenile court for excessive truancy so that social agencies may become active in assisting the problem. Take for granted that any consistently truant child is an unhappy one who is asking for aid by obvious withdrawal and defiance.

35. Make adjustments in the school program where necessary after considering ability, achievement, etc. Inform the parents of reassignments and remedial programs. Give the child daily contact with the school counselor at the start of the school day. Reward him for appearing. Pay him if necessary.

36. Counsel privately with the child, assuring confidentiality, and attempt to find out why he avoids school. If the reason is because the child needs a job, then work out a partial work/school schedule making sure that he can continue to earn credits for his diploma.

Vandalism

37. Since it is incompatible to be destructive and constructive at the same time, start a project where the student helps to build a team clubhouse. Supervision by a shop teacher is usually necessary for this complicated endeavor. Vandalism frequently has deep emotional roots, however, relating to contemptuous attitudes toward schools, stores, neighbors, and general rules and regulations. No simple remedies are effective. Developing pride in a school is a good goal, but it is very difficult to achieve. Vandalism is a delinquency reflecting a deterioration of neighborhood blocks and subcultures.

38. Groups of students in the secondary schools can be permitted to repaint the school cafeteria, locker rooms, and even waste containers in the halls that may have been vandalized by them. If they are known to be vandals like this, they can have a "paint-in" with the custodian supplying materials and supervision. In this case the juvenile court authorities might order

repair and replacement of damaged property, and the offenders may earn "salaries" in school used to pay for the defaced or destroyed material.

SECTION B: OPPOSITIONAL BEHAVIOR

39. A resource room teacher who has also been trained to assist children with emotional problems can be assigned to three to five students from the primary or intermediate grades for a two-hour period. During this day she may give them remedial instruction in academic subjects in which they are weak and also counsel them as a co-therapist with a clinical staff member for their emotional problems. Such counseling is frequently mandated for children placed in classes for the emotionally disturbed.

40. Many oppositional behavior patterns are habits which are no longer functional or no longer serve an original need. Behavior modification techniques are useful in changing such behavior to more acceptable patterns. Teachers and parents may reinforce a child differentially, to help him behave in a manner more conducive to gaining acceptance and recognition than his oppositional behavior was initially meant to achieve. Basically, the child is to be reinforced for increasingly cooperative behavior.

41. For the oppositional child:
    a. Avoid threatening the child.
    b. Substitute activities—await a "healthier" climate.
    c. Communicate understandingly and privately.
    d. Avoid open condemnation before the group.
    e. Make assignments that can be achieved.
    f. Display honest friendship and interest.
    g. Praise good behavior.
    h. Ignore, as far as possible, unacceptable behavior.
    i. Suggest artwork to portray acceptable behavior patterns.

42. The consistently disobedient child may often be getting support from a group of less active followers. These reinforcing followers should be removed by physical separation to another part of the room or perhaps even a classroom change from their

disobedient leader. At the same time, the disobedient child should be given teacher approval during periods in which he performs adequately.

43. If oppositional behavior becomes habitual, the child can be taught compliance by allowing him to choose between two simple alternatives, succinctly stated by the adult. Explanations for the choices should be brief and non-negotiable. For example, the child may choose not to come in the house on time, but in doing so he misses a favorite television show later.

Disobedient to Teachers, Parents, or Authority

44. Set up a program so that there are consequences to being disobedient and rewards for being obedient. The former may deal with deprivation of privileges, and the rewards may be their return, more material objects, or social approval.

45. Planning the work of the class beforehand tends to decrease disorderliness and disobedience. The instructional program should be organized in such a way that the children are actively learning at all times. Essentially, keep them too busy to be disobedient.

46. Self-direction should be encouraged. Although teachers are the leaders in the class, a democratic leader gives children opportunity to make rules and regulations for their own conduct, and encourages pupils to help plan their program and activities. Teachers should be willing to allow children to solve their own problems at their level of functioning, even though it involves allowing the children to make mistakes. Behavior of children is determined in part by the social approval of the group. When the group has defined its own rules of conduct, individual children are more apt to abide by these rules. This procedure gives the teacher an opportunity to remain as a friend and a counselor, rather than as a policeman.

47. Children who are markedly and persistently disobedient are often emotionally disturbed children who might require special education placement. It is highly preferred that exceptional children remain in their regular classes as often as possible in conformity with Public Law 94-142. This kind of placement requires greater effort from the teacher and the peer group. If

the child is to grow up, he will develop more suitably where he can associate with his peer group and not be shunted aside as a person who is incapable of managing himself. Children who are markedly disobedient beyond expectations may also require psychotherapy for them to understand the origins of their own hate and their willingness to do combat with authorities.

48. Except in self-defense, physical aggression on the part of the teachers should be avoided. The teacher might indicate to the child that he is making the teacher angry or reflect the child's feelings, possibly by stating, "It looks like you want me to punish you." If some physical display has to be made, the teacher might hit the desk dramatically, instead of the child.

49. Teachers and parents should not reinforce negative or infantile behavior by continually giving it attention. Such behavior should be ignored, if possible. The teacher should wait for adequate and mature behavior, in order to reinforce the child positively with something which the child feels is worthwhile. Catch the child being "good" and reinforce instantly.

50. The counselor or social worker might provide weekly counseling in small groups to help these children practice expressing their opposition verbally and learn how to alter conditions constructively which are creating their frustrations.

51. Praise all the child's attempts to modify his own unacceptable behavior. Involve him in setting up simple rules, keeping a record in order to note any changes. It is important that the teacher offer praise and support for any minor changes in the approved direction.

52. When the child misbehaves, the nature of his misbehavior should be explained to him clearly, as he may not understand what he did was wrong. Then he should be helped to consider alternative solutions which are more acceptable.

53. The child needs firm limit-setting in the classroom, but he also needs a supportive approach. This may be done through awarding him privileges such as monitoring, passing out supplies, cleaning blackboards, etc., when his behavior is acceptable and through denial of privileges and isolation in a time-out room when he acts up.

54. When the child has a "good day" in school, the teacher

should certainly send a note home with the child to be given to his parents for recognition.

55. The causes of this difficulty are quite varied, but some of it can be understood in terms of the child striving to be an autonomous entity rather than a completely submerged or subjugated personality. Teachers must realize that it is really not a personal affront nor is it a sign of the adult's personal weakness that the child is trying to gain special recognition by being disobedient. If the child feels that the teacher respects and admires him generally, even if he is disobedient, he will be less likely to flare up destructively in the school setting. She must indicate to him that she has greater hopes for his behavior; that she knows he is capable of behaving better than this; and that when he is calmed down and is ready to listen to reason, she will help him progress in school.

56. Some children who are constantly disobedient may be trying to tell the teacher that the material is too difficult for them; rather than admit this, they will disrupt the class and attempt to inflict embarrassment and humiliation upon the teacher. Perhaps assignment to lower-track groups and the lessening of homework would help. A call for tutorial services for the child in this area of academic deficiency would be reasonable.

Marked Carelessness on Tests and Homework

57. Carelessness is the result of lack of interest, lack of motivation and success, and it has passive-aggressive features. It may be necessary to hypothesize the reasons for the behavior and set reinforcement contingencies accordingly. In point of fact, it does not always matter what the cause of the factors are if one can induce the child, through reinforcement, to behave constructively.

58. The teacher should tutor the child in test-taking procedures to insure that he can demonstrate what he really knows without becoming anxious.

59. Given a bright child with some evidence of independence: institute procedures of self-testing, independent of peers, and a series of charted self-competitive records. Delete compe-

tition with the group as much as possible. Emphasize self-competition with child's past performance and graphic records. Go over performance with the child "by appointment," privately.

60. If the child consistently fails to do or to complete homework assignment, the parent and teacher may work as a team. The teacher may write all homework assignments on a 3 x 5 card, and the child must present the card to the parent each evening. The parent checks the card against homework completed by the child and signs the card for the teacher. The child returns the card to the teacher on the following day with the homework assignment. The card technique is abandoned as the child begins to assume responsibility for his own assignments.

61. A child who is careless and slipshod of his work and who performs in a perfunctory fashion is essentially a nonmotivated child in terms of school achievement. Instead, he is frequently motivated to fail. This kind of underachievement is symptomatic of his childlike way of resisting various expectations and pressure that have been placed upon him, not just vaguely by society, but specifically by his own parents and a succession of teachers. Teachers must maintain those value systems which are conducive to academic achievement and are appropriate for varying abilities. Sometimes parents become overenthusiastic about a child's academic work and may put unusual pressures upon him for a variety of personal reasons, often without the realization of the effect of their intense demands. Sometimes a child resents "being used" so he purposely, but unconsciously, tries to do poorly on tests and homework. Such resistance succeeds in irritating everyone much to the child's silent and unspoken satisfaction. This kind of carelessness reflects retaliation against such pressures. Some of these symptoms indicate severe underachievement where a child possesses average or better-than-average intelligence and good health, but is emotionally struggling in the ambivalent problem of trying to grow up and trying to stay infantile at the same time. This may often happen to the son of a reserved, perfectionistic father and a possessing and overprotective mother. The family should seek the assistance of a skilled psychotherapist and also obtain tutorial services for the child.

Negativism

62. The parents are instructed to use both social and tangible reinforcers immediately after the child reveals a positive behavior rather than stubborn negativism. Negativism is often a sign of social immaturity. If it persists beyond the ages of seven or eight, the behavior is likely an indication of a more serious emotional disturbance. Children who are unable or unwilling to comply with rational requests if given by reasonable parents or who throw unusual blocks to their own social and academic development may be suffering from emotional problems. Negativism in its relatively mild aspects is fairly common in terms of an adolescent rebellion. This is often expected by the parents in our current society. However, if the child will not meet his obligations in terms of attending school, performing reasonably in homework areas, living up at least to the minimum of social obligations, participating with friends at least to some extent, the parents should consider referral to a child guidance agency.

Passive-Aggressiveness and Resistance

63. Teachers of a child who is passive-aggressive and nonmotivated in school should clearly recognize that they are usually not personally responsible for the child's condition and should not feel guilty about it. They must see themselves in several roles: (a) Informing the parents of the child's behavior, successes, and failures, (b) providing appropriate academic work within the child's abilities so that he has no genuine excuse for not trying to succeed, (c) encouraging, through the guidance counselor, the parents to seek psychotherapy for the child and possibly for themselves to avoid further difficulties in the higher grades, (d) resisting calmly the parent's complaint that the teacher does not "challenge the child's mind," and (e) reinforcing materially all positive efforts of the child.

64. Provide group counseling sessions regarding school problems on a regular basis for students who are interested and whose parents agree. The leader must be a trained group

worker in order to elicit the anger and redirect it into productive channels.

Provocation to Teachers and Peers

65. This is a problem of irritating others. Children with authority problems who have been inconsistently raised by parents frequently enter into power struggles with authorities and other parent surrogates. They will bait the authority, searching out weaknesses until they find the "Achilles heel." Such a child becomes the nuisance to his teacher who feels fearful and helpless before the child. The child is, in effect, making the teacher feel as helpless as he is made to feel at the hands of his parents. Psychotherapy is one way to help the situation. However, the teacher's handling of the child is critical. First, she must not let the child find her weak spots, not let him irritate her. This may prove difficult because the child is most likely an expert at this. Therefore, she must hide from the child those behaviors which show that he has triumphed over her. In effect, she must forbid him his sense of power at her expense by not showing him that he has succeeded. She must:

    a. Ignore his provocative behavior rather than explode in anger.

    b. Make a joke about his inane comments.

    c. Shrug off his challenges.

    d. Send him out of the room if his wanderings interfere with the lesson until he finds the control to return.

    e. Develop out-of-class activities so that he can be busy out of the range of the teacher.

If the teacher handles the situation calmly, the class will often join her in ignoring the child's nonsense behavior.

66. After the mental test scores and achievement levels have been determined, the teacher may assign the pupil some opportunities to debate with others in his class on subjects of mutual concern. This rechannels his argumentative tendencies into more socially acceptable lines.

67. This is a child who often demands attention from authority figures. Often these children are rejected by one or

more parents. They have learned that they only get attention when they behave poorly. The teacher in this case may be forced to act. This child should be seated close to the teacher so that he can get a great deal of her attention and be called upon frequently to demonstrate his knowledge or skills. If the provocative behavior is severe, the child may require therapy and the family may also be involved.

Runaway Behavior

68. Discuss the reasons for the child's running away with him and check their validity. Provide the names of social agencies to help the child cope with the real causes in a counseling and therapeutic atmosphere. It the situation the child is escaping from is severe and cannot be improved upon, e.g. problems of child abuse, help find adequate counseling services to help him understand and cope with these problems. Runaway behavior may be a symptom of a more serious problem like psychosis, pregnancy in an unwed mother, drug addiction, unbearable tension, etc.

69. For children who run away, one must suspect the possibility of poor parent-child relationships. These may have reached the point where the child feels exasperated and runs away to save himself, perhaps from physical abuse or social rejection. He may be reacting to bitter and traumatic disappointments. It is recommended that the parents contact every friend and relative of the child with whom he might possibly have contact. Falling short here, they should inform the local juvenile authorities to assist in the search for the child. In most cases, if the runaway behavior is a persistent and chronic difficulty, this requires psychotherapy, perhaps residential treatment, and very likely, family therapy. This is a phenomenon which occurs at any social class level; children rarely exhibit a permanent runaway condition. The potential for harm befalling the children is relatively great, so that every available authority should be used in determining his whereabouts. Parents should post notices in "Underground" newspapers to "call home, collect."

70. Sometimes a school social worker, psychologist, nurse

and guidance counselor may be of extreme help to the child when he is returned, so that he may discuss "his side of the story."

71. Transfer the child to a less stressful and alternative environment to offer an educational program devised jointly by the child, parent, and school psychologist.

72. Counsel the runaway student to recognize:
   a. The act is commonplace, at least in fantasy for most adolescents.
   b. It is symptomatic, neither basic to problem solving nor to the core problems that still remain.
   c. The problems involve the behavior of more people than just the adolescent: it is reflective of his parents' problem, not just his, and that the solutions will be complicated.
   d. The consequences of running away are, realistically, to the student's clear disadvantage; conversely, his remaining home usually has very practical, economic, and operational advantages which may appeal to the student's self-interest until he is old enough to take care of himself realistically.

73. Discuss with the parents the need to allow the child new degrees of freedom within the limits of his age. Allow the child to express himself without fear of punishment and find some mutually acceptable areas of responsibility and freedom that all can agree upon.

74. Always alert the parents when the child persistently discusses run-away plans or threats. Efforts should be placed on having them understand better the child's real or imagined complaints. These problems must be modified or the child may execute the runaway he thinks about.

75. If a child returns of his own volition or is apprehended, hold an immediate conference with parents to determine if other problems and possible precipitating factors are present. Discuss the implications of this behavior with parents and student. Also discuss the legal implications: possible arrest for incorrigibility, runaway, truancy, etc. Make a referral to local mental health facility at the first episode, not after the second or third.

Teasing and Similar Hostile Behavior

76. To help a child who teases others to provoke them:
    a. Enlist the help of a small, respected group to include the child and to help him be a member of that group.
    b. Provide opportunities for the child to assist the teacher, but discourage "tattling on others."
    c. Capitalize upon any special aptitudes or knowledge in the child, if any.
    d. Assign him special reports on his area of special interest.
    e. Assign him some task of special prestige.

77. The teacher may instruct her more mature students to react to the child's excessive teasing with "What makes you so mad all the time that you have to hurt other people (or other people's feelings)?" . . . "You must feel mean today; you're trying to make me feel bad with your teasing." . . . "I know I'm (fat, short, ugly, freckled or a lousy baseball player, etc.). I wish I were better, but I'm not." It may be necessary for the psychologist to role-play with peers and teachers to teach this technique effectively, and to help youngsters to react to the teasing in this way. This approach lessens his impact.

78. Include him in small group discussions with his peers wherein they can discuss with him their feelings about his teasing. In many cases peer pressure is effective in such situations. An adult is necessary to provide quiet leadership and direction.

79. It is possible that one parent may be using teasing as an aggressive reaction toward the spouse, and may not realize that this approach teaches the children to be highly skilled in this retaliatory fashion. The parents must understand and investigate their own contributions through counseling.

Chapter VI

ISOLATION, DOMINANCE, DEPENDENCE, AND SEX

A WIDE ARRAY OF behaviors in personal maladjustment are considered in this chapter. Such difficulties are not only present in many school-age children, but are also potentially serious if present in extremes. In contrast to the strident, aggressive child, the markedly withdrawn child avoids conflict, passively accepts life, often fails to develop, and prefers a noninvolved role in school and life. The suggestions for these isolating behaviors range from institutionalization for the psychotic child to simple sociometric seating for the relatively friendless child with minor problems in adaptation. Many of the ideas are adapted for classroom teachers who need to motivate students into the more assertive behavior of social interaction and class participation through adjustment in relationships, teaching style, and simple behavioral techniques.

Dominant or submissive children tend to pose special problems for adult educators and parents since it is normal, expected, and appropriated on culture to be dominant at certain times and submissive at others according to assigned roles and expectations. Clearly the behaviors are not "wrong" or punishable in themselves, since the question is more likely one of degree than time.

Many prescriptions for children who vary on the above dimensions concentrate upon types of relationship therapy offered by the teacher and various behavior modification strategies designed to minimize the extremes. Several treatment suggestions contain the elements of gradual desensitization. The general problems of sexual adjustment are but briefly considered in this volume and are probably palliative rather than depth oriented. Very few contributors to the survey offered ideas for sexual problems beyond suggesting traditional psychotherapy or minor reinforcement procedures. In the main, psychologists rendered prescriptions which dealt with the clearly visible, easily identified, and more readily controllable phenomenon.

SECTION A: ISOLATING BEHAVIOR

1. The teacher should have an early parent conference to determine if withdrawal behavior is situational, i.e. just at school, temporary, etc. If the isolating and withdrawn behavior is quite marked, refer the child and parents to a mental health clinic for therapy after diagnostic evaluation.

    a. Involve the school in small learning group activities with one or two others in the class.

    b. Give shortened assignments, frequent breaks, and free time for talk.

    c. Placement of the child's desk is important, so let him sit near his friends; physical isolation should be avoided.

    d. More time for response should be allowed. Let the child practice his answers at home prior to school and let the teacher ask only from his list of "ready" questions.

    e. Criticism should be minimal and emotional supports and approvals should be maximal.

3. Give the child tasks that involve the coordinated efforts and cooperation of at least two children: puzzles, pick-up-sticks, flash-cards, projects, chores in school, etc.

4. The child might be encouraged to participate in at least one extracurricular activity. Scouting might be a beginning and this should eventually be augmented with group membership in hobby clubs, musical groups, or quiet activities like chess and checker clubs. Perhaps the child can be involved in a noisy cheering section for sports.

5. Reinforcement techniques are most helpful for this kind of problem. Determine what the child might do well, like math or art for example. Have the child do math on the board, draw

and then reinforce heavily for successes. Then, later, have the child teach another one the math on the board or help with the artwork. Reinforcement should be consistently given for the performance of relatively simple, intact tasks at first, but gradually building up other modes of socializing behavior. Obviously the child must be rewarded with privileges which he regards as highly valued. In general, the more disturbed the child, the more primary are the reinforcements necessary to elicit this behavior again.

6. Children who are withdrawn may be so for many different reasons. Depending on the suspected or contributing causes, attempt to change those initial conditions if they are still operating. For example, fearful children often need reassurance and encouragement, friendship of peers and adults, simple tasks or games where success is practically guaranteed, and the support of their parents and siblings. Some fearful and withdrawn children will respond to assertive training done by a trained therapist. This might involve discussing the fear-provoking conditions, selecting a small social task or opportunity (asking another child for help), practicing the appropriate social responses with a therapist, seeing that the world responds more reinforcingly to even minor assertiveness, escalating to more complicated social interactions (asking for a date, trying to get a job), practicing other social activities (dancing, speaking about a topic in class by first reading it aloud at home), getting approval for being assertive, etc.

7. Desensitization to fearful social circumstances may be especially helpful if done privately by a therapist. It may require the establishment of a fear hierarchy and then the use of Wolpe's technique for reciprocal inhibition.

8. Physical relaxation, earlier induced by the suggestion of a therapist and practiced by the client, can be used even when the child is in school. The process of staying relaxed and the awareness of fear circumstances can be learned by the aid of a behaviorally oriented psychologist after a trust relationship has been established. Children in therapy can learn to avoid fright and withdrawal under tension states by the combination of

desensitization, appropriate assertiveness, and general relaxation. Frequently these calmer states can be achieved in only eight to twelve therapeutic sessions.

9. The family physician or pediatrician may suggest the use of mild tranquilizers or other medication for periods of special stress during exams, exciting holiday times, sports events, special performances in the arts, etc.

10. Since a withdrawn or timid child often silently gives himself incorrect and destructive "messages," i.e. "I'm stupid; I can't do anything; What I do isn't really good," he needs to recognize this common tendency in himself through the help of a therapist. To counteract this, he should start saying aloud in therapy the virtues, skills, and good qualities that he possesses starting with obvious and undeniable attributes such as "I am healthy; I go to class regularly; My teachers seem to like me; I have clear skin," and later build up to more complex attributes like, "I am good at art; I can catch as well as most boys; I have lots of friends; I'm good at *blank, blank,* and *blank.*" Such positive self-indoctrination is not only valuable, it is positively inspirational and leads not only to greater self-confidence but to gradual extinction of the self-doubts and fears. Much of this is derived from rational-emotive therapy by Albert Ellis, Ph.D.

11. Play-therapy behavior is especially useful in the counseling office or in private therapy. The person may willingly adopt a new "role" of a more assertive, powerful person and then "act" how he feels this person might act. Practicing this new role begins to help the individual see that he is not restricted to only a fearful and insecure type of behavior and that he could actually survive comfortably with another style that gets better results.

Autistic

6. In a parent conference, refer them to the nearest facility where medical, pediatric, neurological, psychological, and psychiatric services are available in addition to an appropriate educational program. A complete diagnostic workup should be conducted. Urge them to have a copy of the diagnostic reports sent to the child's regular school and offer to meet with the parents after the evaluation to assist in further planning.

Intensive behavior modification programs for shaping or modeling more normal behavior and speech are recommended. A further suggestion is to consider treatment by "Therapy-Play" as advocated and executed by DesLauriers of the Devereux Foundation. Such unique and special therapeutic programs are found most often in residential settings.

7. The teacher and clinical staff as well as the parents should decide if the child can be taught in a regular class or a special class for emotionally distrubed, or if he should be placed in a residential setting. Try to keep the child as "regular" as possible as recommended by "mainstreaming" considerations as allowed for by law for handicapped children.

8. Place the child in a special class for autistic or near-autistic children. Utilize a program of structure with emphasis on personal warmth, self-control, and clear limits. Allow some opportunity for a specific period of the day for the availability of special therapeutic intervention by trained psychologists or similar personnel.

9. After observing bizarre and schizophrenic or psychotic reactions, the regular classroom teacher should accept that she will not be able to contain and help this kind of child in a regular classroom. Children with such behaviors, almost without exception, must be involved in an intensive treatment program at least temporarily. Keeping such disturbed children too long in regular classes may be self-defeating for them.

10. In order to help the parents and therapist, the teacher should keep a daily or weekly anecdotal record of the child's behavior. This should be shared with them. It provides an excellent base line from which to evaluate future adjustment and denotes places of growth or deterioration.

11. During the interim that the parents must retain the psychotic child in their home while they are waiting for residential placement for him, they must provide twenty-four hour supervision of the child so that he does not injure himself or others. Children so upset may be prone to run away, to set fires, to attempt suicide, or to engage in a great variety of actions which can lead them into futher difficulty. They must continue to make every effort to keep their child in contact with reality by spending

time with him, discussing recent events, taking limited and local trips together, and focusing his attention on the realities of the world as they are perceived by most people. There is no point of "entering into" the psychotic reaction of the child with his various delusions and hallucinations. No parent should attempt to be a psychotherapist with his own emotionally disturbed child but can best facilitate help by maintaining genuine interest, support, and affection for the child and cooperating with treatment facilities.

12. Persist with the parents on the need for long-range psychological or psychiatric services even though they need to deny the obvious, i.e. that there is something wrong. Schedule, even with their reluctance, routine appointments to review "progress" or "development." Ask them to observe the child in class first.

13. Place the child with a residential treatment agency that has a wide variety of educational and psychotherapeutic facilities because he may need a multidisciplinary approach to treatment, if he can improve at all.

14. Parents who have had a child recently diagnosed as autistic or psychotic must begin to use every possible resource available to them to find suitable treatment and placement for their disturbed child. They should feel free to call upon the school authorities for initial recommendations, and most assuredly, child guidance clinics, university centers, and their family physician. There are specialists who deal particularly with the severe disorders of children, although it must be recognized that any kind of service incurred is likely to be quite expensive.

Narcissism

15. Give the child some responsibility for helping another less able child.

16. Reinforce, frequently at first, appropriate behaviors when they do occur. Never demand a behavior not in the child's repertoire. Such behaviors can be developed gradually. The teacher should avoid the following:

      a. Verbally backing a child "into a corner" so that he has to "lose face" to comply.

    b. Getting involved in a power struggle with a child in which one person will "lose face" by giving in.

    c. Setting a rule the teacher cannot enforce consistently.

17. When parents become aware that their child is a highly egocentric and narcissistic individual, they may take this opportunity to look carefully at the structure of their own family life. Is this an "only child" who has received so much parental adulation that he is worshipped and adored? If this is the case, then they might begin to provide maturing activities and responsibilities to help him develop and become less self-centered. Initially, he may become responsible for the care of young pets and, in fact, his own privileges must become dependent upon the care of the young animal. Beyond that, he can begin over several months of time to receive various kinds of home responsibilities in keeping with his sex and age expectancies. The parents may begin to inquire from others what are expectations for children in their neighborhood that may be appropriate for this child.

18. If the parents note extreme egocentric behavior and self-centered activities, beyond the age of six or so, then one must question that this is a symptom of emotional disturbance requiring psychotherapeutic intervention for the child. It may be a symptom of insecurity, and possibly a "coverup" for a frightened child. Generally such a child will operate at a more regressed and younger level than his actual age or mental age.

Excessive Fantasy, Daydreaming in School

19. The teacher should interrupt the fantasy and daydreaming by calling the child's name, asking him to recite or contribute often, by standing near him, by touching him, or asking his opinion.

20. Fantasy and daydreaming can sometimes be channeled more constructively into the creation of stories to be read by other children. Numerous illustrations from advertisements can be cut out from magazines. The child is then asked to write a story that the picture suggests. These stories, with the accompanying illustrations, are assembled in booklet form to be placed in the school library or given to children's hospitals.

21. Recommend a "contract" arrangement whereby the child is to complete a certain amount of an assignment (so many sentences, problems) within a time limit and reporting to the teacher as soon as it is completed. The assignment and time limits may be gradually extended and the teacher should reward performance up to the contracted level.

22. Provide tokens, M & M's™, or other candy rewards or privileges for good performance in achievement over previous levels of accomplishment. This may encourage greater interest in school with less drifting into fantasy or daydreaming.

23. When the child is daydreaming, touch, or if necessary, grasp him to bring him back to awareness. Use this carefully in the presence of other children explaining that this is not punishment.

24. All directions should be given clearly and slowly on a one-to-one basis and repeated whenever necessary. The teaching should be based upon simple, specific instructions in task assignment. The teacher should stand near the child and help the child get started.

25. Plan active participation in class: discussions, art, music, sports, and physical recreation for students. Silent reading or solitary research activities tend to encourage daydreaming.

26. Reality must become more pleasant than fantasy. Assign some activity with another child or two; facilitate social adjustment with group projects. Program activities so that there is less opportunity for isolation of individual students.

27. Talk to the child to determine something about the theme of his fantasy. Also, talk to the family to determine if there are any situations at home which might be causing the child to have some difficulty. The main concentration should be on trying to make the school situation such an interesting place that it draws him away from his world of fantasy. By talking to him, and by trial and error, find areas that are interesting to him and try to build activities on these areas of interest. Specifically, in the classroom situation, the teacher can observe him more closely and draw him into group activities by questioning and suggestion. Stand ready to reward him for his achievements when he is able to become a more productive member of the group.

28. Make classroom assignments very short, five to fifteen minutes long, depending on the age of the child. Appoint an easygoing, friendly (but not overwhelmingly or suffocatingly friendly) peer to be a "partner" to the subject, to draw him gently into classroom reality. Have the partner do the school work with, not for, the subject, and maintain responsibility during lunch and recess. Do not scold him for daydreaming. For a young child, one might arrange to have a "big brother" or "big sister" from an upper grade.

29. If the daydreamer happens to be a well-adjusted, brilliant child, then the remedy may be obvious: a major adjustment in the challenging qualities of the curriculum or placement in an accelerated class.

30. A child more fascinated by his private world of personal thoughts and dreams than by schoolwork may be (a) normal, (b) gifted, (c) retarded, (d) deaf, (e) emotional disturbed, etc. A diagnostic evaluation would likely determine the causes of the daydreaming. The teacher should reconsider her own curriculum to be certain that it is real, concrete, challenging, and appropriate. She should also consider if the child's assigned achievement or ability grouping is correct.

Shyness

31. Give the child tasks that require keen attention: puzzles, speed tests, cataloging of book shelves, memorizing of riddles and poems, taking notes of discussion.

32. Only call on the child to recite before class when the teacher has prior knowledge that he knows particular material exceptionally well.

33. Using the theory of successive approximations, a private behavior rehearsal with the child where he practices giving one answer can be helpful. The teacher tells him ahead of time which questions she will ask him. The idea is much like that of practicing for a job interview.

34. Some of the other children in the classroom should be taught the techniques of social reinforcement so that they, too, can listen to and praise the shy child when he performs even minimally.

35. For the child who is reluctant to speak, offer him a piece of candy or cookie. When he has eaten it, offer another saying, "Say 'candy'." If he refuses, eat the candy in front of him and try again. Ask him to say the word again; if he refuses, eat it yourself. Withhold candy unless the child responds by imitating the word or at least making an attempt to make a sound or partial word. If the child fails to respond in three or four trials, of course stop and do something else. This procedure sometimes works with children who are capable of speaking and who talk freely at home, but who have established a habit of not speaking in school by virtue of resistance. Proceed from imitating single words and short phrases to short sentences and more spontaneous speech. Ignore nonverbal communication, gestures, and pointing and ask the classmates to do the same.

36. If there is no pathology, the teacher might try a sociogram analysis in her classroom. Find out whom the child likes in preferential seating. Also move other social isolates into the area since a shy person may also gravitate toward a social isolate whom he may perceive as nonthreatening.

37. This youngster should be included in a group counseling session with his peer group that will focus upon drawing in each member of the group for discussion. The group should be carefully picked to be nonthreatening and its goal would be to focus on the ability to communicate and share feelings.

38. The teacher should avoid placing a child in any situation that will be embarrassing or frightening to him.

39. If the office secretary wishes to be helpful here, she can invite the child to take "Lunchtime Office Duty." The child may count milk money, take messages, perhaps answer requests at the desk, run errands, etc. He may have to observe a mature friend doing these things with him first.

40. Give the child a hand puppet and let the puppet tell what it would like to learn when called upon to read or speak. Let the shy child also be a storekeeper in a school room store where empty fruit and vegetable cans are sold for play money.

41. Solicit home support and cooperation so that the parents do not berate the child for his shyness or become overly

demanding. If the situation does not ease, eventually the parents are to be asked to seek professional counseling.

42. Have the child communicate with others by telephone, out of visual contact with others. Games of varying sorts can be devised which involve verbal communication, say, role playing behind masks.

43. Ask a more mature child to make a friend of a shy child to encourage him in games and activities and also help him in classroom subjects. This might be considered as a "Scouting good deed" and might prove mutually beneficial to both children.

44. First investigate if there is some realistic basis for the child's shyness. Is there a speech defect or physical characteristic which embarrasses the child, and can this condition be corrected or minimized? A great number of once-shy children are now very talkative adults. Therefore the long-range prognosis is excellent.

45. While giving the young child cookies after school, the parents may provide a talking time for him every day. The mother can relate the day's events to the child, tell of her own childhood memories, and listen carefully to what the child offers in return about his day. Just the act of paying attention by the parent is extremely reinforcing.

46. Make a list of the things that are considered valuable and desirable to the child. Set up a point system for talking to parents, other children, other adults. As he earns a point also pair this with a social approval. Give appropriate rewards for points earned to please the child.

47. The parents should ignore the nonverbal communications of the child and never speak for him. He must make his needs known through words or complete sentences in asking for dessert, candy, permission to play, etc. Do not ask the child questions that can be answered with "yes," "no," or a shrug. Be sure that other siblings do not interpret or speak for the shy child.

Perfectionism, Over-Ascetic, and Meticulous

48. Perfectionism is sometimes symptomatic of heightened anxiety and the person who wants everything to be neat, orderly, and predictable to keep his anxiety under control and not

overwhelming. This rather dreadful state of affairs requires behavior therapy as the treatment of choice. The individual will likely respond best to Wolpe's reciprocal inhibition where physical relaxation and a pairing of anxiety-provoking mental images with the therapist's guidance will help relieve tension. Perfectionistic behavior is learned behavior and it can thus be unlearned under the proper new therapeutic conditions.

49. The teacher should be careful not to reinforce the neurotic behavior of a perfectionistic or super-meticulous child by praising him privately or publicly for these traits. The extreme of such behavior usually defeats normal academic and social adjustment. Indicate many times to the child in the class that mistakes are normal and expected and when mistakes occur that it informs the teacher where the children need her help. She should be careful to note that boys may socially reject a meticulous boy as he may appear to be feminine or make them feel uncomfortable. Underneath his controlled appearance, the perfectionistic child is often terrified of being wrong and often guilt-ridden for real or imagined transgressions in the past. Such a child will require an easygoing, calm pace of classroom learning that is fairly well structured and dependable.

50. If the child is copying one parent's perfectionistic behavior but becoming excessive, then the parents should seek professional consultation with a therapist. The child has likely extended the parents' values neurotically and the perfectionistic behavior will become an end in itself. This behavior can also result from excessive guilt feelings wherein the child feels dirty, messy, or disgusted with himself. The child will not "outgrow" this problem; in fact, if may become worse. If parents recognize that they have required meticulous appearance in themselves and, hence, the child, they must first relax their own standards, if possible.

Paranoid-like Behavior

51. Refer the child for special class placement for the emotionally disturbed and seek therapeutic services. Consider residential placement and intensive treatment programs.

52. For the child with milder problems in this area:

    a. Ignore and overlook complaints.

    b. Praise the child for work well done.

    c. Encourage new projects.

    d. Make assignments within the mental ability of the child.

    e. Discuss the problem with the child; he may not be aware of the habit he has acquired of suspecting everyone and blaming others.

    f. Determine if some of his "gripes" are justified.

    g. Confer with parents as to probable causes.

    h. Challenge the student by assigning material including his special interest.

53. Adults should make a special effort to avoid trying to outreason the child on how his perspectives are incorrect, but rather strive to have the child learn to trust them and feel comfortable with adults.

Withdrawn From Normal Social Contacts

54. The teacher should make every effort to reinforce socially any responsive behavior. This may include seemingly insignificant behavioral responses like taking out a book, asking for a pencil or a paper, etc. However, the child's behavior should become more responsive as time goes on. The teacher might try placing him on a point system by giving special privileges after the child has earned "so many points" for more extroverted and socially oriented behavior. Of course let the child help decide on the earned privileges that he is willing to work for.

55. Teach the child to role play: to act as though he were a certain person or felt such a particular emotion; encourage him to focus on the other person, to draw him out or make him feel comfortable; provide for social activity which can cover for self-consciousness.

56. Meet with the parents to recommend counseling through a child guidance clinic or private therapist.

57. Encourage the child to attend groups such as the "Y" or the scouting movement and have a classmate or playmate take him to these meetings rather than have the parents escort him.

SECTION B: DOMINANCE AND SUBMISSION

Boastful, Attention-seeking

58. Boasting and attention-seeking are often overreactions to a deep sense of inferiority. Children manifesting such behavior are sometimes terrified that someone will discover this truth but they are quite unable, without help, to cease this self-defeating behavior. Check with the parents to see if there are parental attitudes or conditions at home that are tending to cause this child to see himself in such a negative light. Assign him to positions of leadership that are within the limits of his ability in school and then supervise him closely to be sure that he is successful and also well controlled. Try him out as a class monitor, safety counselor representative, etc., and see how he responds. Find areas of subject matter that are of special interest to him and let him present a report to the class about this and be sure that he receives appropriate recognition for his contributions. Basically, ignore his boastfulness and story-telling but stand ready to reward him when he tells of real accomplishments.

59. For the attention-seeking child:
   a. Recognize particular skills and divert his energies to those skills where possible.
   b. Praise worthwhile actions and attitudes.
   c. Privately discuss the negative effects upon his peers that his social actions produce.
   d. Assign him to a group in which he must be a follower.
   e. Employ role-playing in life situations.
   f. Use a sociogram in the classroom to place him near his friends at the seat or tables.

60. Ignore boastful behavior; when the child exhibits socially acceptable behavior, give consistent social praise and recognition.

61. Help the child achieve satisfaction through assignments scaled to his ability at which he can be successful. Arrange parent conferences so that sibling rivalries, if contributing factors, may be at least recognized and possibly minimized.

62. Focus daily attention upon the child for reading aloud, "show and tell," passing out papers, taking care of class plants or

animals, and offering token rewards for any successful performances. Meet his needs for recognition and attention by providing him with exactly what he needs: recognition and attention.

Manipulating

63. For a child who is basically dominant and power seeking, the teacher should inform the child very clearly about the school and classroom rules with a note that privileges are lost for infractions. Some children actually enjoy testing the limits and are frankly relieved when they find where they are and that these will be enforced by withdrawal of privileges, a time-out room, or something equally unpleasant.

64. Be very definite in expectations and rules for appropriate behavior in school; try to avoid responding to the child's manipulative tactics. Disappoint the child in his desire to find power over adults.

65. Parents are often both frustrated and guilt-ridden in their relationship with such children. They waver from leniency to severity. Both must work together to set specific limits or ground rules which must be abided by as consistently as is humanly possible. They must never take for granted the child's agreeable and reasonable behavior when it appears. Recognize, praise, and reinforce it consciously.

Overly Conforming and Submissive

66. For a submissive youngster, the teacher should present herself as a nonthreatening person, a helper, and a source for emotional support. She should also try to emphasize the child's qualities and talents by social approval and recognition.

67. Encourage the child to take part in vigorous social activities such as dodge-ball where he can release pent-up aggressive feelings in a well-supervised, controlled play experience. Reward him when he is able to succeed at this. Involve him in class dramatics where he is required to portray an assertive type of character, all the time assuring him that assertive behavior is permissible.

68. Try to encourage original written or oral classroom

work. Do not reward good behavior in class per se, but reward any original ideas or social initiative.

69. Afford this child opportunities to chair peer-group discussions, to exercise a measure of authority as captain of a team, leader, etc., to help the child develop greater self-expression and self-confidence.

70. Encourage the overly conforming child to do things that please himself and not necessarily those which the teacher or others enjoy. Encourage spontaneous and creative pursuits.

71. With very submissive children, the parents should look to see if their own practices are too controlling or their own treatment of the child too fear-provoking. Submissive children are usually fearful. Should the parents be unable to identify the intensity of their expectations on the child, then therapy is clearly recommended for them and perhaps the child.

72. If the conformity is due to maternal overprotection, then the mother needs to review the assets and liabilities of her behavior. The basic motivation is not always love for the child but the reduction of her own anxieties and the satisfaction of her own needs—not the child's. An "asset" is that the child will always be with her and will depend upon her since he will tend to be frightened of the world and not trust himself. Another "asset" is that he is less likely to be hurt in rough-and-tumble sports and may always be a spectator through life, not a genuine participant.

73. The parents should avoid making unnecessary interventions into the child's play or social activities. It is particularly important for them to avoid withdrawing the child from argumentative situations. The child must learn how to assert himself in these situations without interference from the parents.

Rebellious Against Rational Rules

74. The rebellious child often profits from a social modeling technique where he can learn to be both a more effective leader and also a follower. Place a child like this in a subordinate position in a group having a strong leader. The child will perhaps see for the first time appropriate and effective techniques for group work and may realize that he can personally derive

satisfaction from simply being a group member and not necessarily be the leader.

75. It may be advisable that such a child have lunch at home rather than in school for it is often impossible that he have adequate supervision at noon in school.

76. Role playing often helps the chronic rule-breaker see the other side. In a group therapy session, the timid and shy child rarely handles an authority position as well as the boy who was always up against it. Play the scene in the principal's office when the teacher brings in the "bad boy" again. The boy who has been on one side of the desk is often compassionate, gentle ("What am I going to do with you?") and may work out very sensible solutions to his problem when he plays the scene from the swivel chair.

77. Explain to the parents that rebelliousness works very well for the child. Get them to observe the number of times that the child gets attention when he behaves this way and when he refuses to cooperate. Give the child attention only when he cooperates and try, if possible, to ignore times when he is negativistic. If at all possible, use a time-out procedure (noted on page 49).

78. Professional counseling is strongly indicated especially since this symptom often reveals a family in the process of breakdown.

Rivalrous Toward Siblings and Peers

79. Suggest to the parents that they allow each child to stay up one evening each week, one-half hour after all the other children have gone to bed. Each child should have a definite day assigned to him for this privilege and opportunity to be an "only child" assured of his parent's undivided attention for this period of time.

80. Parents should realize that jealousy is a normal reaction to the addition of a new baby. In announcing the coming event, it is best to avoid long explanations or build false expectations. Explain that sometimes the baby will be a nuisance, take up mother's time, etc. "When you feel I don't love you enough, come and tell me." Rivalrous children need to be convinced of the parent's love.

81. The older child should be allowed to express his feelings of anger and hostility about a younger child, but have him direct this against inanimate objects like a child's punching bag.

82. Recommend to the parents that one of them establish a relationship with the child centered on some common interest, a job or hobby, which will not be shared with any other sibling. Let every child have a special time with one of his parents at least every day or so.

83. Undercut jealous behavior by finding activities and areas the child does well in and give praise and recognition. Strengthen appropriate behavior through positive reinforcers. Utilize a time-out procedure when children get into hassles.

SECTION C: DEPENDENCE-INDEPENDENCE, EXCESSIVE

84. This is mostly a parent-child problem and to the extent that overdependency occurs in school, it might be handled there. The principle in working with dependent and fearful children is to set goals for them that lead to independent functioning in other areas. It is also necessary to make these goals in graduated increments to insure success.

85. For dependent children:
   a. Provide role-playing situations for more mature behavior.
   b. Encourage participation in games and sports.
   c. Encourage expression through creative art and creative writing.
   d. Hold student-teacher chats pointing out growth.
   e. Delegate responsibilities of a leadership capacity on occasion.
   f. Group the child with a partner or small group to work on a special class project.
   g. Gear assignments to insure successful completion.
   h. Learn of the child's particular interests and capitalize on this information in oral and written assignments.
   i. Share some burdens with him like, "I know just how you feel"; and reflect on his feeling tone and not offer solutions to his problems.

86. Give the child classroom responsibilities such as water-

ing flowers, taking attendance, carrying messages. Try to encourage the child to participate in extracurricular activities, such as intramurals, teams, clubs, and student government.

87. Repetition of a grade on the lower level might be beneficial especially if such overdependent behavior influences school achievement. Thus the child may gain more certainty in academic skills and start to build self-confidence. However, this has to be carefully balanced against the child's sense of failure through retention.

88. Ask the child how he feels about his own work, rather than the teacher or parents always making a value judgment about the child's work. Let him get involved often in making decisions. Why not reward him materially for, say, every three independent decisions he makes?

89. Be consistent in telling the child that he is capable of performing independently. Ignore his demands for attention that are dependency-related and explain to the child that the teacher will evaluate him only after his work is completed but that he will be helped to accomplish it.

90. For children who are overly dependent upon either of their parents and lack an inner self-confidence, first determine which specific academic area needs remediation. Then supply a tutor. It is often the anxiety about school in the parents that robs the child of whatever confidence he might have, since the parents are least able to communicate a sense of certainty. They should turn over tutoring to professionals who, in addition to remediating subject matter deficiencies, are skilled in supporting children.

91. Encourage the child to become a Boy Scout or "Y" member and to attend a two-week camp program. Consider the camps which match his interests: music, sea scouts, horseback riding, scouting, etc. And, naturally, finances are a major consideration.

92. Require the child to make decisions such as choose between two shirts, ties, or dresses to wear and then slowly increase the selection from two to a whole group. In general, have the child make decisions which are safe and easy to do and then gradually progress to more involved ones.

93. Secure psychotherapy or family counseling for an overly dependent teenager or for the parents who cannot allow the child to become normally independent.

94. Provide an allowance in accordance with the child's age and allow complete freedom of spending.

95. Give increasing freedom to the child to go to parties, movies, walk to friends' homes, ride a bus, or go to ball games. Provide rewards in terms of approval for successful performance.

96. Gradually give the child more significant responsibility: going to the store, removing trash, feeding pets, etc., having each successful performance rewarded on a chart and reinforced significantly every few days.

97. Read the chapters on "Responsibility" in Haim Ginott's book, *Between Parent and Child.*

98. For this child:
   a. Treat him at his age level.
   b. Let him do whatever age-mates do for play and travel.
   c. Permit him to ride, swim, fish, play ball, etc.
   d. Allow greater freedom and responsibility.
   e. Let the child solve most of his own problems.

99. Some teenagers need more activities with people outside the home. Utilize interests in sports, art, or music by enrolling him in a training class. Perhaps he can do volunteer work during a summer vacation or even obtain a part-time job.

100. Parents should avoid interfering when the child has difficulty with playmates. The child should be encouraged to meet problems with his own resources however meager they may appear at first.

SECTION D: SEXUAL ADJUSTMENT

Confusion in Sexual Identification

101. Recommend psychotherapy for the child and have the parents become involved in counseling, probably family therapy. They may wish to answer two questions: Why did the child adopt the opposite sex role and what might be done about this? Some behavior modification approaches and social modeling therapies have been successful with adults depending on the client's desire

for change and the degree of underlying anxiety and guilt.

102. Expose the child to adequate identification figures. If necessary, change teachers and encourage the child's participation in YMCA or YWCA activities and scout programs. If possible, recommend a Big Brother program for such boys. Possibly even hire a tutor whose primary purpose will not be to tutor, but to talk with the boy or girl about school and other matters of interest, and secondarily to tutor in weak areas of academics.

103. If a boy has the problem of incorrect gender identification, do not assign him to a dominant-aggressive female teacher.

104. Pending parents permission, the child with many unanswered questions about sex can be counseled by the school psychologist, counselor, or clergyman.

105. A child who shows excessive concern about love, dating, sex, etc., prior to puberty may be neurotically over-identifying with an older sibling. It seems appropriate for the parents to respond to the child's questions factually but also to promote conversation in other areas to foster more adequate overall development. Persistent questioning about sexual functioning should lead to psychological assessment.

106. With children who overreact to topics about sexual matters, the teacher's role is to be direct, natural, and honest while giving the topic no undue attention. To ignore the topic completely is to try to ignore the obvious.

107. For problems about excessive sexual curiosity:
    a. Be honest with the inquirer to sort out incorrect sexual information.
    b. Provide objective discussion, in open forum, about sex drives and society's controls.
    c. Give adequate guidance and counseling services through group discussion and education.
    d. Avoid preaching.
    e. Avoid shaming the child to produce guilt feelings.
    f. Encourage strenuous physical activity in competitive groups.
    g. Encourage group association in early-dating programs rather than single-couple dating.

    h. Encourage parent-teacher conferences about these problems.

    i. Display affection at home.

108. Assign him regularly for a time each day to tag along with an assistant principal on his rounds, a gym teacher, a custodian, or any other friendly but decidedly masculine faculty member in the hope that some identification will be made with the adult.

109. Help the parents to understand the importance of letting a boy dress appropriately and give him masculine chores to do around the home.

110. In a home where a boy has adopted feminine behavior, it is suggested that the mother withdraw her overly controlling approach to this boy if this is contributory. The father should be encouraged to become much more involved with the boy and engage with him in masculine-oriented activities. The boy must want to become like his father.

Masturbation, Excessive

111. In school, privately inform the child about acceptable behavior in school and ask for his cooperation. Avoid placing the child in a time-out room or he will merely continue this behavior. The basic idea is one of distraction so it might also be helpful to adjust his curriculum to be interesting and to place him in a seat where the teacher may observe his behavior more closely and give clues for his self-control such as a nod, or a mild admonition.

112. For the rapidly growing child, the parents should also check the fit of his underclothing to be certain that the size of the garments has not become too small and uncomfortable.

113. Ask the parents to take the child to the family physician in order to determine if eczema or a skin or rash condition is present. If no medical problem is present, investigate possible personality difficulties through a mental health clinic.

114. Masturbation may be some type of self-stimulating behavior where the child is bored, uninterested, unable to receive proper affection from his home, etc. Certain behavioral approaches would include rewarding the child when he is not touching himself and of course making the educational program

more interesting than his personal, physical stimulation. Perhaps the child does need considerable physical affection from his parents, and this may also be offered by the understanding teacher. Such self-stimulating behavior is more frequently found with brain-injured children or those who are psychotic, but it clearly reveals that the child is forced to attend to himself out of sheer boredom.

Chapter VII

AFFECTIVE BEHAVIOR

$\mathbf{A}$FFECTIVE CONCERNS REFLECT all varieties of emotional life and, when extreme, influence the individual so that social behavior is seriously disrupted. The first concerns in this chapter are in relation to phobic and anxiety responses which permeate the child's life and incapacitate his effectiveness for school work. One of the diagnostic categories responded to most readily by contributors was the problem of school phobia. Although eighty-three prescriptions, a surprisingly high number for one diagnostic cluster, were suggested for this behavioral pattern, only thirty-seven survived the severe editing process in terms of conciseness, originality, etc. School phobia is a common and easily recognized problem usually manifested by young and quite dependent children. It is characterized many times by anxiety, psychosomatic complaints, and an unwillingness to leave the mother and attend school. To change this behavior usually requires not only a grasp of dynamic factors in the mother-child relationship, but also a recognition of the reinforcement potential in the home and the school and a knowledge of the value system of the child in question. It is here where desensitization procedures are often quite effective.

School phobia has a rich potential for both psychodynamic interpretations and behavior modification treatments plus the likelihood of constructive and rapid change. Almost invariably a desensitization approach was recommended by contributors, however many suggestions were based upon recognition of powerful and often resistant attitudes on the part of the parents and the child.

Other diagnostic patterns in this chapter deal with anxiety about tests, school, failure, etc., reactions so common in our society and yet so devastating to those deeply affected. Uncontrollable anxiety is a most debilitating emotion and calls for a series of remedial approaches to reduce or extinguish severe impact. Nor does the solution necessarily require long-term psychotherapy for when the teacher and parents, in consultation with a capable specialist, can execute appropriate strategies, the anxiety does diminish. Such success, of course, depends on many factors referred to generally in the prescriptions themselves.

Many intervention strategies relating to bodily complaints, hysterical behaviors, and depressions of all varieties, etc. draw upon the need for cooperation of medical specialists to rule out organic contributions, provide medication, etc. Relatively few ideas were offered in these last areas of difficulty and some of those will seem superficial in relation to the behavior's complexity.

GENERAL PHOBIAS

School Phobia

1. Allow the parent to bring the child to school and sit near him. Let the child stay in school fifteen minutes the first day with the parent, twenty minutes the second day, etc., in a desensitizing way. Gradually increase the time in the class and phase the parent out of class gracefully by successive approximations.

2. If the mother's anxiety is reinforcing nonattendance, (a) have the father bring the child to school daily rather than the mother, or (b) use school personnel, preferably his teacher, to bring the child to school, and (c) later have the neighborhood children walk with the child to the bus or school daily.

3. A child's absence during a significant block of course work can trigger latent school phobia. Anything which can be done to make school less anxiety-arousing is helpful. Provide extra help for make-up work, private tutoring, and opportunities for personal counseling.

4. Establish some variety of reinforcement schedule at school to reward the child for coming regularly. Make the reward

relevant to the child's expressed desires—use material rewards of consequence if these are what the child will respond to. Explain to the other children that this approach will help their classmate in school and that they too may earn privileges for extra work or may receive special help if needed.

5. In such cases it is best to refer parents to outside agencies for futher evaluation and treatment.

6. Have the teacher provide special tasks that can be accomplished with success. Involve the child in small group tasks and assure that the child can participate comfortably. Tasks should be designed to obtain peer group approval.

7. Tell the teacher that this problem more likely stems from separation anxiety about the child leaving the mother, rather than from poor curriculum or some personal deficiency in the teacher. What can the teacher now think of to make herself a more positively reinforcing person and to enhance the pleasure of the school day? Games? Extra play time if earned for attending? Class discussions of children's fears? Determine by asking the child what it is that he really enjoys doing in the school day. If possible, reward with this.

8. Permit the child to phone home occasionally if he insists. Explore special interests and keep the youngster pre-occupied. Minimize his physical complaints as much as is possible by acknowledging them but treating them casually.

9. Allow the mother to speak often to the child's teacher and principal so that she may overcome her fears that school personnel may be impersonal or unfriendly to her and to her child.

10. Establish a social reinforcement schedule keyed to people with whom the child comes in contact while coming to school, each of whom must participate in his role with the child. When the child finishes breakfast his older brother, for example, will tell the child that he will be his partner in getting to the bus. The bus driver will acknowledge the child's arriving at the bus and will take the child to the school driveway. A principal, teacher, or aide will meet the child and specify that he is the partner of the child who will accompany him to the classroom. A classmate will meet the child and indicate that he is the partner or

seatmate for the morning. Specific people with consistent actions and definitions of role are essential.

11. Allow the child to bring loved objects with him to school such as a blanket or toy. Have high interest activities the first part of class: movies, T.V. shows, puppet shows, live pets, and exciting games.

12. Help the child realize that school and authority figures are not unaware of his needs. It may be beneficial to have a period of time in each school day where children are encouraged to participate in a group discussion of their feelings about people and school. The teacher's role is to clarify and accept the expressed feelings.

13. Once in the classroom the teacher should be ready to make concessions to get the child to favor attendence on a regular basis. For example, she may want to relax the rules for lavatory visitations, seat the child close to her desk (or door if requested), or waive recitation requirements.

14. Since either a change of schools or a prolonged absence due to illness may precipitate a phobic reaction, teachers should attempt to make contact with new parents in the district and their children for "get-acquainted" sessions. For example, brief guided tours may help to desensitize a child in regard to full-time attendance. For the child with protracted illness, home visitations by his teacher may help him keep in touch with classroom activities. Home-bound instruction may be essential if the child is frail or even out of school for a brief period.

15. Involve the parent and teacher in joint conferences so that the parent will learn to like and trust the teacher, the former may transfer her positive feelings to the child and he may accept the teacher as a mother substitute who is comforting and reliable.

16. Each day the child does not attend school, a rigid schedule is to be followed based on the school schedule. The child is to sit at a table and do work as assigned by the teacher via the mother. No breaks other than those allowed at school are permitted and must follow the school schedule. Lunch is prepared in the morning and placed in a paper bag which is not refrigerated. No T.V. or other forms of diversion are permitted until the child completes all homework. The mother should not "nag" the child.

17. Desensitization methods by a psychologist or counselor are often effective for such a phobia with a reasonably cooperative child assuming that the parents are interested in helping.

18. For older children, especially, work along the lines of desensitization and successive approximations toward the final goal. This refers to cases where there is no appropriate medical intervention, and psychotherapy is unavailable or inappropriate. Begin instruction at the tutor's home at regular times during the day or week, increasing exposure to the child's teacher when possible. Alter the physical environment when the child is ready by moving "the classroom" to a nearby library, church, etc. Eventually the instructional period should be attempted within the school proper with the final goal being gradual integration into the school situation. Parents should stay relatively divorced from this technique. The tutor and child together decide when moves should be made. At the beginning of this plan, the youngster should be counseled about the plan, the expectations for him, and his responsibility to guide his gradual integration back into the school.

19. Make every effort, short of physically dragging the child in, to keep the child attending school regularly while remediation of the initial problems continues. Even part-time attendance is better than none.

20. Do not force an extremely anxious child to attend school even though being at home will, unfortunately, provide more reinforcements in a neurotic relationship. Such panic testifies to the seriousness of the problems and the likely defects in the family relationships. Family therapy may have to precede getting the child back to school. Forcing the child back will tell the family that there is no longer any problem, when the problem is only masked temporarily.

21. Interpret to the parents that the school teacher, curriculum, or peers have little or nothing to do in creating the problem, but that it likely stems partly from a long series of overprotective behaviors on the part of a parent at home. These patterns of indulgence, infantalization, and holding the child close are not done consciously by the parent, but do create a great need on the child's part to stay with the parent personally and be dependent. (Omit the clinical interpretation that the child may be fearful that

unconscious desires for harm to befall the mother may actually occur.)

22. Ask the parents for permission to begin therapy with the child to aid in the development of insight or to desensitize the child's fears of separation and the fear of being left helpless and dependent.

23. Ask the mother to become less of a reinforcing person and request that she treat the child more maturely: ask her to (a) stop taking the child to school all the while passing on her own fears and apprehensions, (b) let the child get his own breakfast and decide on school clothes, (c) omit the daily "tearful parting" when time comes for the child to go, and (d) reassure the child that the mother will be home when he returns.

24. Interest the father in playing a stronger role in the family if he has been passive and relegated into insignificance. Have him visit the school, take the child with him shopping on weekends, show his place of work, and contribute his interests at the dinner table. Tell him this in front of his wife and support his new efforts to help his own child to mature.

25. Be sure that the child's physician is informed of this problem especially if there are somatic complaints used by the child as an avoidance technique. This approach by the child is geared to be the most effective way of controlling the mother and arousing her anxiety to become even more protective and infantalizing.

26. Tell the parents that the longer they persist in teaching or telling the child their own fears and apprehensions, keep "babying" the child, and permit themselves to be made upset by him, the longer the problem will last. The child will begin to change after they change, not before.

27. The parent must insist that the child remain in school. Suggest that the parent not "give in" easily to physical complaints.

28. The parent should not discuss the question of whether or not the child will go to school the following day, either with the child or the other parent. This will only serve to increase the anxiety level of all. Act as though this will be an accomplished fact.

General Fears

29. A successive approximation approach may be used in many cases of fear. An example may be in the case of a child afraid of water. Reinforcements may be given whenever the child makes any response toward water. Gradually the child may approach the fear object without being forced.

30. Counseling sessions should be held with the child in order to help him to understand his fear. Fearful situations may be discussed with him in order to reassure him that there is no longer a need to be fearful but that fears are common and usually diminish through familiarity.

31. Grant a child permission to come to his counselor when he is upset. Talking out his feelings, tearfulness, etc., can drain off his anxiety even without much direction from the counselor. If the problems are serious, then the start of an excellent counselor-child relationship has been made if further work is necessary.

32. For fearfulness, use role-playing. Have the child act out the feared activity in the protected presence of a teacher or counselor. When he feels comfortable in the acting out in this environment then have him try the behavior in the actual situation, or some lesser increment.

33. Problems in affective behavior can often be effectively dealt with in peer groups. The teacher can serve as a nondirective leader or facilitator in a class discussion of fearful emotions. This type of sensitivity training is recommended as an integral facet of the educational program. A teacher should first acquaint herself with the technique so that she may successfully operationalize it in class.

ANXIETY ABOUT TESTS, SCHOOLS, AND FAILURE

34. One may agree with the child that he would un-doubtedly do poorly on tests when he reveals his anxiety. This often gives him the first chance not to have to defend himself or feel guilty about not living up to expectations. This clearly is not a cure-all, but since anxiety is the symptom, easing of the anxiety must precede the solution of the problem. In such cases even

agreeing with the child that he has a right to feel anxious can be a vital first step.

35. Teachers should be cautioned against exposing any student, but especially an anxious one, to ridicule or sarcasm. A student reporting that he "froze up" on a particular test should be listened to sympathetically and, if at all possible, provisions shoud be made for retesting under less stressful conditions. Emphasize that the primary function of testing is to promote learning rather than for evaluation. Desensitization by suggestion is also frequently helpful. The teacher may help by having the children relax physically and envision some relaxing pastime. Her voice and behavior should not send signals that she is tense.

36. Have a test-fearful child take a test orally if unable to take it written.

37. Discuss this problem of fear with the parents noting their level of tolerance. Decide whether or not there is too much urging for the child to be as quick or alert as his brighter siblings. Do the parents nag and scold when he is unsuccessful? Is he terrified of possible failure because of parents' attitude? Desensitize the child by discussing how he feels regarding anxious situations; praise often for small successes; put the work on the level in which he can achieve success. Exhibit his work, and expect his cooperation. Help him to accept criticism and to be satisfied to do his best and try to better his own record.

38. A young child who cries easily and resists difficult tasks may have internalized high standards adopted from his perfectionistic or rejecting parents. Suggest that the parents minimize their criticisms, lower their standards, accept the child as a child, and respond positively to his less-than-perfect performance.

39. Allow the child to set up easy daily goals at first. This will allow the child to decide which weaknesses or strengths he wants to work on specificially and will give him some responsibility for his own behavior.

40. For anxious children, grades or marks should really be eliminated as they create unnecessary anxiety in the child and his parents, and are often used negatively by the parents who punish

the child for poor performance. If grades must be used in a traditional system, then grade these children leniently.

41. Request that the administration establish a genuine nongraded primary as the environment least stressful for children. This minimizes or eliminates grades, unrealistic pressures on teachers, children, and parents, and has countless other advantages for grouping and individualized instruction.

42. An anxious child who experiences considerable rejection and failure will not work well under pressure or in competitive situations. Such a child should function more effectively in small groups. Parent tutoring should be terminated immediately.

43. Counsel with the youngster concerning fears of tests. Parents are to provide a special place for studying. The teacher or counselor may develop with the youngster some good study methods and acts as a reinforcing agent for strengthening study habits. A "study-buddy" system is helpful in preparing for tests if the other student is capable and service-oriented.

44. Promote in the child an awareness of the need to be "test-wise." Provide a schedule of conferences with the child or with his entire class to explain how tests are used and how the scores are only a relative measure of strengths and weaknesses. Practice with the child by using easy tests to begin. Offer remedial help in areas of subject deficiency.

45. This type of anxiety is sometimes brought about by overambitious parents who fail to recognize the child's limitations, needs, and suffering. This type of patient will need help in arriving at realistic expectations and being satisfied with the child's best efforts. Thus, parent counseling is in order.

46. Anxiety can be highly disrupting so it cannot be shrugged off. Neither is it amenable to a common-sense approach of pointing out the inappropriateness of the anxiety. Depending on the severity, two lines of approaching desensitization are available. For relatively mild or recently appearing anxiety, overpreparation and then facing the crucial situation is often sufficient. For deeper or more entrenched anxieties, progressive desensitization with a competent professional is indicated.

DEPRESSION—MILD, MODERATE, SEVERE

47. In the classroom, seat the depressed and unhappy child near the teacher and make a special effort to involve him in class activities. Try to have him assume specific tasks such as passing out papers, being a helper, etc., to keep him alert and interested. Keep him too busy to brood.

48. Encourage the parents to explore medication from a family doctor. Seek the causes of the depression: death in the family, bitter disappointment, repressed hostility?

49. Such a child should be referred immediately to a local mental health center. He will not likely perform effectively in the classroom due to his emotional problems and little improvement will occur until these are resolved. This child will not do well on time-tasks in school. Breaking up long assignments into small segments may be beneficial. Continued pressure will be detrimental; omit home tutoring. A warm, supporting teacher-pupil relationship will be essential.

50. For depression, obtain behavior therapy to train for different behaviors: Utilize assertive training to help the child control more areas of his life and produce effects upon others for his own advantage. Also, reinforce consistently and heavily all spontaneous or requested behaviors involving activity, work, action, play, movement, conversation, projects, discussion, and participation. Offer tokens for any variety of action taken to be traded for money or desired possessions or privileges. The child should have obligations and responsibilities to groups and parents. Interrupt the child's depression with instruction, demands, and assignments; and set time limits for completion of work.

HYPOCHONDRIA AND PSYCHOSOMATIC COMPLAINTS

51. Seek the source of the child's bodily complaints. He may have an ulcer and his stomachache is derived from test anxiety and fear of failure. Place the child in a less demanding curriculum even if he is bright, as he obviously cannot tolerate the stress.

52. For a child with migraine headaches, relieve the tension

from the child's daily routine. Reduce all sources of perfection-istic standards. Give the child more freedom to express his own ideas among siblings and/or classmates.

53. Discuss with the parents the critical medical and psychological aspects of this behavior and refer for psychiatric help, assuring the parents of the need and then working with them until the child is in treatment. Attempt to alleviate the causes where known to lessen the problem until therapy begins.

54. The child should not receive any secondary gain from his symptoms if this pattern is to diminish. Requests to go to the school nurse should be evaluated carefully, and pampering should be minimized. However, the teacher should be supportive and give him the opportunity to talk about what is upsetting him.

55. This type of complaint often comes from students with considerable anxiety caused by academic and parental pressures. The social and emotional pressures are frequently caused by a demanding parent. This parent should focus on the child's health and adjustment rather than on grades or the ambitions of the parent himself. Family therapy is recommended.

56. Persistent and minor somatic complaints should be treated as a budding school phobia, especially if these occur at the beginning of the school week or during test time. In conference with the parents, a referral to the family physician is in order. If the child is healthy the child should be in school. The parents should "take his temperature" on the morning of a day of complaint to let the child see that they are interested in him. However, a united front should be presented to the child by both parents insisting upon regular attendance. The child should be reassured that he can see the school nurse if he becomes ill at school. The school nurse should be alerted to the case to see that the child is returned to the classroom if not really ill.

IDENTIFIABLE EMOTIONS: EXCESSIVE GUILT, SHAME, INFERIORITY

57. Bibliotherapy is often most effective in dealing with transient emotional problems. There exists a wealth of books related to well-known problems experienced by many children.

For example, if a child is concerned about his small physical stature, a newly born sibling, being adopted, etc., he can read about it. If there is interest in sexual reproduction, masturbation, etc., then the first step is to have correct information to dispel myths and ignorance.

58. An especially sensitive teacher may develop a mental health unit in class which deals with people's feelings. This unit might emphasize particularly the emotion with which the subject is having difficulty. She should encourage all the children's verbalizations about their feelings. Perhaps the teacher or the children might invite the school psychologist into the classroom to talk about people's feelings and the reasons for them.

59. For feelings of inferiority in a child:
   a. Inspire confidence in his own ability.
   b. Supply work to help him "catch up" with the group.
   c. Test specific areas of achievement and devise a program at these levels.
   d. Capitalize on strengths shown by tests and interview.
   e. Let the child do something for the teacher.
   f. Express appreciation for effort.
   g. Appoint him to "head" a committee.
   h. Include him in a spirited special panel on "emotionally charged" topics: crime, pollution, etc.
   i. Include him in a group whose work merits special recognition.
   j. Send a note home telling of good effort.
   k. Involve the child in class discussion, questions, activities.
   l. Make observation projects involving social behavior— in the cafeteria, halls, downtown, in theaters, etc. Teach him to watch for desirable and undesirable behavior in others.

60. Some children feel inferior or behave badly or ineffectively in physical education class, art, and similar areas because of lack of coordination, feelings of shame, etc. For example, in gym some children may be embarrassed because of their size, weight, or general ineptitude. Give some special "tutoring" in how to shoot a basket or to perform some tumbling activity; the children

may develop more confidence. Many children dislike these special areas, not because they cannot do well in all or some aspect of the program, but because they fear ridicule—real or imagined. Such a child might be asked to help score or keep time until he develops some skill in the activity.

Chapter VIII

COGNITIVE DYSFUNCTION

I F THE COGNITIVE processes are disrupted for practically any reason, a multitude of special stresses are placed upon the child in school. Expected to perform at a presumed or measured ability level, the ineffective child cannot in fact use his ability to full potential to reach adequate achievement. His teacher or parents, hoping for normal functioning, initially tend to ignore the subtle problems in the child's thinking process, his confusions, misinterpretations, and loss of drive. His inability to think abstractly and to deal symbolically in both verbal and quantitative spheres often has more to do with his lack of an organized process than with the intelligence level itself. Major problems in reading, arithmetic, spelling, and writing may occur, not for lack of initial motivation or sound instruction in school by dedicated teachers, but for detectable deficits in cognitive equipment or its functioning.

Special limitations may arise from developmental delays, a lack of cognitive experiences, and the presence of emotional problems and conflicts. The resulting underachievement (as determined through an achievement expectancy from intelligence test scores) adds to the child's problems, since the treatment often attempted by well-intentioned teachers and parents is to apply "pressure" for accomplishment or "challenge" in his academic work. Although some children with full neural equipment, resources, and motivation can learn under some pressure like this, many children with liabilities in cognitive functioning become significantly less effective as pressures become cumulative and anxiety dominates his affective state. In addition, such children receive far less reinforcement for the achievement which they can muster—and so the cycle of defeat begins.

Significantly, it is here that the role of the diagnostic-prescriptive psychologist may come to bear, especially in a teen relationship. The psychologist may psychometrically tap the child's assets and liabilities in the learning areas with the help of educators and other specialists and then help to account for his problems and explain them via many theoretical routes to the interested teachers and parents. Naturally, the team members must prescribe appropriate remedial programs deemed to be effective for the child's future. In general, instruction should be aimed at teaching him through his strongest modalities within the regular class while intensive remedial work is offered in a tutoring or special facility. Some cognitive dysfunctions can be remediated by individual or small group programs while others seem impervious to change, i.e. extreme dyslexic conditions apparently due to organic deficits.

Psychogenetically derived cognitive dysfunction, such as passive-aggressive behavior, is sometimes emotionally satisfying and necessary to the child for unique reasons dealing with survival in a conflict situation. Cognitive problems are revealed as a result of more subtle strategies on the part of the child to evade the standards of others. These are based apparently upon unconscious and tenuously recognized reactions against unrealistic aspirations of the parents according to psychodynamically oriented professionals. The difficulty may appear to be a reading problem per se, which assuredly requires instructional assistance, but its source is rooted in the child's rebellion and saps his desire to achieve in school. If anything, the child is truly an expert at failure or near-failure behavior. This variety of resistance is manifested in the child who resents being "used" by the parents for their own aims, although they frankly feel that they have had only his best interests in mind. Obviously no single prescription will untangle this series of confused messages between parents and child. Counseling or therapeutic contacts, often involving long-range commitments, are often necessary to clarify the issues, develop mutual understandings, or establish reward systems for productive behavior.

When considering these kinds of ineffective behaviors of the child, the reader is asked to attend not only to the legitimate prescriptions for these problems of learning in the reading or arithmetic area, but also to be attuned to the other treatments which attack the basic difficulty: strained interpersonal relationships.

The last section of this chapter deals with additional disruptions of the cognitive process ranging from problems with reality contact and fantasy to distractibility and on to memory problems. Some of these difficulties may require extensive psychological and medical assessment and treatment. No problems are dealt with exhaustively, yet the creative clinician may determine a basis of operation here by considering a general range of treatment approaches for the respective problems.

Strictly in the educational domain, educators and psychologists will continue to learn of better and more experimentally valid instructional techniques and curricular programs. These should be substituted for the ones listed in this chapter which will tend to become outmoded or simply nonproductive.

SECTION A: LEARNING FAILURES

Learning Inhibition Due to Emotional Difficulty

1. It is recommended that a comprehensive psychoeducational evaluation be executed to determine the full range of the child's problems and the possible causes leading to those difficulties. Such a study is essential to help determine the several remedial strategies which may be necessary to assist the child. It may be essential that psychotherapy be recommended to affect the emotional difficulties in the case often accompanying the child's learning problems in school.

2. Begin by establishing a reinforcement schedule at school rewarding the child's completion of his work. Offer short assignments that the child can and will probably finish. When possible, give tailor-made homework that is within the endurance and interest span of the child. Find out through interviewing what interests the child has and attempt to match these with the curricular experiences and assignments.

3. The counselor or psychologist should work with the child with the parents' consent, to focus on the emotional problems on a one-to-one therapeutic basis possibly by engaging in values clarification counseling sessions to help the student sort out priorities and to review the contradictions in stated beliefs and behaviors of the child.

4. The teacher may take occasion to spend special time alone with this child. These times together can involve a review of academic strengths and weaknesses and may allow the child a chance to ventilate feelings of distress and guilt about his academics. This is predicated on the teacher having an excellent personal relationship with the child.

5. The child who has problems in self-control and limited motivation in school will function best with the teacher who is both firm and supportive. In addition, such a child needs specific directions and concrete materials to help him organize his energies and focus on the required tasks. The teacher should be aware, however, that despite her best efforts, such a child may go through periods of inefficiency, moodiness, and depression. She can continue to express her interest and her optimism about the return of his "good days" of acceptable work and she will be sure to notice even small increments of efficiency. A teacher or parent should not destroy this newly formed maturity, by comparing it with past immaturities with questions like, "Why don't you always work that well? Why didn't you do that well before?"

6. If the child has several teachers during a school day, they should decide among themselves with reasonable unanimity how the child is to be treated. They then present the child with a consistent expectation of behavior to which he should adhere. This should create a model that is less confusing and less anxiety-arousing than if the staff all had different standards for him.

7. To assist the child who has difficulty in holding his attention, the classroom should be made as free as possible from distracting stimuli. This might encompass a study carrel, a seat near the teacher with student friends near him or perhaps an "office" which is surrounded by a screen.

8. The teacher should try to reorganize the learning tasks so

that they are clearly defined, for example, "We are going to read this next paragraph to find out what happened to Billy's father. I will ask one of you to tell us what happened."

9. Perhaps this child could be transferred to a special education program such as Distributive Education.

10. Since anxiety tends to increase as the day progresses for failure-prone children, the more difficult studies might be taught in the morning. A shortened school day and perhaps a part-time job might be helpful for all the students disinclined to work at school. This is useful only to the older adolescent in view of work laws and the amount of skills needed for the employment of adolescents.

11. For a teenager who has an alcoholic parent, a referral to Alateen is in order. Here the child can receive supportive help of peers and a professional adult when reviewing common problems.

12. The librarian and an English teacher could cooperate in providing a list of readings as a form of bibliotherapy about parent-child relationships, peer trouble, divorcing parents, sibling rivalry, etc., as the problem so dictates. Most counseling offices have such literature available at the reader's level. Good information can sometimes help clarify problems.

13. Teach to the child's instructional level, i.e. one or two grade levels below the achievement test scores. That is, if the child scores low sixth grade on a Standardized Reading Test, his instructional level is about low fourth or low fifth grade and that is where he should be placed for group reading. In math, one must diagnose the errors made on the arithmetic test and teach those concepts that lead to correct solutions which the child must practice. The teacher should consider the possibility that previous failures have made learning tasks very distasteful and now arouse anxiety. Development of a classroom routine that includes a minimum of difficult tasks and guarantees a high probability of success experiences might help break this defeating cycle of failure. For a truly upset child, try to discover the source of emotional difficulty and conflict. Use other children in the class or in the upper grades for tutoring such an individual. Secure or devise educational games aimed at overcoming learning difficul-

ties by discovering areas of interest, or at least relative competence, and use these as a core in centering the studies.

14. Send the child part-time to a Resource Room or Learning Center in the school where individual diagnostic and remedial work may occur at a more favorable atmosphere of small teacher-pupil ratio.

15. All pressure should be removed if possible from the emotionally conflicted youngster while in the learning situation. The teacher should emphasize only those areas where the child feels at least minimally competent. Gradually, the child is placed back into the mainstream of academics only after he is ready and able even though this may take from one to three years. Though it is true that small amounts of tension do aid normal learning, the mostly disturbed children are frequently too overwhelmed with anxiety or other emotional reactions to learn effectively because of interference. They frankly pay more attention to their inner fears and difficulties than to the external world of facts and relationships.

16. Call the child's name, praise his attending to the subject, reward correct responses, and minimize the input of error. No teacher could be effective until the child is paying attention to her.

17. As a method of increasing a child's self-confidence, the teacher should call on the child for recitation only when the teacher is relatively sure that the child will know the correct answer.

18. The teacher might work towards increasing a child's self-esteem by giving him jobs that make him feel important. Successful experiences should be maximized by giving him new materials in small doses. Areas of strength should be highly commended. He should be given support when he experiences failure by acknowledging the difficulty rather than glossing over it. For example, "You seem upset and angry because you couldn't do all the arithmetic examples. It will take some time before you get all of them. You were able to get several of them right. I'm happy that you're trying so hard."

19. Reduce critical remarks by looking for positive aspects of behavior where the child can be genuinely commended. The

elevation of low self-esteem is quite important.

20. A summer tutorial program is probably appropriate for the child who does not benefit from regular class instruction during the year. Naturally the child's resistance to such extensive school work must be taken into consideration.

21. Punishment for lack of motivation is probably inappropriate and should be replaced instead by positively reinforcing creditable work. The general rule-of-thumb is, the more disturbed the child, the more primary is the reinforcement to be selected for use. Thus a truly disturbed child might best respond to food reward, candy, physical affection, and those with relatively minor problems can often respond to teacher praise and approval if the relationship with her is positive. Should the teacher "yell" at the child when he is daydreaming and criticizing, this may actually reinforce that behavior just because the child received attention, even though this is negative attention. Research into behavior modification in classrooms has clearly verified this principle countless times. The difficulty is to control what is a positive reinforcement in the classroom.

22. For the parents who wish to help their underachieving child, it is necessary to explain that the child's instructional level is at least a year or two below the test-score level and that their role is to reinstruct him or reinforce him in areas where he is actually competent and comfortable. Parents should not try to teach the child new material. When it is the child's moment to read to the parents or recite a spelling list, they should guarantee that the material is simple enough for him to be successful and see pleasant responses when he performs for them. For parents involved with their children's school difficulties, a professional psychologist or related person may explain that certain needs must be met (attention, recognition, achievement, peer group approval, affection) before the child is able to approximate his full potential. They must seek ways to meet these needs. Such an approach must be preceded by a clinician administering projective testing and a clinical interview to the child to tap out the significant needs that have not been met.

23. A summer camp program involving full-time residents may be helpful to the child with emotional problems. Here the

entire structure of the camp is ready to accept various outbursts and have sensible ways to divert destructive behavior. Many of these camps are quite stimulating, well-organized and essentially therapeutic, and even the children testify to their gain and confidence after these experiences. The parents are to be helped in understanding that emotions can block learning as clearly as intellectual, physical, and health problems. Naturally it is necessary for mental retardation to be ruled out through psychological appraisal. The parents must understand that punishment practices must be replaced to a great extent by a more positive approach and that some emphasis can be put on deprivation of privileges. Perhaps a tutor can be employed by the parents. They must understand that the child does not consciously or willfully do poorly as a "get even" tactic, but in fact may be unconsciously rebelling against excessive parental pressure or expectations. It is important that a psychological study be done to evaluate this aspect of the problem.

24. Sometimes vocational school placements might be appropriate for a child facing considerable learning difficulties. These are especially good if there is also a learning disabled class available part-time in a vocational program. Although this is continually debatable, request of the parent that the child be fed only a tiny breakfast so that he will respond better to food reinforcements as rewards for school learning in conjunction with a behavior-shaping program designed by the psychologist. Denial or restriction of primary rewards is a debatable practice even though it has often been effective in modifying the child's behavior. If the child is restricted in some normal reward, he can become quite resistant to the program. A timer with a bell or alarm clock can be used for the child who has some difficulty in meeting responsibility of homework assignments. A signal will indicate a time to begin and end and a definite study period of time is established. This will eliminate the child's resistance to parental "nagging." The parents may provide some food or treat at the close of the study period.

25. To reduce the emotional conflict experienced by a child, it may be helpful if the parent spends more time with him in activities without other siblings being present. Furthermore, the

most anxious parents should stop trying to teach the child or threaten the child with punishments. The calmer of the two parents is more appropriate. When both parents are calm, they should spend time with the child engaging in pleasant conversation and simple duties. Perhaps he can be allowed to make some decisions about his activities in the day and the parents revealing that his opinions have merit.

26. Those parents who infantalize their child should be referred for guidance in a mental health clinic or private practitioner. It would be well to point out the relationship between their lack of discipline and indulgence to the child's poor achievement. For poor performance, deprivation of privileges should follow, but this is very difficult for a loving indulgent parent to execute, and such a parent may need outside assistance.

Pseudoretardation

27. The pseudoretarded child has often been indoctrinated by the advantages of acting like a helpless and dependent infant. Often he enjoys the indulgent behaviors executed by parents because of their concentrated attention on him. However, the child knows that if he learns things too well or rapidly, the indulgence will end. In order to break up this pattern of stubborn behavior, it should be pointed out to the parents that their reaction is reinforcing and insuring the continuance of the child's dependency. The teacher should give the child no help in class beyond what the class gets as a group and not respond to his helplessness. She instead should respond to his own initiative and motivation. When the child appeals for assistance when it is actually not required she might say, "You can do that, let me see you do your own work today." For the parent who refuses to see that the child is not as incapable as he pretends to be, it could be pointed out that a "very expensive" private school might be appropriate for the child. This "suggestion" might help them realize that a shift in their behaviors is now merited since the private costs are often prohibitive. Such parents may well need counseling to understand the roots of their own indulgence of the child. Often it is related to their high state of anxiety and their

feeling that anything they might do will "harm" the child or that they may lose his love. It is a complicated problem that needs professional investigation.

28. The pseudoretarded child should be maintained in a regular class, certainly not in a class for the mentally retarded. He should be provided with a typical amount of verbal information and discussion without the demand that he take part. The school psychologist will never permit a pseudoretarded child to enter the retarded class as this is unethical and illegal and, of course, may result in a self-fulfilling prophecy damaging to the child.

29. Sometimes in the case of pseudoretardation, the child does not want to supersede one of the parents who is particularly defective in school learning much earlier and may not want to surpass such a parent. It is necessary for this parent to be very clear about reinforcing the child for school success, and counseling may be necessary for both of them. Certainly a powerful behavior modification reward system should be established by a counselor or psychologist for a child like this. Most teachers, even with behavior modification training, do need to have a consultant to discuss a behavioral program in detail.

Underachievement—Passive-Aggressive Behavior, or Poor Educational Background

30. Classroom assignments for the underachiever should be well structured at the instructional level and not the ability level. The problem is frequently one of motivation or a special learning disability which requires psychological evaluation. It is essential for the professionals to understand the parameters of the problems so that they can select appropriate remedial strategies. An excellent psychoeducational evaluation is crucial.

31. Students at the upper elementary level who show average achievement or slightly below that should be released to tutor younger children in the primary grades also demonstrating underachievement. In terms of peer group tutoring, students with learning problems seem to relate well to others who are experiencing similar problems and end up reinforcing their own skills.

32. Some underachieving children display considerable

interest and enthusiasm in isolated subject areas: sports, cars, baby care, etc.. Capitalize upon these interests by seeing the child complete assignments in these areas if possible. Hopefully with the introduction of new materials, positive attitudes may generalize to the regular subject areas.

33. A special program for underachieving youngsters should be developed after there is a general agreement about the criteria for selection by the staff and psychologist. It may be difficult to eliminate the number of children eligible since approximately one out of five children in a typical classroom manifest learning disabilities let alone underachievement for that or other reasons. In the urban schools and in the low class neighborhoods, the underachievement frequently includes over 50 percent of an individual class. Such a program for underachievers, the teachers might well function in a nongraded team-teaching situation backed up by intensive remedial programs. The children should have varying class sizes of no more than three to fifteen pupils at least part-time. The project method is often employed in science and social studies or as remedial techniques are used in reading and math. Intensive tutoring should be also available, and diagnostic evaluation should preceed such specialized training. It is possible that government or state funding might be accessible to mount such a comprehensive program. It is essential that the programs be quite individualized for each child even though they can be grouped should they manifest common problems and similar instructional levels.

34. To focus on the affective side of underachievement, several such pupils can participate in group discussions with a counselor. That person should be flexible and understanding, be capable of reflecting their frequent feelings of self-condemnation and failure, and allow them to ventilate their frustrations and negative attitudes towards adults and the educational programs. The end result is to help them diffuse their anger and anxiety and to see that they themselves are an integral part of this problem and must attack it directly rather than project blame on others. Extensive sessions in values clarification will be quite important, as it is necessary to understand how one not only desires certain goals but must behave in a way commensurate to achieve those goals.

35. The teacher or counselor may obtain the confidence of the child by being genuinely concerned about his underachievement and his feelings about this. It is appropriate to discuss the child's potentials as well as his weaknesses with him as he is vividly aware of the latter. One starts by planning a realistic program at a level where the child is working comfortably and by developing a reward system by earning so many tokens or marks in one week that may be "cashed in" for special school privileges or rewards at home. The parents can be included in this planning and can supply a prize. A reasonable goal should be set so that the child does not become initially defeated the first week. Give him a healthy amount of "points" just for agreeing to participate in the reward program.

36. Secondary and social reinforcers are ultimately the best for a typical classroom; however, start with something that is extrinsically rewarding, e.g. M & M's, a small candy bar, a game with the teacher or friend; graduate slowly to more subtle and social reinforcers such as the teacher's verbal approval, smile, a note home, peer approval, etc.

37. If the student is deficient in writing by virtue of some visual motor problems and has difficulty in handling written assignments, give him oral examinations or let him tape-record his responses on a cassette tape.

38. If at all possible, do not let the child be wrong in response to a question given in classroom. The teacher should be willing to provide plenty of "hints" to almost guarantee that the child "gets it" correctly. When he responds correctly, obviously she should praise him.

39. The parents should be kept informed about the particular and individualized assignments given to the child. Sometimes these must be given via a telephone message by the teacher as the child sometimes "loses" the notes from the teacher to his parents. Earned privileges are dependent upon completed homework assignments for underachievers.

40. The parents may inquire of school personnel about a list of approved tutors in certain subject areas where the child is deficient.

41. An underachiever may have a slow pace of life and may

require extra attention and additional time to complete assignments. Naturally a physical examination is required to rule out contributing medical problems.

42. If the student has some problem in handwriting, perhaps typing may help him with his written assignments more effectively or perhaps another family member may do the typing for him.

43. As noted in other academic areas, a peer tutoring arrangement may be helpful especially from an older child who is service oriented.

44. Parents may eventually need to recognize that the problems of many underachievers are deeply rooted in psychological conflict of trying to stay dependent and "babied" on one hand, while also trying to become independent and mature on the other. Although the recommendation for psychotherapy for the child and his parents may be warranted, it is an idea that relatively few parents can accept or afford. Most parents will resist therapy until they have exhausted all of their own strategies and those of the school personnel. Therapy cannot be pressured onto parents.

45. Sometimes group therapy in the school setting can be effective with underachieving children if motivation and personality problems interfere with learning. Obviously, parental permission is essential as well as a high degree of competence on the part of the therapist. The therapist must select the group members and not the administration or the faculty.

46. To help the child get started, often a reduction in the level of expectation for the underachiever is necessary. He might learn to work more comfortably within this new frame of reference which deals with helping him at a very low instructional level and reinforcing for any and all efforts on the part of the child as he tries to achieve. Certainly the teacher offers considerable encouragement after the child makes some progress. Many such children are demoralized by their past defeats and it may take many months of personal assistance and encouragement to get them to "try one more time."

47. It should be obvious that differentiated assignments are needed for individual underachievers, even those who are quite bright.

48. The underachiever, if possible, should be provided with a quiet, private place to study at school or at home and the parents should set aside a time each evening when he is supposed to do homework. They are to reward with some "treat" for him when he accomplishes his assignments.

49. With the assistance of a specialist, a reading program should be developed which taps all modes of sensory input like various visual motor activities, the Gillingham-Stillman for association difficulties, the use of tactile methods such as recessed letters and numbers, raised letters and numbers, sand tables, sandpaper letters, etc. Use analogy games for auditory-vocal associations. The regular classroom teacher or Resource Room person should talk with the specialized reading teachers or teachers of learning disabled children to see what methods they use.

50. Suggest to the parents the reading of a book by Bricklin and Bricklin: *Bright Child, Poor Grades*, New York City, Delacorte Press. This book, which is essentially psychodynamic in orientation, expresses well the dilemmas and problems faced by underachieving children and outlines vividly the contributions which parents may inadvertently make in the life of the underachiever. In most cases, psychotherapeutic interventions were necessary for the child and family.

51. Perhaps a transitional first grade for children manifesting learning problems should be used by the school. Children in this class may have intense perceptual problems, come from unstimulating environments, or confusing bilingual backgrounds, be generally "immature," reveal low test scores for readiness in addition to many observations by teachers in the kindergarten program. Due to problems of short attention span, such children may be able to tolerate only a shortened academic day which may have more physical activity, recreation, play, and rest. Many such children are still operating as late nursery school or kindergarten-level children and we must suit the program to their current functioning. They may later make more rapid gains once their problems are minimized.

52. Provide shorter assignments, such as fewer spelling words to learn, fewer arithmetic problems to do, making sure

several are easy or already known. Set time limits within which the work should be done, preferably longer than should be necessary so that the pupil can "beat the clock" as well as have a relatively successful experience.

53. Give marks and report card grades on the basis of effort and production, rather than marking in relation to the class. Help the parents to understand what the marks mean. Perhaps no marks or a different method of reporting like a conference with parents, would be better yet.

54. When the pupil begins to do better work, or even when there is sporadic improvement or even a single good piece of work, be sure his effort is well-recognized by putting it on the bulletin board, sending him to show what he has done to the principal, his last year's teacher, or anyone else who is interested in him and who will respond positively to his accomplishment.

55. The teacher should lower the academic expectations to guarantee a long series of academic successes by determining first where the child is providing a program at such a low level. She will not give the child assignments or class work he cannot or will not do just because the rest of the class gets them. Obviously children are all different and underachievers in particular need different assignments. The underachiever is different; the child knows it and so do the class and his parents.

56. If academic underachievement is due to neglect, physical or emotional problems, the case may be referred to welfare officials for assistance and possibly evaluation. The school nurse or the school social worker may visit the home to appraise problems there and in all likelihood the school psychologist should be involved with a comprehensive psychoeducational evaluation.

57. Increased parental pressure toward achievement is likely to result in minimal productivity. It seems essential that production in the school should be dealt with by the teacher and the child, with the parents exerting no pressure, but offering commendation for effort. If the child does not produce, the teacher may introduce such sanctions as loss of free time, but nothing is to be said at home. If no results occur in a reasonable

period of time, say, one semester, then therapy is usually warranted.

58. A capable child who fails to produce may feel overwhelmed by what he perceives as excessive demands. A "contract" approach may be helpful—that is, the child and his teacher plan together what specific assignments he will complete. Appropriate rewards for completion and/or sanctions for noncompletion could be determined during such planning, so that the child has the security of knowing what to expect.

59. In private, talk with the underachiever realistically about his strong and weak points and inquire about what he thinks the trouble is and what he can do to aid himself. Help him set initial academic goals that are achievable for him. It is extremely simple to be more logical and more rational than the underachiever. Try to limit the opportunities for making him feel even more ridiculous than he already does.

60. Get excited about his productions. Carry him along on enthusiasm alone. Tell him that his efforts are just between him and his teacher and his results will not be sent to the parents, his personal jury set for conviction.

61. Always have parent conferences to keep them informed of progress or lack of it; be specific with them in observations and document comments if possible.

62. Ask the child to work as a personal favor to the teacher if there is a good relationship. Personalize the request and indicate the hope that he will do one task well today in the academic line. Tell him that he can relax all the rest of the period, perhaps the day. Request these half-hour productions for a week or so, expecting no more. Then try for a forty-five minute spurt with some rewards available to him. Let him relax the rest of the period in class. Inform the class why.

63. Retention in school grade almost never benefits the child and has, unfortunately, a ring of revenge and condemnation. The child who profits from this retention is one who has had total remediation of the problems that made him "fail" in the first place. Do not threaten the child with retention when discussing his deficient work and poor habits. The superior and normal student will be scared out if his wits and will be well-motivated by

threat of retention, but, frankly, it is never needed for a person like this.

64. Many underachievers unconsciously do not want to succeed and are trying deliberately but unconsciously to fail. This academic and vocational suicide is a way of fighting a battle for independence, mostly against certain kinds of parental expectations or when locked in a sibling rivalry. Underachievers are still worthy of praise, respect, and fair treatment.

65. Set up with the child a "study-buddy" system with his neighborhood boyfriend to exchange study sessions at their homes on a schedule.

66. Give skill training to the child privately in good grooming and personal care; teach him how to shake hands, how to dress, and to become friendly with others. Give him the chance to clean up his hands and comb his hair. React positively even to minimal efforts. He may perceive himself as perceived by others.

67. The teacher may strive to be the child's "different" teacher who avoids criticizing or feeling angry at his underachievement. The child feels guilty enough at the conscious level; more guilt will not help the matter. The teacher will avoid creating more anxiety in the child than is already there. Even though he may cover his feelings, his anxiety is always present even though he has an attitude of nonchalance and seeming indifference. The teacher will make every attempt to really like the child and respect him even if he does not improve. She will attempt to offer him the qualities of friendship—a good friend knows your limitations and likes you anyway.

68. Do not sit the child next to superior students, but rather with average students whom he likes and who like him. Ask them, with his knowledge, to "keep him on the track" in a friendly and helpful way in terms of desk work, writing down assignments, and reminding him of due-dates on reports and projects.

69. Teachers should make themselves available to underachieving students before or after school at least one day per week for individual help. Some children should get consistent, individual help, possibly ten minutes a day to review homework.

70. For underachievers, a vocational program might empha-

size arts, crafts, business, home economics, and shop courses that may make use of an underachiever's strength and underplay his weaknesses. It should be recognized that just because a child is poor in academic subjects it does not necessarily mean that he will be particularly good in use with his hands or particularly skilled in motor functions.

71. The underachiever from a poor cultural background may be rewarded for progress with tokens which can be "cashed in" at the end of the day for candy privileges or special rewards. To insure accuracy and neatness, tokens could be added or subtracted from the child's "bag of tokens." In one school in an urban setting where this was tried, it was surprising to find that some of these children were cashing in their tokens for school materials in order to continue schoolwork at home. They were buying construction paper, paste, and even mimeographed assignments.

72. For such children from an economically deprived background, they face a number of unrelenting problems: no place to study, distractions, parents not interested, health difficulties at home, etc. Since teachers usually stay a bit later than most pupils, the school could assign one special room for those children who wish to study after school to complete assignments and request a volunteer teacher or parent to monitor it. Such students could be invited to make use of such facilities after school. Naturally it is to be done on a permissive basis and it could be called a "homework clinic."

73. If a child forgets his homework, he should be allowed to make it up during recess or after school. This should not be done as a punishment, but the child should be made to see that he can control whether or not he goes out to recess, and by not doing his work he is hurting himself.

74. Lowering the academic expectations is not always a means of helping an underachieving youngster. Frequently the problem is the lack of interest and motivation. This is particularly true of the high ability and gifted youngster, who is bored with many of the classroom's typical assignments. Using his areas of interest in giving him assignments which gain him status with his peer groups frequently is a successful method to motivate this student.

75. A child living in a disturbed family circumstance may have learned the relative security of silence and passivity. Although counseling and family therapy might be recommended to such parents, it is not surprising that most reject it. The main work has to be done with the child in the school setting and the staff must make every effort to win the child's trust and confidence.

76. Many parents, anxious because of the child's under-achievement, insist on providing instruction at home and request the teacher to provide specific things for the child to do. Instead of letting them help with reading or arithmetic which require new teaching, suggest that they review old spelling words, well-known number facts, and perhaps read a story that the child has always enjoyed. The parents should try to reinforce old well-known skills and not develop new ones. Much of what they are asked to do should cover subject matter which the child can handle fairly well so that both parents and child can experience the satisfaction of success. All such work should be quite brief.

77. If underachievement problems develop, sometimes a change in teachers, even mid-semester, can alleviate the problem.

78. At the secondary level, the students who are in academic difficulty might be allowed to come into the guidance office for remedial help. During a study period, they could meet with a peer-group member who is proficient in the area of difficulty. The child usually feels more comfortable with a peer-group member than with the teacher and may come daily for such assistance.

79. As a temporary relief for the child, ask the parents to stop asking the child about school. Give him full responsibility for his homework and school assignments and consider hiring a private tutor.

80. Sometimes a boarding or a prep school provides the necessary structure and environment needed to change the behavior of a serious underachiever. The move to a private school has disadvantages and advantages since it is a major change in the child's environment. This needs to be reviewed in depth; loss of freedom, relief from tension, loneliness, the chance for a new start, etc. All these pros and cons must be weighed by the child

and his parents together before a decision is made. Not all children profit from such experiences.

81. Use a reinforcement chart. When the student has earned a certain number of points, he may take the chart home where it is turned in for some prearranged activity with the parents, such as playing a game with them, baking a cake, going shopping, or earning money towards some valued possession.

82. If the child's difficulties in verbal expression suggest a need for broader experience, the parents may need to spend more time reading to him and talking about what was read, discussing about television, conversing about real-life experiences, helping him describe his own actions.

83. Perhaps the parents can start a school scrapbook to be filled with the children's school drawings, good test results, and examples from his daily work. The child could be encouraged to bring home work regularly to be added to the scrapbook, and the parents may react favorably as they occasionally look through it with the child.

84. For children who are completing a year of attendance of kindergarten but are not academically or emotionally ready for the first grade, the child might be enrolled in a transitional first grade or nongraded primary class. The parents obviously must be involved with this decision.

Reading Underachievement

85. Materials available to aid the child with reading and language difficulties include:
   a. Kinesthetic Alphabet, Products, by H. R. Stone.
   b. Language Building Cards, Sound Identification Cards, and Something to Say During the Day by Interstate.
   c. Peabody Rebus Reading Program, and Peabody Language Development Kit, by American Guidance Service.
   d. Sounds and Patterns of Language, by Holt, Rinehart and Winston.
   e. Vallett's Psychoeducational Resource Programs Nos. 37-41, by Fearon Publ.

f. Words and Patterns: A Spelling Series, by SRA.

86. Encourage the child with reading problems to learn through movies, T.V., other visual aids, records, tapes, lectures, field trips, and listening in class. Reading is just one way to obtain information.

87. A remedial reading program should be attempted using a very highly structured, multisensory and phonic program, such as the Gillingham-Stillman method, and should be intensively instituted. A reading program as is offered by a University Reading Clinic should be seriously considered. The child may require an adjusted program in the regular class but retention should not be considered unless it is clearly going to be of benefit for the child.

88. Underachievers may find it more relaxing to use large-print books, as these seem to be less threatening than the material written in standard print. The large-print *World Book Encyclopedia*, for example, is used more often by children who are apprehensive about opening a regular reference book.

89. Programs available to aid in the instruction of a child with difficulty in reading include:
   a. Listen and Read program by Educational Developmental Laboratories.
   b. New Phonics Skill texts in the Merrill Phonics Program.
   c. Open Highways Program by Scott, Foresman.
   d. Reading for Understanding by S.R.A.
   e. Reading Thinking Skills by Continental Press.
   f. Sullivan Associates Programmed Reading, by Webster Division, McGraw-Hill Book Company.

90. If a child is severely deficient in reading, he will certainly need a placement in a remedial reading program with teaching emphasis on the visual, auditory, kinesthetic, and tactile (VAKT) approaches.

91. A severely dyslexic child should be taught as though he were a blind child. All too often, such an individual is cut off from many educational experiences because so much effort is used in teaching him to read. Unfortunately it is difficult to make this diagnosis because some children who are apparently dyslexic

end up being at least partially remediated. The aim of this special recommendation to treat him as a blind child is merely to provide intensive education also through the auditory channels.

92. For a resistant child who refuses to do the drill and repetition necessary to master basic reading concepts, he is given readiness work at his level and the teacher insists that he does it even if he misses out on recess. The work is steadily increased as the child realizes that he has only the alternative of missing pleasant times.

93. Use a language laboratory approach with cassette tapes for reading in science, social studies, and English.

94. A careful diagnosis by a reading specialist or psycholinguistic consultant may be essential. Dyslexic children are usually visually or auditorially perceptually handicapped or have unusual language impairments or perhaps some combination. Have the visually perceptually handicapped child use phonics and the auditorially perceptually handicapped child begin with a sight vocabulary and then develop some phonic abilities.

95. Even materials in shop class must be adjusted to a very low reading level for disabled readers. A ninth grade boy reading at the fifth grade level must have a shop manual written at this lower level if he is to succeed in interpreting the work. This might be an interesting "translation" assignment for a superior student looking for a work project.

96. Children with reading comprehension problems might have the Merrill Skill Texts offered. When the child begins to find some success with them, give praise and tangible rewards occasionally. Too much praise is tawdry and sometimes backfires. The child should not be permitted to disturb the learnings of his classmates and should be dealt with sternly to conform to reasonable class norms of social conduct.

97. For those unable to read efficiently, perhaps they can be offered a "bookless curriculum." This incorporates various modern technology to replace reading skills that are both uncomfortable and inefficient. Various auditory media, records, cassette tapes, and language laboratory techniques are used if properly structured. The goals should include the child's ability

to think critically, the transmission of culture, etc. Other considerations for the child might be interesting guest speakers, books on tape, field trips, discussion groups, training in the artistic areas, etc.

98. Let the child point with his finger at words in the reading book. Removing his finger may force him to lose his place since he may have some distractibility problems and visual tracking problems. Later when he is a good reader he will probably discard the use of pointing.

99. Parents should never "give the answer" to an underachieving child doing his homework but rather should make the child look it up after giving him guidance. If necessary parents may suggest that the child find it "somewhere between lines 4 and 7" in his reading book.

100. It is quite appropriate for parents to obtain some simple Dolch® games which can be used in a benign manner to reinforce classroom learnings at home with their child.

101. The child may be allowed to read from five to fifteen minutes aloud every day and have the parent help him "sound out" new words. This provides him with auditory as well as visual and content clues. Let the child read simple stories so that there is no effort, yet much pleasure in reciting aloud. Let the child read a comic book, as this is better than no reading at all and in fact may stimulate reading speed and greater interest later on.

102. If at all possible, the parents should be as relaxed as possible and not reveal to the child that they are anxious about his reading problems. They should reassure him that his problem is very common and that, although progress is slow, he will eventually learn to read well if steady efforts are made by all concerned.

Arithmetic Underachievement

103. Helpful material for individualized remedial instruction in arithmetic includes:
   a. Basic Mathematics: A Programmed Instruction by Appleton-Century-Crofts, Meredith Corporation.
   b. Self-Teaching Arithmetic by Scholastic Book Serv-

ices of Scholastic Magazine.
c. Vallett's Psychoeducational Programs Nos. 44-46, Fearon Publ.

104. Extensive drill in addition, subtraction, multiplication, and division tables might be useful to the child deficient in arithmetic processes. This new material is to be taught in class while old and easy information is practiced at home.

105. Lined paper turned sideways is sometimes a helpful device for the child who has difficulty writing the numbers for arithmetic problems in straight columns and rows. Sometimes graph paper is helpful or the child may line his own paper with a ruler.

106. With older children money is often an instructional breakthrough if they are old enough to value it. Use the cafeteria milk money for the arithmetic class to make things realistic. Real dollars make the problems quite interesting to children. Try to relate money to prized objects seen in store catalogs.

107. Try unusual materials to arouse the children's curiosity over basic quantitative concepts: their own height and weight, the *Guinness Book of World Records,* students' sports records, etc.

108. Simple flash cards produced by children in the class can be useful to aid learnings. Testing can be done by a child's friend in the classroom.

109. Remedial work in arithmetic can be assisted by the use of a calculator. These relatively inexpensive devices often interest a youngster and in many cases encourage him to work with numbers which have previously been unpleasant. An added specialty would be an audio-calculator for school subjects but this is currently quite expensive.

110. Break the arithmetic work into smaller units, not less work, but less exposure for any one period of time. Other children may respond to the Cuisinaire Rods, an abacus, domino sets, etc.

111. After repeated failure in arithmetic, children, though they may have mastered the basic processes, tend to lack motivation. Provide very long but simple problems such as:

$$\begin{array}{r} 888 \\ -333 \\ \hline \end{array} \qquad \begin{array}{r} 321{,}742{,}134{,}521 \\ +\ 134{,}151{,}341{,}237 \\ \hline \end{array} \quad \text{or} \quad \begin{array}{r} 892{,}678{,}542 \\ -\ 151{,}265{,}321 \\ \hline \end{array}$$

Children will initially deny their ability to do such problems. After it is demonstrated to them that they can work them out, they appear eager for such "hard" problems.

112. Parents of preschool children, as well as those in kindergarten and the primary grades, should be encouraged to play arithmetic table games with their children (Old Maid, Chutes and Ladders, Picture Lotto, Picture Domino). Aside from the value of pleasant social interaction, the children (who may have to be helped at first) soon show ability to count, recognize colors, perceive similarities and differences, to learn to wait for their turn, and to experience success and failure.

Spelling Underachievement

113. Recall—use three steps: (a) recognition exercises, (b) partial recall, (c) full recall. Reduce the word list to a success level; maintain a chart of successes.

114. Provide a star chart where each student receives a star when he does as well or better than he did the week before. This is more motivating to children than requiring a grade of 100 percent which many of them may never earn.

115. Use Vallett's Psychoeducational Resource Program No. 43, by Fearon Publ.

Writing Underachievement

116. If the child reverses letters, take one of the common reversals such as "B," and use the tracing technique on this letter only. At the same time the letter is traced, have the child say aloud over and over, "Down from the top, up half-way, and then swing to the right and around." Pair the verbal instructions with the act.

117. Use programmed handwriting materials and give short written assignments. Teach typing at any age over five, especially for bright children as this is not only fun, but it is sometimes easier than cursive writing.

118. A full-size pencil is often much too difficult for any child with a writing problem. Cut the full-size pencils in half or use a regular size pencil if the child prefers rather than a giant one.

119. For remediation in the writing area, consider the use of the following material: Vallett's Psychoeducational Resource

Program No. 42.

120. The Skinner and Krokower material, Handwriting with Write and See, published by Lyons and Carnahan, is a helpful program that could be profitably utilized for handwriting problems.

121. If a child places his paper in an extremely rotated position, the paper should be taped to the desk and, by small increments over several months, it can be rotated to the proper writing position. Care should be taken not to allow the child to alter his body position once the paper has been taped.

SECTION B: THOUGHT DISTURBANCES

122. Many of these children feel a great need for routine and well-defined rules and work instructions. They are often able to work for only brief periods of time, as they are so prone to daydreaming and emotional withdrawal. It is sometimes helpful to give them specific assignments and to set a time limit. When the time is up, collect the paper and give the next assignment. When the daily routine is to be changed, it is helpful to explain the change well ahead of time, and to discuss carefully what can be expected to happen, for example, when the class takes a field trip or a special guest visits the classroom.

123. For children with severe emotional problems and thought disturbances they might be placed in a class for only five or six children of near-age for instructional purposes. Older ones may participate in gym, music, etc., and any other subjects they can handle in a regular class. Some children's behavior is too bizarre to be aided in public schools or through home instruction, so residential placement is essential. Psychotherapy is essential in this case after ruling our neurological deterioration.

124. Children who are in special classes for the emotionally disturbed generally come from homes where parents and children need psychological treatment. However, parents often resist this recommendation, or when they attend clinics they frequently terminate due to lack of cooperation or lack of understanding on their part. Yet, a psychotherapeutically trained school psychologist or counselor may aid the child if the parents do not object.

Concretistic Thinking

125. Emphasis should be placed upon common elements in class identity and on analogical thinking. In giving directions, the teacher should initially stress the concrete, rather than the abstract, until the child's ability to deal with abstractions improves. Visual and auditory clues should be given as much as possible and instructions for any new learning situations should be on an individual basis. Such thinking is often characteristic of the retarded, obsessive, or psychotic child and, hence, a differential diagnosis is necessary by a clinical team.

Problems in Reality Testing: Extreme Fantasy

126. The major task of the diagnostician is to determine the content, patterns of illogical flights, and stimulating cues to the fantasy. The stimuli leading to the fantasies should be shared with parents, and a contrast drawn between the parental responses and the child's reality-irrelevant responses. The goal: referral for psychotherapy. The requisite: parental acceptance of the fact of the child's distortions beyond "a good imagination."

127. The child will most likely require a psychiatric evaluation and therapy. Such an emotional condition will significantly interfere with his overall adjustment and academic progress. Therefore, no specific academic techniques beyond the normal are to be recommended at this point. Rather, his progress or lack of it will be determined mostly by his emotional status. Classroom activities should be structured so that this child knows exactly what is expected of him.

Distractibility, Short Attention Span

128. An isolation booth or "office" should be set up in the classroom where this youngster can be placed when his hyperactive and/or distractible behavior becomes too severe. Such a booth would cut down upon impinging stimuli and allow the younger to calm down. It is important that the use of such an "office" be made a positive thing in the classroom rather than a punishment. Such an isolation area could also be used in the home setting.

129. Because of short attention span the child may need to have academic work given in small units followed quickly by approval from the teacher when the work is adequate. She then gives another immediate assignment of the next small unit of work.

130. Drill periods must be of short duration but frequent. Certainly visual aids may assist. The work must be highly motivating to capture the child's interest which should be at the child's instructional level.

131. Give opportunity for tension release through light muscle activity between periods of study and work.

132. The teacher should provide positive reinforcement for any acceptable "study-response." This may start with any responses that approximate study behavior, such as getting out a pencil, opening a book, etc. This should lead to additional "study responses" that can also be shaped via consistent reinforcement procedures. Let the child suggest what is an appropriate rein-forcment for him.

133. In order to focus this child's attention, use a narrow horizontal opening or window cut out of a cardboard or paper in order to isolate the material in reading which the child is working on.

134. Proximity control techniques are suggested for an inattentive student. A tap on the desk, a touch on the shoulder, or even a name called could help him refocus on the classroom activity.

135. Limit distractors: do not seat the child near windows, colorful bulletin boards, or open doors. At times, allow the child to work quietly by himself in the back of the room, not as punishment but as a means of helping him complete his work. The teacher might also turn the child's desk toward the wall if there is no study carrel in the classroom.

136. The parents have possibly "oversold" education, striving, and learning and the child may have exaggerated this trait by incorporating the values into a compulsive need to excel and to be perfect. The parents should gradually take pressures off the child, begin to lessen their intense interest in his academic success, let the child know that he is cared for regardless of his grades.

137. The first step would be to isolate the source of the problem. A neurological examination with EEG evaluation may identify brain damage requiring medical attention. Rehabilitation services or physical therapy may be required if there is damage to the central nervous system. If the etiology is psychological essentially, some form of psychotherapy and special education should be considered.

138. Play games with the child that require concentration and attention and try to get others to play with him also. For example: start with three objects on a tray, look at them for thirty seconds, then tell or write about what was on the tray. Gradually increase number and complexity of directions.

Disturbances in Memory and Awareness

139. For serious disturbances in memory and recall, refer for psychiatric consultation with a clinical team. It is very likely that serious memory deficits may require placement in a learning disabled classroom. In all probability a neurological pediatric examination should be required.

140. For a child with problems in memory, first inspect all school records for indications of physical impairments of the child. Ask the parents to obtain a complete physical evaluation for him, including audiological, ophthalmological, optometric, psychiatric, and neurological evaluations. The possibility of vitamin or mineral deficiency as well as other contributing physiological or dietary factors should be weighed.

Overachievement Associated with Tension

141. At times children with average or above average intelligence utilize excessive energy in obtaining academic achievment above and beyond what is ordinarily expected of them. Often, overachievement is done at the expense of the development of social skills. The teacher may guide such a child into areas where he can obtain social recognition by his peers. The child should also be encouraged to enter extracurricular activities of the school such as chorus or any clubs that might be available. Through these activities the child will be confronted

with social problems and hopefully will break the binds of his isolated "bookworm" method of escaping potential social rejection. Some overachievers stress academics in a rivalrous competition to overpower another child or fear that parents will reject them if they do not perform "perfectly" in school.

INTEGRATIVE BEHAVIOR AND OTHER PERSONALITY DISTURBANCES

T HIS CHAPTER DEALING with integrative behavior refers essentially to those emotional problems laden with elements of anxiety and poor impulse control and, from a psychoanalytic point of view, exaggerate the use of defense mechanisms for emotional control. Under these circumstances, the individual does not work in harmonious coordination; he may behave one way but feels or intellectualizes another way, or adapts irrationally to his internal stresses by erecting impenetrable defenses. From a reinforcement orientation, the same behavior allegedly results from the simple fact that such behaviors, however they began, have been consistently or intermittently reinforced by being satisfying or useful to the person, i.e. helping him gain control over his environment or receive desired attention, recognition, etc. In particular, controls for impulsive behavior are noted in this chapter and deal briefly with some classroom management and behavior modification approaches regarding distractibility and hyperactivity.

Intervention strategies for the more pronounced personality disturbances regarding stereotypic behaviors and varieties of prepsychotic and psychotic adjustments are noted in the last section of this chapter. The obsessive-compulsive deviations dealt with are too extreme to be considered as developmentally normal. Often perceived to be unconscious in origin, ritualistic behaviors take on an irrational appearance to both the child and the adults in his life and reveal the individual's attempts to control unacceptable impulses. The overt behaviors themselves are recognized as irritating and illogical even to the child, but must be executed to reduce anxiety. Some clinicians seek the original source of such obsessive-compulsive symptoms, while others find that certain behavior therapies effectively control and extinguish the entire problem by, for example, negative practice without resulting in symptom substitution (Ullman and Krasner, 1965). Such behaviors provide a professional battleground for different theoretical orientations and treatment strategies.

In the main, most suggestions dealing with serious disturbances rely upon the participation of a professional therapist rather than a teacher or parent. Other approaches for additional personality problems are only briefly listed, testifying perhaps to the fact that such complicated behaviors are difficult to remedy by anything less than major environmental manipulation, intensive therapy, or both.

SECTION A: IMPULSIVE BEHAVIOR

1. A child who is low in impulse control, regardless of etiology, may respond to a behavior modification program which will reward him for increased self-control. Explain the system to the school administrator, the child's parents, and other children in the class before it begins as well as the child himself. Thus, after observing the child and obtaining a baseline rate about how many times he, say, gets out of his seat, or hits others, or speaks out of turn, then present him with a chart of each day and a set of potential reinforcements. Depending on the need level of the child, these may be candy, M & M's, stars, tokens for free play, or anything the child finds rewarding in the school setting. Reexplain the behavior shaping program to him again indicating that he will be rewarded for increased self-control by specifically paying attention, completing his class work, staying in his seat, etc. Pair the reinforcements with teacher praise, eventually use intermittent reinforcement, and later just verbal approval. Much of the carefully executed work in behavior modification in classrooms has been quite successful if monitored by a knowledgeable school psychologist in cooperation with teachers and the child in question.

2. Lower the achievement goals and expectations for a child who loses self-control easily so as not to exceed his tolerance threshold. When the child reveals he is comfortable with the work, then let him operate there and saturate him with success. Ask the child when he is ready for more difficult work and let him decide when he is ready even though other groups may move ahead.

3. Make sure that the child understands the reasonable expectations for self-control and point out to the child that he can control himself and has proved it previously while the teacher states specific recollections.

4. For children who lose control of their impulses, the teacher's reaction may range from withdrawal of privileges to placement in the time-out room in the classroom.

5. Where an impulsive child attends a departmentalized school, the teachers may decide upon a common set of rules for him. These should be written down for the child and parent to see and agree upon. This cooperation in adults prevents the child from playing one set of rules of one teacher against another in the next class. When the child is getting restless he may be permitted out of his seat to get a drink or go to the lavatory or visit briefly and quietly with a friend.

6. The child with problems in impulse and self-control may need the evaluation of a pediatric neurologist who may consider medication to relieve the problem. The child may also require (a) special education placement for emotionally disturbed children, (b) firm and clear limits for his behavior, (c) appropriate academic goals within his ability and current achievement levels, (d) constant monitoring by the teacher to help him focus on the lessons at hand. Both of his parents are recommended to obtain counseling to assess what part of their own behavior may be contributing to their child's problems.

7. Other teachers in the school should be informed to be patient with an impulsive and easily distractible child. A brief staff meeting should be held to explain the past history and present behaviors while the teacher shows the child's photo enabling easy identification.

8. For the ultratalkative child:

   a. Privately tell him to be aware that control is necessary.
   b. Involve him in all class activities.
   c. Set limits beyond which the child may not go.
   d. Establish the idea that behavior beyond certain limits will merit its own consequence: usually withdrawal of privileges.
   e. Use the child's name whenever possible.
   f. Provide opportunities for him to relate interesting and unusual experiences.
   g. Assign special, challenging projects that require concentration.
   h. Use the child as a teacher-aide to assist a student who has been absent.
   i. Investigate home discipline and authoritative processes involved; suggest moderation from extremes.
   j. Evidence a vital interest in the child's work, not his "hot air." Focus on production.
   k. Learn to listen about the theme of his complaints: being ignored, rejected? Attend to him only when he produces some acceptable work, however minimal in length, and when he is well controlled.

SECTION B: STEREOTYPED BEHAVIOR

9. A complete physical evaluation for consideration of endocrinological disorders is recommended. Stereotypic symptoms may also be associated with brain injury as well as functional disorders.

10. Stereotypic behaviors like head-banging, eye-poking, rocking, head-nodding, finger-flicking, and repetitive grunting sometimes respond best to behavioral approaches: (1) mild aversive therapy (lemon juice squirted into the mouth), (2) overcorrection, or (3) primary reinforcement when self-controlled.

11. Although the more serious problems will likely require residential treatment, mild manifestations may permit the child to attend special classes in the public school for emotionally disturbed children. Such children need to be kept in contact with

reality, partly through daily school experiences where there are tasks to accomplish and people who must be attended to.

Compulsive Behavior

12. Such behavior is difficult to minimize without therapeutic intervention. The teacher and parents can only offer palliatives, such as minimizing or discouraging perfectionism, deemphasizing criticism, and perhaps pointing to their own imperfections as "normal." In treatment, the execution of the ritualistic behavior may be requested, perhaps demanded, so that the extinguishing of such behavior may begin as a form of negative practice. In this circumstance the behavior must exhaust itself so that tension is no longer present and the individual no longer feels anxiety which leads to the inappropriate behaviors. A behavior therapist is the clinician of choice although medication may help to reduce the anxiety levels. In all probability a clinical team should evaluate the child's circumstances.

13. The teacher should become aware of the underlying disturbances. She might meet with the parents, nurse, and psychologist who review dynamics and the relative uncontrollability of the compulsive behavior. The problem is that when the child is not permitted to execute such behavior he gets more and more tense and anxious. Her role as a teacher then is to remove stress from the child's school life as much as possible, protect the child from ridicule of peers, and help him to continue learning anyway.

14. The parents should understand the contributions to a typical compulsive behavior and perhaps alter their own behavior where necessary: reduce drives for perfection and discuss easier goals and more comfortable expectations for their child. They should enter counseling and place their own child in therapy also. They might be taught behavior-shaping techniques so that they can undertake an active part in the child's treatment, i.e. only attend to the child when he is not compulsively engaged.

Perfectionistic Behavior

15. The perfectionistic child is usually very much afraid of

failure, e.g. his perfectionism is often an vercompensation for his perceived inadequacies. This concept, when applicable, should be explained to teachers and parents. Attempts should be made to help the child achieve in class at a level commensurate with his mental ability, to find friends who are interested in him and who will sit near him, and align him with a supportive teacher interested in his general welfare. It is recommended that the child be taught by the school psychologist how to relax in the classroom and try to avoid becoming tense and anxious. This calls for weekly counseling sessions dealing with progressive relaxation.

16. Perfectionism is a special learning adaptation to great anxiety and stress. Since it is learned, it can be unlearned. Wolpe's reciprocal inhibition should be instituted by a behavioral therapist wherein the individual client is helped to develop a hierarchy of fears and anxiety situations, then taught how to relax physically, and then participate in a pairing of relaxation and recall of anxiety-provoking circumstances. This "relaxation therapy" has been very helpful in cases dealing with phobias, anxieties, fears, perfectionism, traumatic events, etc.

SECTION C: TANTRUM BEHAVIOR
BEYOND EARLY CHILDHOOD

17. Require that the child leave the room until he can act more cooperatively and agreeably. If necessary, physically remove the child from the situation. Audiences are necessary for the continuation of tantrums. To attend to a tantrum in any way is to reinforce and sustain it. Tantrums are short-lived when no one attends. This requires a time-out room.

18. After the time-out room procedure is finished and the child has reduced the tantrum, it is necessary to talk with the child to inquire about what made him upset and to try to change circumstances which provoked these behaviors if possible. It may be that the child has not acquired a tolerance for frustration and this may be built up gradually. If the teacher finds that isolation seems to lose effectiveness for self-control, arrangements might be made with the parent for the boy to spend the remainder of the day at home. The child's own desire to return to school with his

classmates may be sufficient motivation to develop better self-control.

19. A child manifesting tantrum behavior, not neurologically based, often responds to interest shown by an authority figure or adult friend on the school staff. Such a person meeting with the student would provide an opportunity to vent feelings and uncover clues that initiated the tantrums. An administrator or counselor could fill this role if trained in interviewing skills.

20. If temper tantrums are associated with migraine, insomnia, vertigo, etc., then a pediatric neurologist should be consulted to examine the child. There is a possibility of epilepsy or a variant of brain injury in this behavior. Psychomotor seizures are sometimes revealed by uncontrollable temper tantrums. Such seizures may respond to anticonvulsive medication rather than a form of psychotherapy or behavior therapy. It is likely, however, that people with psychomotor seizures may need to have counseling in regard to their self-concept in addition to medical intervention.

21. The tantrums may be a function of the child's confusion of changing rules which reflect a permissive attitude one time and a strict one the next time on the part of parents or teachers. Set clear and consistent expectations appropriate to the child's age.

SECTION D: HALLUCINATIONS

22. For auditory or visual hallucinations, have the teachers, parents, or classmates consistently interrupt the child during an hallucination and force him to concentrate or focus upon one element of reality. For example, ask the child a specific question; make him maintain eye contact.

23. For such a child, contact medical personnel, both neurological and psychiatric, since these symptoms can be derived from pathology in either specialty. Rule out drug-related behaviors and addiction and consider therapy in a residential treatment program for possible psychosis.

24. If at all possible, explain reality to the child and interrupt his hallucinatory behavior by calling his name, touching him, and ordering him to complete some task. Do not "enter into" the hallucinatory or psychotic behavior or try to inquire about the

various creative sensations that he is receiving. Focus instead on the external world rather than his private problems.

SECTION E: DELUSIONS OF GRANDEUR OR PERSECUTION

25. Confrontations with the child in class should be avoided whenever possible even though the child may make statements which seem distorted. It seems best that the teacher accept these statements, but not act upon them, and at a later time point out privately to him the expected behavior and the reality as the teacher sees it. Certainly one must investigate if there is an actual basis to the child's complaints, e.g. gang retaliation. The child who persists in such behavior should be referred for a diagnostic evaluation.

26. Ask the child which teacher he feels most comfortable to be with; if possible, assign the child to that teacher and reduce interpersonal stress with adults. Avoid a "showdown."

27. Making the assumption that the child is in contact with reality, everyone who deals with him needs to be open and frank, pointing out reality features of every situation the child might question, in advance wherever possible. "Sick" behavior should be ignored, and realistic assessment of situations commended. Problems of this intensity need to be evaluated by a mental health clinic or private practitioner.

SECTION F: MALINGERING

28. Teachers should plan strategy with the school nurse after seeing evidence of malingering (feigned illness at specific times or in specific situations). While teachers need to be concerned lest the child is physically ill, they should be conservative in their response to the child's dependent and helpless reaction. Suggest that the child put his head down for a few minutes, distract him briefly by some physical activity, or perhaps review the reasons for his behavior, i.e. lack of skill, inability to perform, or some extrinsic factor. He should not be permitted to find a visit to the nurse as an escape but should return to his work obligations. Ordinarily any child using such drastic methods is in need of

more professional help than the school usually can offer. The causes of this symptom vary widely from psychosis to negativism to social rejection and should be treated according to its determinants.

29. Assign work appropriate for the ability of the child that can be completed in the time given. If these conditions are possible to meet, insist that the work be completed before the child begins another activity, be it recess, lunch, or academics.

30. Make the child clearly see the penalty for not working. Associate the malingering with the loss of a favored activity.

Chapter X

MENTAL RETARDATION

W ITH THE ADVENT of Public Law 94-142, renewed emphasis was placed on the valid classification of retarded children according to several important criteria. No longer can an evaluator examine any client legally by a single, all-encompassing intelligence test without accounting for the other significant variables through further measurement. Affecting such a diagnosis would be a child's minority membership, visual and auditory perception, record of development, measurements in achievement and intelligence, learning style, health, and most importantly his level of social competence or adaptability. Further consideration would include the selection of valid tests and expert administration.

Competent psychologists have appreciated these and other variables long before the new law, while psychologists of questionable training and/or execution are no longer able to ignore multiple criteria. In the 1970s, Mercer (1978) initiated considerable research efforts to help insure that more valid diagnosis would include assessments of the social and family milieu of the child and an objective assessment of social functioning within those important realms. It would be pleasant to report special and extraordinary refinements in the current batteries of tests for cognition, perception, development, etc., but such is not the case. Many tests are still inappropriate to the same degree for particular groups or individuals, others rely on old or inadequate norms, and some "standard" tests have always been inadequate in the first place. Psychologists functioning more frequently with younger and more handicapped children now rely on tests with better standardization procedures and with a view to assess in particular sets of clients, i.e. the Bayley Scales of Infant Development (1969) and the French Pictorial Test of Intelligence (1964). Struggles on the issues and the assessment of the mentally retarded will likely continue through the present decades as refinements in research and social awareness evolve.

According to Kessler (1966), mental retardation is a symptom of underlying disturbances varying from neurological deficits to cultural deprivation to psychological disturbance. Some see certain varieties of mild retardation as temporary when due to remediable psychological maladjustment (Rubin, 1980), while others (Sarason, 1969; Baumeister, 1971) see retardation as relatively permanent when resulting from genetic abnormalities and brain injury. It behooves the evaluating psychologist to consider all these possibilities in conjunction with a clinical team. The causes should be determined, arrested if possible, and remediated appropriately.

Although special education classes are theoretically established for children with genuine and relatively permanent retardation, all too often those enrolled are later more correctly diagnosed as being learning disabled, being pseudoretarded, having aggressive behavior problems, being dyslexic, being psychotic, and even of having above average intelligence (Garrison & Hammill, 1971). The prescriptions in this chapter, however, are geared for the genuinely retarded and are to be used by their teachers and parents when so recommended by a specialist.

The retarded child is, first, socially incompetent to some marked degree (Doll, 1941) in that he competes or adapts socially far below the social level of age-mates, fails to grasp their rules and complex subtleties, prefers to operate at a simpler level, etc. The social incompetence is often viewed as "general immaturity," by teachers or parents. Such a child is never a gang leader or club president of normal children, nor is he capable of executing complex roles or adapting to social circumstances as well as his age-mates. There are always social limitations or else the child is not truly intellectually retarded.

A second criteria involves the fact that scores on individual intelligence tests are consistently below approximately a 75 IQ and indicate subnormal functioning and adaptability. This judgment proceeds on the assumption that the tests are adequate to the child's cultural and social experience in the sense that they are normed on his population, that he did not recently emigrate from a foreign country, etc. Such measurements obviously depend also upon the skill of the examiner in establishing rapport, the socioeconomic level of the child's home, the richness of his cultural and educational experiences, and the presence or absence of neurological and psychological problems. To a certain degree, the intelligence level may represent an index of efficiency for the individual, at least in the academic setting.

Third, a genuinely retarded child is consistently behind his normal classmates in academic achievement and learns very slowly. Although many work up to the expectations for their mental ages, most are at least three or more years below regular grade level in achievement when over eight years of age.

Fourth, it is not unusual to find some degree of brain damage or cerebral dysfunction in the retarded child. This etiological basis is not always readily detectable but may be revealed through sensitive medical and psychological examination or may be hypothesized as influential in causing the developmental delays accompanying retardation. Such damage, if it has occurred, has likely affected the central nervous system through insult before, during, or after the birth of the child rather than through hereditary contributions, although the two may clearly be related in some cases. Much mental retardation (Sarason, 1969) apparently is derived from exogenous factors. Retardation "caused" by severe to mild cultural deprivation is such a complicated topic that it cannot be adequately attended to here. That such retardation can occur is no longer a primary question, but the precise process by which it does develop is still under consideration. Lack of stimulation, low auditory and visual inputs, low expectancy, and minimal demands on the child for creativity and learning are probably all contributing factors as are deficient diet, absence of medical care, and general neglect. If intervention and remedial procedures are not introduced early in the child's life before he suffers from the above problems, the probabilities for normal adaptation are markedly lowered.

The best-known definition of mental retardation has been sponsored by the American Association for Mental Deficiency and is noted as follows:

> Mental retardation refers to significantly subaverage general intellectual functioning existing concurrently with deficits in adaptive behavior and manifested during the developmental period (Grossman, 1977, p. 5).

SECTION A: MILD MENTAL RETARDATION (EDUCABLE)

Mainstreaming and Placement

1. Young mildly retarded children might best be placed twice in kindergarten, a nongraded primary, or transitional grades rather than in a class for educable retardates. They need individual or small group tutoring and work at their own preschool levels. They should be kept with younger, normal children, in general, as they can profit from interacting with regular class children and may respond positively to normal competition and social expectations. It is always possible that a young child diagnosed as mildly retarded might later be diagnosed as some other classification and not be verified as retarded. In a class for educable retardates, such young children may function at a lower level because standards are often too low to require their best efforts. Whichever placement is made, it must be done with agreement of the parents who may resist too early a placement in the educable program and who are not sure if their child is genuinely retarded. In this sense it helps the parents accept the real possibility of later educable retarded placement when they discover in a year or so that the child truly cannot keep up academically, intellectually, or socially with his normal age-mates.

2. Strive to integrate the retarded students into as many regular school activities as possible in assemblies, sports, clubs, special events, visits to cultural centers, and academic experiences. Arrange with a regular class teacher to have the retarded children to sit with her children during lunch time. Plan gym, playground, and joint activities with other classes of comparable age.

3. Keep a five- or six-year-old child of suspected mental retardation in the kindergarten, rather than exclude him from

school, for a year or two in both morning and afternoon sessions. This may maximize his input of stimulation and training. Request an evaluation of him prior to placement in first grade or a retarded educable class.

4. If a child is waiting for a placement into a retarded class but remains in a regular class temporarily use an accepting, sensible, bright child to help him with tutoring and whatever lower-level assignments are given during the delay. Give him desirable jobs to do in the room and around the building so that the child may feel pride and receive recognition. The concept to be learned is that although the retarded child is slow to grasp academic material, he is still capable of contributing and being a respectable class member.

5. For the educable child, his regular class teacher should offer a sustaining program until the special class placement becomes available to him. It is reasonable to remove the regular class obligations for academic work and offer assignments and instruction at the mental age level of the child. If, for example, a sixth grade teacher has such a child and he reads at a second grade level, she should certainly offer appropriate second grade materials on loan from a primary teacher. The delay in placement may still be an opportunity to help the child learn.

6. If there are no placements readily available in the retarded classes, the child should still continue to attend school in the regular classes but in the lowest sections of academic work. Understand that the retarded child may be larger, older, and less capable than the majority of his classmates. Point out areas in which he should be given recognition, such as good grooming, posture, manners, cooperation, etc.

7. Teach him to count accurately to twenty, recognize letter names, do work in class on dittoed materials, or activities which are appropriate for his mental age. Do not let him do what the other regular children do in academics, even if he requests such high level material. Chronic failures with consequent feelings of inadequacy and frustration are much more damaging than using class materials different from those of other children. Do what makes educational sense for the child and help him accept it. If the teacher gives him work beyond his ability, even with good

motives, it tells the child that his limitations are unacceptable to her and should be ignored. These limitations may be perceived by the child as too awful even to consider and too hopeless to discuss honestly. It may be inconvenient to be retarded, but it is not, and should not be regarded as, a disgrace.

8. Put the child in a special education program where he can begin his readiness activities without undue pressure. If he is around seven, eight, or nine years old, he should respond to most readiness experiences ordinarily found at the kindergarten or even nursery school level.

9. Prepare the children in the special class for a newcomer, especially if he has a physical handicap too. Tell them what the child looks like, his special assets, and interests. Perhaps the children can decide on ways to make the new child feel welcome. It might be well for the child to visit the class prior to official enrollment.

10. The classroom teacher should be especially alert for any indications in the youngster's functioning which might indicate that the child is not genuinely retarded. Tests presently available for diagnosis do not adequately identify the pseudoretarded who come from culturally deprived and language handicapped backgrounds. Pseudoretarded children need another educational program, without doubt, as they can be socially and perhaps educationally thwarted by being incorrectly placed with the retarded.

11. If the child is not ready for formal school placement, then nursery school placement should be considered, or even a shortened school day schedule. The child still needs social and emotional interaction with peers.

Curriculum and Instruction

12. In the educable retarded classes, individualize instruction as much as possible by learning the levels, skills, and limitations of each student in each academic, motor, and social area through personal observation, achievement testing, and reliance upon psychometric evaluation. Teach the children at their respective levels to overlearn, to master the predetermined academic material within their abilities. Set the level of expectations on the par

with the child's ability or development in that area, be it academic, perceptual, motor, etc. Special help, individual or in small groups, should be given in areas of marked deficiency by the teacher, educational aide, or specialists.

13. To aid reading readiness in a multisensory approach, use some visual-kinesthetic items that are three-dimensional with felt, sandpaper, or smooth or rough leather. These make fine training items for discrimination of similarities and differences in prereading experiences.

14. Lettering in clay helps the retarded child to learn kinesthetically. He should print letters, later words, in clay in block print with left-to-right direction. Then he should trace the letters and words with his fingers and a pencil. This approach is also good for the remediation of letter or word reversals. Older children should have access to tachistoscopic training for reinforcing their left-to-right orientation.

15. Isolate each concept that is to be taught and test the child to be sure he understands it before moving on. Make quite sure that the child understands position words: inside, outside, on top of, and the routine action words: running, climbing, jumping.

16. A nonreading retarded youngster should have an intensive readiness program starting with experience charts, signs and labels. He can begin to read stories when readiness is established and should be interested in drawing pictures, telling about them, and writing stories. Perhaps he can be able to make booklets of stories which he has been told and which he has read from charts. He should be able to take trips to further his experiential background. He might wish to begin to read preprimers and later handle primers. To assure success, this child should know approximately ten words by sight before he is given the first book.

17. Probably the most important information about the retarded child from the psychologist's report is an approximate mental age which indicates with reasonable accuracy where the child thinks, understands, judges, and reasons. Obviously this mental age will always be less than the chronological age and gives the teacher an excellent clue about the operational and social level of the child. This mental age indicates his readiness level and suggests a level that one might eventually expect his

academic achievement to function near. Should the child be offered material that is more than a year or so above his mental age, it is likely that tension, anxiety, and withdrawal may occur when the child faces continued stressful failure. The child may reject material far below his mental age because it is too childish and simple for him.

18. The retarded educable child should be placed on a set schedule; tasks which demand creativity and originality should be minimized.

19. Each child should be allowed to work at his independent level much longer than average students so that overlearning may occur readily. A grasp of well-learned knowledge reinforces the child's feeling of competency and reduces the feeling of inferiority.

20. Provide the child with as many multisensory experiences as possible to develop all learning tracts. Have the child identify objects by sight, feel, sound, taste, smell, and touch. Do things with—and without—vision. The same may be done with sound and smell. Guess the names of objects and describe many qualities and characteristics.

21. Allow as much time as possible for this child to express himself verbally since he is apt to respond negatively if he is urged to respond too quickly or perfectly. Do not permit him to use body language, grunts or finger pointing as substitutes for verbal expression.

22. Be certain that the child's attention is in focus prior to giving him a verbal command or some assignment in class. The child should be facing and looking at the teacher, otherwise he may not respond to her directions. Directions must be well-structured and in the language level of his mental age. The words must be clear, simple, and explicit. The verbal instructions must also be spaced evenly and spoken only at an average speed. Long instructions require an excellent auditory memory that almost no retarded children have acquired.

23. At the level of initial reading skills, a basic sight vocabulary of from seventy to ninety words should be established. This paves the way for phonetics and visual analysis. These words are in the preprimers and primers and are learned by the child in the following ways:

a. Through picture clues: the child tells the story from the illustrations, getting the thought of the story, preparing titles for pictures, by preparing a booklet of pictures that are given titles, labeling a list of room duties, health suggestions, rules, matching colors and color words, etc.

b. Through context clues: the child is taught how to guess a word from the meaning of the rest of the sentence or paragraph. The teacher may ask guiding questions about the content of the story, have the children guess what comes next. These will be excellent crutches the child should use at the beginning stages of reading.

c. Through configuration clues: certain words may be recognized by differences in appearance, the length, height and peculiar characteristics. Such crutches may be discarded by the child as soon as he begins to employ other techniques.

24. For a child in the readiness stage of reading, he might greatly benefit from acquiring a background experience by excursions, trips, filmstrips, etc. Within the home and the school, he should have many opportunities for verbalization. There must be constant correction of pronunciation to the ability level of the child. He should develop visual readiness by matching: colors, shapes, sizes, forms, and numbers, and work with simple jig-saw puzzles, use peg board designs, etc. Auditory readiness experience might consist of following simple directions, listening for rhyming words, supplying words to finish rhymes, mimicking sounds, guessing the identity of voices, etc. Kinesthetic readiness: learn to cut with the scissors and to color with crayons by staying within a definite area by tracing a teacher-made drawing, connecting dots, fitting forms together, finger play, and learning to go from left to right on a page by use of picture sequences.

25. Plan a curriculum that is relevant to the child's interest and experiences, utilizing such educational aids as audiovisual material, programmed instructions, tape recordings, films, trips, etc.

26. Use concrete teaching techniques, such as the Fernald Visual-Auditory-Kinesthetic-Tacticle system, to present initial

letters, sounds, words, etc.

27. Use the Sullivan Programmed Reading Materials as distributed by the Webster Division of McGraw-Hill or Behavior Research Laboratories for the elementary and secondary age students. Then set up reward systems to motivate progress. With programmed instruction, rewards can be given by the frame, by the page, or after the completion of a successful test. Rewards must be very satisfying.

28. Use as many sense modalities as possible and stimulate with concrete materials when possible. For example, in spelling: repeat the word vocally to develop the auditory modality; memorize the word visually for visual memory development; practice writing the word to develop the tactile sense and assist in fine muscle control.

29. Having an "office" in the classroom would be beneficial in eliminating or reducing certain distractions. Such an "office" should have a desk and seat facing the wall with two screens on either side, and should be free of distracting visual and most auditory stimulation. It can be used as a retreat when a child is overwhelmed or excited or when requiring privacy to learn.

30. Make every effort to keep the retarded child in an appropriate, meaningful retarded class program at the high school level. School counselors should be especially active in establishing part-time job placements that are supervised by sympathetic, reasonable employers. Keep each child in school until nineteen or more years old to insure that each one has reached maximum development and received maximum value from the special educational-vocational program. Contact the local agencies to help, especially the Bureau of Vocational Rehabilitation, Goodwill Industries, hospitals, farms.

31. Plan the curriculum largely around living needs: health, home and family decisions, getting along with others, counting, making change, budgeting, cooking, sewing, crafts, manual activities of a practical nature, leisure activities, safety, and prevocational activities. Discuss feasible vocations and the personal traits needed in these jobs.

32. It is good educational policy for some or perhaps all retarded children to attend school in the summer, part-time, since

they need to work closer to their maximum potentials than most others. This may violate a tradition, but an exception can be made to provide continuous socialization and education for retarded children. Young children, in particular, may welcome such an experience. Older children may have to be weaned away from the television set. If teen-agers are appropriately employed, this activity could be considered as a legitimate reason for nonattendance in the summer.

Perceptual Training

33. Programs suggested for the mildly retarded to remediate perceptual deficiencies:

    a. Detect: A Sensorimotor Approach to Visual Discrimination by Science Research Associates.

    b. Cheves Program; Dubnoff School Program; Erie Program; Fairbanks-Robinson: Pathway School Program by Teaching Resources.

    c. Frostig Pictures and Patterns; Frostig Visual Perception Exercises; Junior Listen and Hear by Follett Publishers.

    d. Kinesthetic Alphabet by R.H. Stone Products.

    e. Peabody Language Development Kit by American Guidance Service.

    f. Perceptual Testing-Training Guide Kit for Kindergarten Teachers by Winter Haven Lions Research Foundation.

    g. Something to Say All through the Day; Sound Identification Cards; Language-Building Cards by Interstate.

    h. Sounds and Patterns of Language by Holt, Rinehart, & Winston.

34. For perceptual-motor training at a basic level, the programmed handwriting course, Handwriting with Write and See, by Lyons and Carnahan should be helpful.

35. In the area of perceptual dysfunction, have the teacher consider the Cratty Programs of the Vancouver Schools Program for better motor coordination. The teacher should inspect the programs of Kephart, Ayres, Getman, Myklebust, and Barsch.

Reading for this group should stress associative-type patterns as set forth in the Sullivan Materials, Gillingham-Stillman (Orton), SRA, Fairbanks-Robinson materials.

36. Visual perception training should be initiated, not for all retarded students necessarily, but rather for those so deficient. For younger children, examination on the Frostig Visual Perception Test should precede training on the Frostig Visual Perception Exercises. Research results here are mixed and debatable. In view of the extraordinary number of visual perception handicaps in retarded children (those with learning disabilities, and those with some indication of minimal cerebral dysfunction) it is strongly recommended that each child so handicapped receive a comprehensive evaluation from a developmental optometrist. Such an individual is particularly attuned to the functional aspects of the child's vision dealing with focusing, distance, perceptual skills, alignment, the coordination of eye muscles, factors of fatigue, near-point, refraction, and especially visual perception training programs. The reasons many group-administered or teacher-administered visual perception programs have been unsuccessful with both groups and individuals is that they have not been highly individualized for the child in question and are too global to have effect. A developmental optometrist, by contrast, can make a highly definitive examination and prescribe training experiences both in his or her training facility or for the specialist in the school that are attuned to the child in question. In general, ophthalmologists are not concerned with the learning aspects of the child and the functional difficulties in terms of remediation through training.

37. With retarded children having severe perceptual problems, stimulate visually and auditorially but keep visual and auditory environments uncluttered. Play with the child with one or a few objects in one modality at a time keeping the stimuli simple. In vision, use materials having clear, definite shapes and outlines.

38. To assist the child with visual-motor coordination, provide him with primary, lined paper over which an onion-skin paper may be placed and held in position. A specific alphabet letter, number, or the child's name may be on the bottom paper.

Have the child trace on the onion skin following exactly the printed material beneath.

39. The child should be given a reading marker which blocks out most of the reading page, leaving a small space where a limited number of words can be focused upon at one time.

Social Training

40. A retarded child will need many instructions and demonstrations to learn social skills. Imitation and reward and approval through this practice may prove quite successful but will also be repetitious in nature. The child should be taught how to ask for directions, tell a strange adult about being lost, recite his or her name, address, and telephone. The child should learn how to ask for help from adults, introduce parents, shake hands, and handle the simple amenities of life. Conceivably these can be taught in the school program and supplemented by the interest of parents.

41. Make some prestigious school job the exclusive domain of the special class. This helps to reduce the disparaging comments of nonretarded age-mates. The job might be that of running audiovisual machines, mimeo operation, a supply or equipment room, or care of animals in the school.

42. Request that the guidance counselor discuss private concerns and problems with the teenagers on a regular basis. The counselor and teacher need to keep each other informed of their respective and congruent plans for each special student, be the considerations social, academic, or vocational.

43. To enhance the pleasure of the school day, have the children grouped by sociometric principles; let the children sit and work near their friends. Preferred seating arrangements can be used as incentives and rewards for teacher-determined work performance or self-control.

Vocational Training

44. For older educable retardates, the school program should continue to be geared toward practical endeavors with a heavy vocational and socialization flavor. Considerable practice and

role playing should be done in applying for jobs, answering the telephone, completing application blanks, increasing mobility via different modes of transportation, using money, etc.

45. After prevocational experiences, begin a more advanced vocational experience selecting specific activities within the world of work to provide the student with real jobs: salad-making, bus-boy, and other restaurant responsibilities, janitorial jobs, car wash, laundry and hospital work, gardening, farming, and sheltered shop, all of which are often suitable for the mentally retarded as initial experiences.

46. Enroll both boys and girls in a basic home and appliance care program which is designed to give them a working knowledge of simple repair and maintenance. Since some of the retarded people will marry, they should receive intensive training in child care, simple medical knowledge, home nursing, house care, cooking, and of course prevocational and vocational training and supervised field experiences.

Medical Assistance

47. Each retarded child should have a complete medical evaluation plus an eye and ear evaluation prior to enrollment in a special class. Request this of parents or seek to determine if funds are available elsewhere through contacts with agencies. Each child should also receive a speech evaluation and the teacher and parents should discuss the results and possible recommendations with the specialist. Retarded children with suspected minimal cerebral dysfunction or brain injury should be evaluated by a neurologist with the consent of the parents and the advice of the child's physician.

48. Request through the parents the sustaining interest of the medical doctor if the child appears to be excessively hyper-active. Does he consider medication or some other approach to be effective?

49. If a retarded child seems particularly sluggish, tired, or unresponsive, the parents should be urged to obtain a complete physical examination for him through the child's physician.

50. Emphasize physical education aspects such as body balance, laterality exercises, fine and gross muscle coordination,

and individualized programs of physical education as created by the gym teacher. If some students appear to require physical therapy for coordination, poor posture, etc., then so inform the parents to discuss this with appropriate personnel, medical or otherwise.

Behavior Modification Approaches

51. Behavior modification techniques will be very helpful in establishing a more accepted level of performance—a level which should require work on the child's part. Daily work assignments should be tied to a specific amount of work performed, at a specific level of accuracy, with specific and tangible rewards or tokens. Often a large problem is motivation to learn since nonreinforcing defeats have preceded. Sometimes a child has learned that a minimal performance is acceptable. He must relearn acceptable modes of behavior which would lead to maximal performance on his part. The teacher can encourage motivation by offering rewards of value to the child: food, candy, tokens, free-time, a special seat, money, etc.

52. For a nonverbal retarded child, the teacher should present him with situation where talking is necessary, as in requesting lavatory permission; when he responds (in whatever way) he should be positively reinforced. Gradually he should be reinforced only when he responds verbally. Eventually, more and more requirements can be imposed and tangible rewards given quickly.

53. A bagful of coins of each denomination is useful in teaching changemaking and purchasing. Symbolic purchases can be made of boxes constructed to look like grocery products, toys, etc. This can be worked in a shopping day game or can be converted to be used as a store to obtain gifts for reinforcements of good classroom performance as determined by the teacher or group. Tokens can be made in several denominations corresponding to our monetary system and given for successful growth in self-control, mastery of simple number facts, etc. Combinations of tokens can be used to make purchases in the classroom store or larger privileges on the playground, or to purchase candy rewards.

54. One important approach to extinguish disruptive behavior, if possible, is to ignore it totally and not permit other children to remark about it. They too must be instructed to ignore the child who is having temper tantrums, otherwise they may inadvertently reinforce it. This procedure is to be matched with considerable attention, tokens, praise, and class recognition as well as the teacher's approval for quiet work, good self-control, class seatwork done well, etc. Naturally the rewards must suit the child's value system. Be consistent in rewarding for approved behavior at least one or two months, trying to ignore inappropriate behavior unless it is harmful to the child, his classmates or has some destructive aspects to it. Obviously it is impossible to ignore a child who is cursing or insulting some other person. Some of these extinction procedures might best function in a residential treatment home rather than in a public or parochial school setting. Before beginning such a reinforcement or extinction program, it might be helpful to record base-line behavior which is to be changed. Tokens accumulated may be turned in for special privileges or some reward that is appropriate for the child's needs.

Teacher Expectancy

55. Expect slow progress in the special class. Do not express disappointment by word or gesture over the slow progress, lack of it, or forgetfulness of a retarded child. Accept him as he is and attempt to modify only those aspects of him that are within reasonable control. Do not reject him. A sign of rejection or disappointment will almost invariably substantiate his own self-appraisal as worthless and hopeless.

56. Accept the observation that many, if not most, retarded children are often achieving as well as their mental ages and previous experiences permit. If anything, retarded children tend to overachieve rather than underachieve their mental age expectations. The teachers may frequently take credit for this functioning level because of their individualized work with children in the class. Obviously it is an interdisciplinary effort in addition.

57. Levels of expectation should be kept consistent with progress. Yearly group or individual achievement testing, evalu-

ation of perceptual abilities, and assessment of sense organs and health should be a routine part of the class program. Proper records of plateaus or growth in achievement should be kept on each child to aid instructional decisions and provide data for parents and professional personnel.

Helping Parents

58. With the parent's understanding, place the child in a class for educable retarded children, even if it takes a year or more to obtain their consent. A knowledgeable professional, preferably the person who made the diagnosis, should inform the parents with sufficient detail and explanation all that retardation implies, how special education may help, and what education cannot solve.

59. An otherwise normal child, accurately diagnosed as educable retarded by the team consideration of a physician, psychologist, neurologist, educators, etc. should be placed in a special education class for the retarded in his local school district. The placement must be appropriate to his chronological age and mental age and the teacher must be a competent, trained and mature person. This placement must be preceded by understanding and general acceptance by the parents who are willing to continue aiding the child in his educational and social development. Children diagnosed as mentally retarded should have been so classified by virtue of verified social incompetence compared to age mates, consistently low or subnormal intelligence, exceptionally poor school achievement for age, developmental delay in motor, perceptual, social, physical or language areas, and the confirmation of knowledgeable physicians. Classes for mentally retarded children should be reserved only for genuinely mentally retarded children. Those to be excluded from entrance into such a program are pseudoretarded, dull-normal, aggressive behavior problems, psychotic and neurotic, blind and deaf, learning disabled children of average or low average intelligence, poor readers, and culturally disadvantaged.

60. The parents should be made aware of the child's retardation after a complete evaluation and diagnosis has been made. Interpretation should be made in terms of the child's

behavior and mental ability at that time. One should avoid attempting to predict the child's future with accuracy unless it is an older or severe case. Parents should understand that special programs should help the child to mature at his slow rate without undue frustration. Parents should be informed by the psychologist or physician, not the principal or by letter.

61. Help the parents by gentle, honest reasoning to realize that early placement in special classes is easier for the child now than later. The child will accept it as the parents accept it.

62. Children placed in retarded classes should receive comprehensive psychoeducational evaluations every two or three years, not just to determine eligibility, but to inform parents of growth and problems and to provide a basis of further planning with the teacher.

63. Parents of retarded children should especially encourage independence in the child's dressing, eating, playing, socialization, and self-care. Efforts should be made to toilet train the child completely. Discipline, expectations, and training should be consistent. Make sure that the child knows why he is being rewarded. Both parents should agree on what the child should learn and how to reward him.

64. The parents should be helped to understand that the child will still require a great deal of patient help even after he has been placed in a retarded class and that the school personnel services or some agency professionals may assist on problems dealing with child-rearing practices, discipline, jobs, dating, teenage values, and marriage.

65. Enroll the child in a local club, "Y," or church program under the sponsorship of the parents for retarded children. The child will become active outside of school at a social level with other children, and develop awareness of sexuality, dress, behavior, community projects, etc.

66. Permit the child to make specific choices regarding clothing as one of many ways to help the child become as independent as possible.

67. Provide the child with a list of routine tasks at home which are carefully laid out in sequence for designated times. If listed by pictures of the jobs, each can be checked off by the child

as accomplished. What reward system will the child respond to? Use this as incentive.

68. If parents are uncertain about plans offered by a school diagnostic team, tell them to take the child to a clinic or hospital qualified to assess these difficulties to satisfy themselves about the ability of the child. Then, presuming verification, they should return and permit school personnel to place the child appropriately and set up a program that will be of the greatest educational value to him.

69. After the school personnel have revealed that a genuine problem is present, request the parents' permission to conduct an extensive psychological study. Discuss the findings with the parents after telling the school personnel. If this is the first occasion on which the parents have been informed of this condition, offer and strongly recommend a program for parent counseling. Consider the child for placement in a retarded class. Advise the principal and teachers of the outcomes of all such conferences.

70. While discussing the evaluation with parents, include options for day care, home training, and residential placement. Offer counseling until a reasonable plan of action is formulated.

71. Spend time with parents explaining what mental retardation means in terms of educational efforts and planning and what are more or less the realistic levels of expectation. Offer interested parents some relevant reading materials on mental retardation. Insist that parents visit the special classes, not only at their own child's level but the subsequent groups. Have the parents write questions to discuss with the teacher, psychologist, speech therapist, etc. Keep the parent interested in what the child is doing.

72. Explain to the parents before placement of the student in a class for the retarded that the child will be periodically examined by the school psychologist and will be removed and placed in another program if he should subsequently show improved abilities. Do not encourage that such is likely to be the case, but indicate only that the child is never permanently assigned or dismissed from further consideration by school authorities.

73. Most parents find some relief from guilt when they learn of the great number of families who share their problems, of the many factors which can interfere with normal birth and development, and the great likelihood that their child was damaged by causes over which they had no control. Except in cases of obvious genetic contributions to the retardation, be certain that the parents are informed that in the great majority of cases mental retardation comes not from heredity, as the layman often believes, but from damage to the brain before, during or after the birth of the child. The medical professional may be better equipped to determine etiological conditions and should be contacted if the parents wish to determine initial contributions.

74. If a parent shows a marked reluctance to admit her child to a retarded class, request the mother of another retarded child in the same room to make a social call on the new mother to discuss the educational program.

75. In helping parents to accept their child's intellectual limitations, explain the special and routine methods used in class to aid learning. Point out the advantages potentially gained from placement in this class and the educational plans for their child in particular. Indicate at some later time that comparable education in a private or residential school could cost several thousand dollars yearly, but is available to them at no special cost in the public schools.

76. Parents have a right to know what the school personnel know about their children. With the exception, perhaps, of disturbed or irrational parents, the teacher and psychologist have obligations to inform them of general test findings and their observations in an effort to share knowledge and plan cooperatively with parents. It is to be expected that some parents will attempt to blame the teacher for the child's lack of normal progress and his slow comprehension.

77. Parents need reassurance that learning for young retardates is possible, but that reading skills, as parents expect on a brief story, will not occur until the chronological age of, say, eight or nine years under the best of teaching and encouragement. Some portions of learning may indeed by enhanced by teaching machines, reinforcement schedules, etc.

78. Traditional report cards for retarded children are inappropriate unless they are tailor-made for each child with ratings that are clear to the children as well as the parents. Parent conferences, at least a few times yearly, and especially on complicated cases, are strenuous for both the teacher and the parents, but are much more effective in helping to focus on real issues and problems. Nevertheless, each child should be rated or evaluated against his own previous performance and informed clearly of his own progress. There may well be children who are too emotionally devastated to have any kind of report card.

Home Activities with Parents

79. To help develop language facility in a retarded child, the mother may have him sort objects and learn the names of each. Talk to him, explaining categories such as fruits and vegetables in the store. Have the child memorize the names via repetition. In motor development, aid the child with gross motor activities, such as those used in nursery school. Use jumbo crayons, Play-Doh, ring toss game, and bean bags to adapt the equipment to the child and not the reverse.

80. The parent should take the child to the library to borrow books appropriate to the mental age of the child. She should read to the child using the content of the book as a means of helping to develop vocabulary by discussion and recall. As a rule of thumb for the educable retarded child, select:

    a. Preprimers for chronological ages six through eight.
    b. Primers for ages seven through ten years.
    c. Primary Readers for ages eight through eleven years.
    d. Second and Third Grade Readers for ages nine though twelve years.

81. Advise parents not to punish their child for poor academic achievement. Advise them not to deny the child food or the use of a toy as a means of forcing the child to learn. Rather have them reward good performance than punish poor performance. If the parents get upset when trying to teach the child something, suggest that they train for a simpler level task well within the child's comprehension.

82. Emphasize the educability of their youngster, urging that his present capacities are to be judged roughly on the basis of his current mental age. Specify that educational gaps not only will persist but will broaden with increasing age. Tell them that it is improbable that the child will "catch up" or "snap out of it" even with the best of medical and educational care.

SECTION B: MODERATE MENTAL RETARDATION (TRAINABLE)

Placement

83. Place the moderately retarded child in the trainable class if his level of functioning is too low for comfortable adjustment in the educable level. Have the physician send a report to school personnel about medical information that would be helpful to know about the child. Is physical therapy advised, a special medical program, or reduced activity?

84. The consideration for institutionalization is always a highly individualized matter and depends on many factors which must be weighed by the parents. Often they need help here to consider: the amount of medical, therapeutic, or education care required, the emotional stability of the other children in the home, the strength of the marriage relationship, finances, local services, religious preferences, age and ability of parents, degree of parental guilt feelings, etc. One large factor is the degree of emotional disturbance and potential destructiveness of the child and the parents' ability to cope with him. When all of these topics have been explored with a professional person, the parents may consider trial placement or adaptation to their child's problems at home.

Instruction

85. Recognize that the child will probably be unable to achieve literacy. Teach self-help skills and plan for a semi-sheltered environment.

86. Emphasis should be placed upon helping the child to develop adequate self-help and self-care skills. These might encompass physical hygiene, appearance, proper eating habits,

etc. Special emphasis should also be placed upon developing communicative skills.

87. Behavior modification techniques have been effective frequently with these youngsters in eliminating unwanted behavior (or eliciting desired behavior). Negatives: nose-picking, rocking behaviors, masturbation in class, scab-picking, shouting, punching, tantrums, pouting, unwillingness to work, cursing, poor eating habits, dependency, enuresis, etc. Positives: being quiet, working alone, walking to the bathroom, not disrupting others. Consult the psychologist for strategies.

Social Training

88. Place the child in a day care center if possible. If toilet trained, attempt to have him attend a nursery school. Give specific training in behavioral objectives developed from a list based on development sequences.

89. Provide a specific object upon which anger and frustration can legitimately and habitually be expressed when necessary. Large rubber inflatable toys, a large but not too heavy punching bag, plastic models, and a decorated cork panel for bean-bag throwing could be used. It is usually necessary for each child at any one time to have his own exclusive use of such an object.

SECTION C: SEVERE MENTAL RETARDATION (SEVERE AND PROFOUND)

90. If a severely retarded child is a continuous threat to the safety of younger children or to himself, institutionalization may have to be arranged with parent consent. Most severely retarded children in recent years have been living in their homes and in some cases both their parents and siblings have testified to the benefits which they, themselves, have derived from this experience.

91. Tell the parents tactfully but clearly about (a) the noneducability of the child, (b) his very limited trainability, and (c) the need for continuous supervision at home or away. Ease whatever guilt may come into play by convincing the family that the separation is, in fact, an act of real sacrifice based on their

concern and love for the child and their desire to do whatever is best for him also. Caution the parents about the possibility of neglecting the needs of their other children at home.

92. In regard to institutionalization, the basic decision for such placement rests with parents or a legal guardian. Inform them that the decision is never simple. Discuss all the advantages and disadvantages; help them recognize that there are other persons to be considered, particularly normal siblings. The age of parents is a factor not to be overlooked since there is always the possibility that the retarded child could outlive his parents.

93. If a residential treatment or custodial home wishes to use behavior modification toward better socialization and functioning at higher levels, establish a complete token economy. Give tokens for good habits that can be traded in for primary reinforcers such as candy, beds, and other creature comforts. In some cases, the primary reinforcers will need to be administered directly because tokens are too much delayed. Perhaps, over a period of time, tokens can be associated with primary reinforcers, thus eliminating the need to administer primary reinforcers directly.

Chapter XI

SPECIFIC LEARNING DISABILITIES

A S IS NOW BETTER recognized, specific learning disabilities encompass a large group of related special learning problems which have only recently evolved into a clearer focus for professionals. Previously, specialists in medicine, psychology, language, and education had emphasized their respective concerns, for example, in vision, audition, or speech as they investigated their particular interests (Clements, 1966). In the last three decades, however, a professional merger of interests has developed which has a common meeting ground: specific learning disabilities of children. Now available is a pooling of ideas, talents, and research possibilities (Brutton, Richardson, and Manuel, 1973; Johnson and Morasky, 1980; Ross, 1976; Sapir and Wilson, 1978; Seiderman, 1976, 1979).

A resulting emphasis has generally devalued a concern, almost an early obsession, for the discovery of a medical etiology and medical intervention and has changed instead and upgraded its focus to an educational adaptation and remediation with a fuller concern for its psychological impact. As Myers and Hammill (1976) have correctly indicated, several new theories, assessment instruments, and research perspectives have been developed in an interdisciplinary effort to help such children.

Who these disabled children are varies with the definition suggested.

A definition of specific learning disability was made by the National Committee to HEW in 1968 and was revised for inclusion in Public Law 94-142 as follows:

> Specific learning disabilities means a disorder of one or more of the basic
> psychological processes involved in understanding or in using language
> to listen, think, speak, read, write, spell, or do arithmetic calculations.
> The term includes such conditions as perceptual handicaps, brain
> injury, minimal brain damage, dyslexia, and developmental aphasia.
> The term does not include children who have learning problems which
> are primarily the result of visual, hearing, or motor handicaps, of mental
> retardation, or environmental, cultural, or economic disadvantage
> (Federal Register, Education for All Handicapped Children, 1975).

With increasing emphasis, by educators primarily, on remediation and not causation, it is apparent that the educational
domain will carry the major work of intervention in terms of
learning, as specific learning disabilities are currently understood. In addition, however, has come the eminently reasonable
belief that learning disabled children definitely need and can
profit from group and individual psychotherapy or counseling
approaches aimed at enhancing their self-concepts and helping
them accept responsibility for some of their own behavior as
learners and people. Many such children have denigrated themselves to such an extent that they are truly lacking in motivation
for another assault on the academic world.

Reviews of research have indicated that the field is understandably debating whether or not particular kinds of remediations are
effective for particular disabilities, concerns highlighted by the
general absence of tightly controlled, experimental studies. The
issues are not yet resolved and are certainly not considered in this
relatively brief chapter. Most if not all of the suggested approaches must, of course, be regarded as experimental in nature
and thus available for research inquiries.

It is presumed that the reader is familiar with the terms used in
the subheadings of this chapter. More comprehensive texts have
been written about such terms and the issues involved with
learning disabilities (Hammill and Bartel, 1978; Lerner, 1976).

This chapter is divided into the main headings often noted in
the literature about specific learning disabilities: (a) visual
perception, (b) auditory perception and language skills, (c) motor
coordination, (d) several subsections relating to control of
attention, and (e) specific ideas for the considerations of teachers
and parents.

A final consideration: as new and experimentally verified programs and strategies are developed through research and field practice, ineffective prescriptions noted in this chapter should be readily discarded.

SECTION A: VISUAL MODALITY PROBLEMS

Visual Perception

1. Different geometric designs of forms are drawn on the blackboard. Have the child touch those forms which are alike; those which are different.

2. Sort blocks according to shape, size, color, angle.

3. Place cardboard cutouts over corresponding shapes.

4. ,Match a picture and a concrete object.

5. Try outlining important figures (area of map, figures, etc.) with felt pen or dark pencil. Trace on onionskin paper.

6. Offer a mimeographed copy of board material which can be used at the child's desk rather than have him translate from the front or side board. Reduce visual shift and distance.

7. Find all things of one color in the classroom.

8. Cut many geometric forms. Find all the red triangles, green circles, etc. Outline shapes in black.

9. Look at a picture. Find the tallest object, the shortest, the largest, etc.

10. Trace around template with finger, crayon, pencil.

11. Reproduce design on: (a) pegboard, (b) ceiling tile with golf tees, (c) board with nails or tacks.

12. Reproduce forms with match sticks, objects with tinker-toys.

13. Do jig-saw puzzles, first with a simple design, then with more than one design. Have each design separated and sharply outlined against a relatively undetailed background.

14. Match words in manuscript, capital letters, and cursive writing. Circle all the "e's" or "w's" in a newspaper page.

15. Give a child a green block and a red block. Have him follow these directions: (a) Put the green block in front of the red block, (b) Put the red block on top of the green block.

16. Use a cut-out cardboard which exposes only one word or

short phrase at a time for the child who skips words or who has trouble focusing attention.

17. Put lines between the words for the child who tends to fuse words.

18. See how many particular words or letters can be crossed out on a page of a newspaper. Reward for fewer errors on future trials.

19. Use Fernald's kinesthetic method.
   a. The teacher writes a word with a felt pen on plain paper using blackboard-size cursive writing.
   b. The child says word as he traces it first with his finger and then with his pencil.
   c. He repeats the process as many times as necessary in order to learn to write the word without looking at the word.
   d. He writes the word and checks it.
   e. After he learns the word, he files it alphabetically in his own word-file box.

20. Words can be traced or written on a rough surface (rough drawing paper, paper towels, or sand paper) with a crayon.
   a. First trace it with eyes closed.
   b. After learning through the tactile method, trace with eyes open.
   c. After learning a word, it is typewritten and placed into his own word-file box for flash cards.

21. Have the child find and underline each word in a different color.

22. Perceptual training may be recommended and executed by a developmental optometrist.

23. Consult *Handbook in Diagnostic-Prescriptive Teaching,* by Mann, Suiter, and McClung (1979).

Visual Discrimination

24. Match all things of about the same shape or size in the classroom: round, square, smaller-than-a-book, etc.

25. Describe objects or pictures and discuss functions.

26. Determine how two symbols are alike or different.

27. Sort objects by size and color, e.g. marbles, buttons, discs.

28. Match letters, numbers, and block designs which are the same.

29. Put picture puzzles together. Variation: cut own pictures for puzzle and reassemble for magazine covers and advertisements.

30. Cut out comic book pictures. Arrange sequentially.

31. Cut up magazines for examples of textures: smooth, rough.

32. Use magazines and newspapers to underline all the "b's," and the "s's," etc,

33. Cut particular words out of a newspaper or magazine each time they appear. Mix them up and place them in a pile and then ask the child to match like words even though they are printed differently or are reversals, i.e. left, felt; was, saw; how, who.

34. Some children have a diffuse or global visual perception rather than an accurate perception of detail and so base word recognition on only one or two characteristics, such as beginning sound, or general configuration. Emphasize visual detail in verbal discussion of words . . . How is the word "house" like the word "horse"? . . . How is it different? Also, provide many activities which require the child to look at separate parts of words. Circle the small words in the big word . . . Guess what word I'm writing . . . What is incorrect about the way these words are written, etc.

35. Use a ditto or typewritten sheet with numerals or letters in a column on the left side. Have these same symbols with variations typed (written) in a horizontal row. Ask the child to circle each symbol that is like the one in the left column. Example:

b—a e k j b i o l w l p 2 , c - 9 w b * p b a
p—u w e c @ v * k l p m , w e q o p V b p f t
e—u , m c 3 $ q D o p l h i E e d c s a t o c
8—1 x 3 8 23 8 0 ½ 2 w d 5 4 9 90 23 43 33 8

Figure-Ground

36. Match pegboard design. Increase the difficulty.

37. Use Visual—Perception Exercises appropriate to this

disability. See reference by Mann, Suiter, and McClung (1979).

38. This child may be distracted by many words on a page. Cut a slot in a cardboard marker, so that only one word shows at a time. Have child move the marker from left to right as he looks at each word. Use reading materials with few words on a page if possible. Use a marker to keep the place on the page, or ask child to point to each word with his finger as he reads it.

39. Outline in felt pen essential features for the child to help his discriminate a figure from its background. Gradually introduce more complex pictures and use less outlining.

Space Relations

40. There are so many prepared materials available that specific exercises are not listed here. See resources listed:
   a. Perceptual-Motor Teaching Materials by Teacher Resources.
   b. Alpha Book Re-Markable Products by Kleeco Products.
   c. A simplified Readiness Program in Visual Discrimination by Parkinson.
   d. Frostig Exercises by Follett Publishing Company.

Visual Memory

41. Look at sequence of objects of pictures; close eyes and try to recall them verbally.

42. Use a kinesthetic approach to reading and spelling.

43. Work with colorful materials so that the child's attention will be less distracted by other classroom activities.

44. Games to enhance visual memory.
   a. Two children have from two to six objects. One child places the objects. Second child observes, and then closes his eyes, while the first child removes one object, then the second child tells which is missing. The second child takes a turn. Reward improved accuracy.
   b. A child rearranged objects when other child's eyes are

closed. He then has to replace them in an original order.

c. A child touches an object. The next child touches that object and one more. The next child touches the previous objects in order and then adds one more, etc.

d. A child leaves the room. One child of the class goes to cloakroom. Child returns and identifies one who went to the cloakroom.

e. Describe an object and have a child guess what it is, i.e. "I am thinking of something little and white with long ears and a short tail and pink eyes. What is it?"

f. Describe the clothes and appearance of a child. Another child tries to guess who is being described.

g. Let a child look around the room for a prescribed period (15 seconds). Then he turns his back and the teacher asks questions, i.e. "Who is wearing a blue dress?" "Who is sitting next to _____?", etc.

General Instruction in Visual Perception

45. Under ordinary circumstances, subvocalizing can be a hindrance to reading quickly. In the special child's case, however, he may need to subvocalize merely to understand what he is reading. The teacher should permit him to continue. The child needs to learn to read with comprehension before he can learn to read with speed.

46. Quadrille paper, with horizontal and vertical lines, is recommended for his handwriting and arithmetic work in the classroom.

47. Written assignments should be short, highly structured, and preferably limited to one area at a time, i.e. spelling or syntax or penmanship. Let the child dictate some of his assignments or homeword to be written or typed by someone else if the student is more talented orally than visually. Use paper-and-pencil tracking exercises, such as the Michigan Visual Tracking Self-Instruction Workbooks for eye-motor control and sequentialization. Ten to fifteen minutes, three to five times per week, will be helpful. Use the EDL Controlled Reader at reduced speeds for training in following and tracking for both oral and silent reading. It may be

helpful to let the child tape-record his reading occasionally in order to call attention to pacing and skipping.

48. Permit and encourage the child to use his finger, a pointer, or place marker to keep track of his place during silent and oral reading.

SECTION B: AUDITORY MODALITY PROBLEMS

Auditory Perception

1. Teach good listening habits.

2. Give individual help privately where there are few distracting noises.

3. Use a record player, tape recorder, etc. with earphones.

4. Listen to a record, keep time by beating a drum, clapping hands, or clicking sticks.

5. Teach the child to sit still, concentrate, and look at the speaker. Reward for good attending skills.

6. Build auditory "set" with whisper activities.

7. Listen for differences in sounds between paired words: sat - set, tap - top, and such pairs found in tests of auditory discrimination.

8. The teacher may start a sentence and the child may complete it.

9. A child may indicate when words rhyme:
    a. When listening to poetry read by the teacher.
    b. By adding a last word in the second line.
    c. By adding a rhyming word in response to, "I am thinking of something in this room that rhymes with door."

10. Games using beginning sounds:
    a. Name three words. Have a child identify two which start alike.
    b. "Tell me a word that starts like . . ."
    c. A child may bring in pictures of objects which start with a given sound.

11. With closed eyes, identify outside or inside noises, and sounds on records. Examples: a pencil being sharpened, a light turned on, a window closed, a shoe dropped, a voice.

12. Categorize sounds: pleasant, unpleasant; those which make one happy, sad, afraid. Imitate animal sounds.

13. Use choral poems and stories.

14. Read stories and question listeners for comprehension.

15. Listen for words within words: restless.

16. A child may make his own recording on tape and listen for his errors.

17. A child may draw pictures of things with a given beginning sound.

18. Provide concrete experiences so he can perceive what he hears: "soft, hard; cold, warm; stop, go," etc.

Auditory Discrimination

19. Children may close their eyes and listen to sounds around them; then point to the direction from which each comes and identify it.

20. Children may listen for differences in sounds: high—low; loud—soft; fast—slow; etc., (use musical instruments, footsteps, etc.).

21. Children may listen to, distinguish, and identify specific sounds:

    a. scissors, hammer, broom, saw, bell.

    b. clapping, snapping fingers, clucking tongue, humming.

22. Have the children listen for gross differences in words. Ask questions: "Do we ride a penny?" "Can we climb a letter?"

23. Have children look at two pictures and choose the one named turkey—turtle; eggs—ax; etc.

24. Ask "Which is it?"

    a. "Which grow on chickens? Feathers or sweaters?"

    b. "Which is an animal? A puppy or a puddle?"

25. Always verbalize experiences with the child, i.e. when traveling, visiting with the class, taking a field trip, talk about what is seen. Do not allow child merely to visualize experiences.

26. Read stories to the child and ask comprehension questions about the story.

27. Purchase musical records (child's and teenager's) and encourage the child to hum and then sing by imitating the record.

28. Purchase records for the child which include different sounds (animals, trains, etc.) and have the child discriminate these sounds.

29. Use ITPA curriculum techniques in areas of auditory memory, general and sequential, auditory closure, etc.

30. Spelling exercises and Spelling Bees should be used, but having only words with which the child can be relatively successful.

31. Use the "Look—say" method to teach beginning reading.

32. Use the Fernald VAKT system for teaching reading.

Auditory Reception

33. Ask "yes—no—maybe" questions, such as, "Children should have shoes," "A red light means GO," "This barber gives the best haircut in the world."

34. Verbal directions are given and the child complies. For example, "Go touch the table and the chalkboard," or "Touch the back of your head with your left hand." "Simon Says" is a good game for practicing this skill.

35. The child should listen to a sentence, paragraph, or story and retell the story or answer various questions. It may be helpful to advise the child what to expect, such as the names of the children or how many boys, and so on. As the child improves, the complexity of the task is gradually increased.

36. Review the techniques suggested in Chapter II.

Grammatic Closure

37. Auditory sound blending is a closure function. The teacher may present a word with syllables or letters separated by a short time interval (b-a-b-y, c-a-t). Sound blending experiences may have to be introduced using pictures as visual cues. The separated word "b-a-b-y" is presented several times and the child identifies the correct picture. Another exercise involves sound blending words that represent objects in the room. "Find something on the desk with this name—p-e-n." A related sound blending activity may utilize a sentence with only one word

sound blended. "The boy ran up the 'h-i-l-l'." The child may identify this word through context clues. Gradually all visual cues are removed.

38. Teach the child an uncompleted sentence such as, "This is a very nice _____ ." After the memorization process is completed, walk around the room pointing at objects. The child says and completes the stimulus sentence. For example, if a plant were designated as the stimulus object, the child would respond, "This is a very nice plant." Each word is presented in the proper order and repetition is mandatory.

39. Teach the child to give a specific word response to a stimulus word. For example, the child always responds with "elm" to the stimulus word "tree." After this pairing of words is thoroughly established, a second pair is introduced, such as the stimulus word "big" and the response word "large." After this second pair is thoroughly ingrained, the two sets of words can be interchanged. More sets can be added gradually.

40. For the child with a sound blending disability who is unable to synthesize a whole word from its individual sounds, place four to six pictures of three-syllable words on the chalk ledge and say, "Bring me the bi-cy-cle," separating the syllables. Repeat this exercise until the child can do it accurately and easily. Repeat this type of exercise, using first two-syllable words— "Touch the ta-ble." Finally, teach the child to synthesize phonic elements in a given word; e.g. "d-e-s-k," "c-u-p."

Articulation

41. Repeat sounds in isolation or attached to meaningful situations (e.g. imitation of a fire engine).

42. Furnish sound effects for a story told by the teacher, e.g. "The little engine came down the tracks—ch-ch-ch-ch".

43. Whenever possible, appeal to the senses when articulating a sound, e.g. voiced "th":

    a. "Look at me as I make the 'th' sound." (Visual)

    b. "Put the tip of your tongue between your teeth and gently bite. Blow a stream of air, and feel it tickle your teeth and your tongue." (Tactile)

    c. "Listen to how it sounds." (Auditory)

44. Relate to motor skills, e.g.
    a. "How would you draw a picture of O-O-O-O-?"
    b. "If your hand is up when you hear (high) eeeeeee-eeeeee, where is it when you hear (low) eeeeeeeeeeee?"
    c. Have a child write letter or letters for the "th" sound as he says it over and over.

45. Use a mirror to show the child how he looks as he makes specific sounds.

46. Use a tape recorder so child can listen to himself.

47. After the child knows sound in isolation, encourage him to use it in words, sentences, stories, and conversation.

Auditory Memory

48. Repeat digits, words, sentences, starting with series of two.

49. Play games such as, "I'm packing my trunk. I put in a _____ ," and add more items one by one.

50. Have children follow a series of directions.

51. Play restaurant with children remembering "food orders" to give the cook.

52. Give simple directions which the child can remember; increase the number of directions as his ability to remember increases.

53. Read a story which is short, repetitive, and filled with action. Let the child retell it, recall ideas and details.

54. Games which require memory. For example:
    a. "I went to a farm. I saw a horse, a pig, a sheep, and a goat. Now tell me the names of the animals I saw."
    b. Present a series of words that have some relationship. Have the child repeat words in correct sequence. For example, apple, peach, orange, banana, or red, yellow, blue.
    c. Songs, such as "Old MacDonald Had a Farm," which require adding items to the original are useful here.
    d. "On my way to school, I saw..." (listing a number of things).

55. Write words while saying sounds. Dictate simple words containing short or long vowel sounds, diphthongs, or conso-

nant blends. The child should identify the sound and write the word with its correct spelling.

56. Use a listening center with recorded or taped stories.

57. The teacher may describe colors for simple pictures while the child closes his eyes. He then draws the picture using described colors.

58. Give the child a set of numbers from 0-0 printed on 2" square cards. Call out a series of 2, 3, 4 . . . and ask the child to form the sequence. Increase the difficulty of the task by introducing letters and then words; start with two variables and gradually increase the number.

59. Prepare a tape which names several easily drawn nouns like "house." Children listen and draw the object. Gradually increase the complexity of the description, e.g. a small house with three windows and a tall door, etc.

60. To help a child follow a sequence of verbal directions and improve auditory memory ask him to: hop to the door, turn out the light, turn around twice and skip over to a seat. For a child with severe problems start with only one direction and as he is successful, increase the number of sequential steps.

61. Use prerecorded cassette tapes of children's stories for school and home. Let the child record his own voice through a short story he made up or his description of an interesting event.

Auditory Discrimination of Consonants

62. In an alphabet game, ask about what in the zoo begins with c-k (give hard c sound). Write answers on the blackboard. Continue by naming letters of alphabet, and by using other categories, e.g. hardware store, clothing stores, cupboard, museum, railroad station.

63. In a mailman game, make cards containing a single consonant or consonant blend. A child pretends that he is the postman and passes the letters out. Each child stands, reads his letter, first by name, then sound, lastly gives a word starting with that sound.

64. Dictate a word in which a specific consonant is in beginning, medial, or final position. A child must indicate its position. If done with a group, each child may make three

numbers (1-2-3-) and circle the number which shows the position of the letter.

65. For a Go Fish game, made commercially or by a teacher, use cards in pairs (or sets of 3) containing words or pictures which begin with the same sound. Players are dealt six cards each and work for sets by asking another player, in turn, for a card starting with the sound of the one he holds. If successful, he has another turn, if not he takes a "fish" from the cards remaining in the center of the table. The game ends when one child uses all the sound cards in his hand.

66. Reado-LoHo cards, commercial or teacher-made, are played like Bingo except that each square contains a consonant, blend, or word depending on the level the child has reached.

Auditory Discrimination of Vowels

67. For a short vowel game, make an apple on oak tag for each child. Write short words containing the short "a" sound, e.g. hat mat cat, on each apple. Ask questions about the words. "What rhymes with hat?" (mat); "What scratches?" The same game can be adapted to other short vowel sounds.

68. Make up words that have one vowel sound and write them on cards for verbalization.

Auditory Vocal Association

69. To categorize or classify objects, "Name all the birds (cars, farm animals, household items, etc.) you can think of." Then reverse the process by asking of what category three similar items are a part; for example, a plow, pitchfork, and tractor.

70. Build the concepts of "Same and Different" by asking the child how two or more things are alike: "In what way are a horse and a cow alike?" Initially, concrete likenesses (legs, eyes, tails) are encouraged, but gradually more abstract similarities are developed (both live on a farm, work for man, and are animals).

71. Cause and effect questions can be employed, such as "What would happen if . . .?" Examples include, "If a faucet handle broke, what would you do?" "What would happen if a dog and a cat were put in a room together?" "If you saw a lady fall, what would you do?" "Why?"

SECTION C: COORDINATION

Gross Motor Coordination Deficits

Running

1. Walk to a drum beat with arms bent—quicken the beat to approach running speed and tempo. Exaggerate arm motion.

2. Hold child at hips so that his hips are ahead of his toes. Tell him to run as soon as you let go or else he will fall down. Tell him to practice pushing his hips forward to run faster.

3. Use bean bag relay races or timed races against himself or one other person. (Review Chapter II for exercises here.)

Jumping

4. Have a child jump from one foot to the other—forward, back, and to the side.

5. Play Jump the Creek: put two chalk marks on the floor or use jump ropes instead of chalk. Start jumping with both feet together over the narrow part of the "creek." Bend knees for greater distance.

6. Use blocks of wood or cardboard box to jump over. Lengthen and build higher.

Hopping

7. Hop to hand clapping or signal.
8. Balance on one foot and then hop up.
9. Hop to a beat on one foot and then the other.
10. Use hopping in relay races. Have couple hop holding hands in a race.

Skipping

11. Stand on one foot, skip forward, then on the other foot. Quicken the tempo by beat or verbal command.

Balancing

12. Have the child mark an "x" on a blackboard at eye level then stand several feet from it. Tell him to look at it very hard,

then instruct him to raise both arms outstretched to the side and finally one foot. Tell him to bend his upper body over his balancing leg (to the side—not forward). If the child is right-handed it is usually best to balance on the left leg, but also try the other leg. Another hint is tell the child to press his toes down hard.

13. Put one foot ahead of the other heel-to-toe and balance on one foot.

14. Stand for ten seconds by tiptoe on both feet.

15. Stand on one foot and swing the other foot forward and backward and from side to side, and then with eyes closed.

16. Walk on tiptoes, stopping on command.

17. Walk on a balance beam.

18. Balance heel-to-toe with arms up and out to the side at shoulder height.

19. Walk heel-to-toe without a tape marker but toward a spot to concentrate upon. Walk in as straight a line as possible to it.

20. Walk a line 1 inch to 4 inches wide heel-to-toe, concentrating on looking at the end of the line or tape. Start off with a wide line or tape.

21. Walk a low balance beam by heel-to-toe.

22. Encourage movement through space to stimulate balance. Use swings, rocking-chair or rocking-horse, seesaws, spinning, tricycle riding; walking and turning to various directional commands.

23. Vary the throwing experiences with a bean bag; throw at a target, for accuracy and distance.

24. Keep a record of how many catches in a row a child can make and reward him. Change to smaller balls gradually, because they are harder to track in the air.

25. The physical education teacher should scrupulously avoid placing a clumsy child in a situation where his coordination problem will be exposed to his peers. For example, asking the child to catch a fast baseball will be exceptionally difficult. The teacher should observe the child closely to determine what physical skills the child does have. For example, some special children are larger than other children and are physically strong.

This child should be allowed to demonstrate his physical strength often. Participation in quick moving sports may be omitted for this child.

General Coordination

26. Walk, run, march, dance, hop, and skip to the rhythms of piano, song, or clapping.

27. Creep with opposite hand and knee striking the floor at the same time.

28. Walk up and down stairs using alternate feet.

29. Stand with hands at sides. On command have a child jump and spread feet apart while he claps his hands above his head. Employ various exercises.

30. As a child walks have him point with his left hand at his right foot, then as he takes his next step point with right hand at his left foot around the room.

31. Utilize group games such as Looby-loo, Simon Says. Create an obstacle course involving walking, crawling, and climbing.

32. Try body stunts such as rabbit hop, duck walk, tumbling, etc.; use rings, ladders, pushups, hoops, jungle gym.

33. Walk a line four inches wide, eight to twelve feet in length, in a heel-to-toe manner.

34. Provide means for child to measure and record improvement in individual skills.

35. Identify body parts by touching after instructions.

Fine Muscle Coordination

36. Use clay, drawing, coloring, weaving, folding, cutting, lacing and tying, block building, etc.

37. Fit objects together, nested cubes, peg boards, simple jigsaw puzzles, cut-out stencils, reproduce block designs, use pick-up sticks.

38. Sort cards with different letters of alphabet or numbers.

39. The teacher may demonstrate shapes with hand and arm, beginning with a circle, the square, etc.: in the air, on the board, on paper, on a line. The teacher may hold the child's hand

and help him carry through on movement.

40. Stringing beads in a reproduction of a pattern. Use a bolt board using bolts, nuts, and washers of various sizes to aid in fine coordination in a speed and accuracy task.

41. Use games such as jacks, marbles, peg board. Tinker Toys, Lincoln Logs, block city, Chinese Checkers, and tic-tac-toe with marbles on a wooden board or on clay.

42. Use the Montessori Dressing Frames for snapping, large buttons, shoe laces, zippers, and bow-tying.

43. Use a Play-doh, stringing beads or macaroni; sewing with yarn on cards, burlap, or felt.

44. Color within heavy dark lines the outline shapes in picture ads, while progressing to coloring books. Discuss staying within lines.

45. Give practice with scissor cutting.

46. Follow dot drawings, shapes, and letters (telling first what will be drawn); use tracing books.

Laterality and Directionality

47. Identify the body parts of themselves, other children, and in pictures.

48. Imitate movements made by the teacher accompanied by verbal directions, e.g. "I lift my left leg." The teacher may do movement in "mirror image" or with her back to class. Students may also lead.

49. Stepping Stones: 6 inch squares of cardboard—ten black, ten red. Black: left foot; red: right. Arrange squares so that a child must take steps of different lengths and in different directions. Put a black ribbon on the child's left foot, red on right. Instruct the child to walk on squares with corresponding colors.

50. Play games such as "Here we go, Looby-Loo," and "Simon Says."

51. Point, in addition to saying, "Start at the upper left-hand side of the paper." Give verbal and visual directions simultaneously.

52. Practice traveling using road maps and constantly noting direction.

53. Have children draw left to right lines in mazes, making fences, roofs, etc.

54. Move beads on a horizontal string or abacus from left to right while counting; return beads in a group.

55. Write in cursive rather than with script, since it is harder to make reversals.

56. Trace hands on paper, labeling which is left and which is right.

57. Learn the left and right sides of the body by practice. Keep score of number of correct responses daily.

58. To help body directions and crossed laterality, have child touch his left ear with his left hand; touch left ear with right hand, etc. Later, introduce mirror games:

    a. "Look in mirror. Touch your left eyelid on your face."

    b. "Touch your left eyelid on the face in mirror."

59. Trace figures in both directions. Trace in both directions with left and right hand. Reproduce the entire figure to left of the midline of the body and again to the right of the midline of the body.

60. Place story pictures in sequence from left to right.

61. Mark where the child is to start on the left. Put a cross or dot on the left side of paper. Use lined paper. Reward the child for following instructions.

SECTION D: GENERAL BEHAVIOR

Disorganized

1. Use highly structured routines and materials.

2. Give clear, explicit directions. Provide a calm atmosphere.

3. Try programmed materials; break tasks into small component parts.

4. Teach the importance of outlines, carefully arranged notebooks, and the value of lining up columns of figures carefully.

5. Plan a daily routine that is adhered to rather specifically.

Problems in Logical Sequencing

6. Ask the child to jump over boxes arranged in a size order.

7. Have him fit varying size cans into one another.

8. Cut out comic strips and require him to put them back in a logical sequence and explain his decisions.

9. Have him complete an unfinished story.

10. Unscramble mixed up sentences, play scrabble.

Distractible

11. Isolate the child to complete a specific, single task of short duration, then put materials away immediately after use.

12. Use a "One Word Wrong" game: Have children listen to a sentence that has one word in it that spoils the meaning. Let volunteers put in the right word:

    a. "Mother put salt on the berries to make them sweet."

    b. "Jane washed the dishes in the mailbox."

    c. "John put a star on the letter and then mailed it."

13. Use a study carrel to protect students from distracting sights and sounds.

14. Sit the distractible child directly in front of the teacher. Parents permitting, give the child ear plugs or cotton to reduce auditory stimulation when he takes tests.

15. Have such a child complete one task, but put all materials away before starting next task.

16. Avoid medical sedation to improve attention span; the areas of hyperactivity and distractibility are most controversial. Try to calm the child down by reward system and truly interesting curricular content.

17. Permit him to use card or frame to focus attention on single line, problem, or paragraph.

18. Give specific assignments prior to library research. Topics should be highly specific.

19. Sources of stimulation and distraction: To the hyperactive child, a major source of distraction is another child. The teacher should place the hyperactive child next to the teacher's desk with his back to the light and to the rest of the classroom.

What the child cannot see may not distract him. If the teacher will get a refrigerator carton, cut a hole in it for a "door," and cut a few other holes in it for ventilation and arrange for a light, the box can be used for a "study booth." The hyperactive child can be encouraged to use the "study booth" as a quiet place to do work. If the booth is ever used as a punishment or "quiet room" the whole purpose of the booth will be defeated. Accordingly, the teacher should permit other children to use the booth as they want or as a reward for good behavior.

20. Use a reinforcement to reward the child for longer periods of concentrated work. Approve verbally of in-seat behavior.

Perseveration

21. Give a five-, three-, and one-minute warning before a change of activity.

22. Have the child move physically to a new task.

23. Play games such as Musical Chairs, Simon Says, Red Light-Green Light.

24. Play Copy Cat: in this game the children copy the teacher first with no verbalization on the teacher's part; then she gives the proper command each time with an appropriate action; finally, teacher stops her actions and gives only commands to initiate the children's appropriate actions.

25. Give a warning before the end of class, or test time. Set limits in advance to length of report or composition. Always interrupt the perseverating child.

Hyperactivity and Impulsivity

26. Set firm limits to behavior for self-control. Give verbal approval and token rewards for better self-control.

27. Have children engage in such purposeful activities as copying patterns on peg board, inserting toothpicks in salt shaker tops, writing in clay with stylus, sewing, and other

constructive activities.

28. Help student plan specific steps in order.

29. Discourage wild guesses.

30. Encourage use of outline before writing or speaking from notes, etc. Help them depend upon external guidelines first.

31. Reward them systematically with candy, M & M's, peanuts, tokens, marks on charts, etc. (anything the child feels is worth working for) for any specific progress in self-control of impulsivity. Research has clearly indicated the powerful effectiveness of behavior modification techniques for this circumstance.

32. Be reluctant to approve of medically induced sedation — a controversial issue.

33. Assign the child tasks of useful activity such as delivering messages, collating mimeographed materials.

34. Try to channel activity constructively by frequent opportunities to exercise.

35. The teacher should see to it that the hyperactive child gets plenty of rest at home. Fatigue symptoms are only another source of stimulation for the hyperactive child. Allowing the child to "run it off" on the playground only works with a limited number of these children. As a consequence, the teacher should see to it that the child does not get exhausted on the playground. Keep the recess period short.

36. The hyperactive, overly distractible, and distracting child can sometimes function more effectively for a short period of time. When placement in an appropriate special program is not immediately available, (a) have the child attend regular class for an hour, then return home. Sometimes this can be gradually extended, (b) have a "crisis or helping teacher" available to remove the child from regular class when his behavior is too disrupting. Usually one keeps the child only a half-day, the "crisis teacher" tutoring him when he is out of his regular class.

37. A low rocking chair and small table can be placed in the rear of the classroom with pictorial types of magazines, *National Geographic Magazine,* or various comic books on the table. When the child feels that he can no longer sit at his desk or chair, he can quietly go to the rocker, look at the magazines or just rock

while the other children study. The teacher's permission is not required for this action. Explain the need for this to the other students.

Difficulty With Abstractions

38. Play games of "How things are alike" and "How they are different."

39. Have a large box of objects that can be placed in categories, e.g. fruit, food, eating tools, school supplies, toys, etc., then have children pick out objects belonging to a specific category.

40. Sort blocks by size, shape, color, one quality at a time.

41. Name parts of a whole; e.g. house: door, window, room. . .

42. Point out similarities and teach him to group things in different ways. Where possible, use concrete materials.

Poor Body Image

43. Use a full-length mirror in a grooming lesson for children to see themselves.

44. Have a child make a like size tracing of a classmate's body, then with his own.

45. Have a child stand facing teacher at distance of about ten feet and have teacher say, "Touch your shoulders." "Touch your hips," etc.

46. Use songs such as, "Put Your Finger on Your Nose."

47. Have the child lie on his back with his hands on his sides; ask him to spead his feet and move his hands touching the floor; return them to the original position. Vary the exercise with moving one arm and one leg; rather like Angels-in-the-Snow, but on specific command.

48. Have a child crawl over, under, and through an obstacle course while stating what he is doing, "I am going under the table." This exercise also helps to develop related concepts.

Low Frustration Tolerance

49. Present all tasks in carefully arranged sequences from easy to difficult. Give frequent reassurance.

50. Begin with one or two pieces of a puzzle, then more.

51. Try to anticipate when the limit of frustration will be reached so as to change the activity beforehand.

52. Whether emphasis should be placed on accentuating child's strengths or improving the weak areas depends upon child's emotional status. If self-confidence is low, the former might be advisable; if child is reasonably confident and enjoys challenge, the latter could be of greater value. The approach could be altered at any time depending upon child's self-concept about the tasks to be attempted.

SECTION E: SUGGESTIONS FOR TEACHERS OF LEARNING DISABLED CHILDREN

1. Many teachers talk too much in a classroom because they feel that they must direct all the activities of all the children at all times. Continual direction by the teacher tends to force the children to disregard her. When a teacher gives directions infrequently and at appropriate times, children will learn to listen and pay attention to her better. A loud or excitable voice of a teacher tends to produce confusion in a classroom, whereas a calm voice and manner may help to obtain calmness from the children. A loud voice should be reserved for emergencies.

2. The routines of the class should be kept simple. Complicated procedures lend themselves to disobedience and disorderliness in the classroom. How the children should enter the classroom, where to sit, how to pass and collect papers, and other similar routines should be organized systematically and simply.

3. Since children requiring remedial help often need to repeat a particular lesson often, it may prove advantageous to order two sets of workbooks, cut them into individual pages and organize them sequentially in file folders according to the specific function with which they deal. An individual page may then be presented to a child in a clear plastic enclosure on which he may write or draw with a felt pen. The markings can easily be removed with a damp tissue and both the plastic enclosure and the workbook page can be reused many times. Handwriting may also be taught in this manner, inserting a teacher-made handwriting sample rather than using an original workbook page.

4. In the case of a youngster under medication, educate both teacher and parents about the necessity for consistency and timing in administering the drug. Supply the teacher and parents with a simple checklist of symptoms so they can monitor the youngster's behavior for these signs: drowsiness, excessive sleeping, loss of appetite, increased hyperactivity, sleeplessness, irritability, lack of motivation, etc. If these signs are observed, advise the school nurse or doctor and request a recheck on the drug.

5. Form groups within the school setting with a teacher trained to aid children with slight learning disabilities: visual, auditory, associative. Encourage the teacher to read in the field and to take courses.

6. Parents and teachers should be informed that "hyperactive" behavior can be reduced considerably in mildly brain-injured children through reasonable discipline, the same behavior being present in some children who are not injured at all.

7. When a child is placed in a class for children possessing minimal cerebral dysfunction, he has undoubtedly experienced much academic frustration. Initially the child should be given work which he is able to complete with little or no difficulty. This illustrates to the child that he is capable of obtaining goals which his teacher assigns to him. In effect it is giving the child a sense of academic attainment and will set the stage for future learning.

SECTION F: SUGGESTIONS FOR PARENTS

1. Assuming potentially average ability, do not treat the child differently than other children; discipline him appropriately and consistently in proportion to his capacity to control himself. Avoid attributing all misbehavior and all poor achievement to the neurological deficit.

2. Children diagnosed as "Learning Disabled" should have not only medical, otological, optometric and ophthalmological examinations but also neurological ones. A psychoeducational evaluation will assess the functioning intellectual and achievement levels, the psycholinguistic assets and liabilities, and the personality structure, and will also provide remedial ideas to modify what is modifiable, be it in the home or school setting.

3. The term "Minimal Cerebral Dysfunction" may be

educationally irrelevant to educators but has special significance for the attending neurologist, the assessing psychologist, and especially the parents who have, previous to the diagnosis, likely been blaming their disciplinary practices for their child's condition.

4. Assure parents that they are not to be blamed for the child's lack of more optimal development, since he may not have fully adequate neurological equipment; often he has a good chance of improving with appropriate training as well as with general maturation.

5. A child whose disability is not severe enough to warrant special education placement may benefit from concentrated effort in the regular classroom. The physical education program should stress eye-hand coordination, e.g. walking a balance beam or doing cross-lateral activities, if that is part of the child's deficiency.

6. A major hurdle to overcome is the feeling on the part of many parents that they have produced a "defective" child, and that the child's problem is their fault. Strong feelings of guilt can often be attenuated by an honest, straightforward approach to the real problem. Several counseling sessions may be necessary in order to fully explain the etiology, presenting symptoms, and future educational planning. Parents should be made to understand that the problem is not their "fault," and that they can contribute to the positive adjustment both in school and at home. The reasons for the child's behavior should be carefully explained and discussed. They should also receive realistic suggestions concerning future educational and vocational planning.

7. Manipulative and construction games as prescribed by the teacher or psychologist should be provided in the home so that the youngster will have experience with this type of rehabilitative material.

8. It is often important for parents to realize that much of this child's acting out behavior is a direct result of frustration caused by his inability to perform as he wishes. Parents should not expect more of him than he is capable as they should recognize that he has the emotional control of a much younger child.

9. Strive to aid the parent to recognize and accept: (a) the commonness of minimal brain damage and CNS impairment, (b) the ramifications on learning functions (fine motor coordination, concentration, some rote tasks, activity levels, verbal and behavioral perseveration), (c) variance from such gross motor impairment as the cerebral palsy child, (d) educational accessibility through specialized classes, manipulative materials, and equipment and unique training experiences, (e) the major expenditure of effort and time should be on effective learning/ teaching techniques, not upon the manipulation of or training of the central nervous system.

10. Sometimes youngsters display the behavioral characteristics typical of children with minimal-cerebral dysfunction, but there is no medical or psychological evidence to support this diagnosis. With some of these youngsters, a trial on medication has proven successful.

11. Interpret the general characteristics of such children so that past behavior as well as future progress will be understood, for example, the tendency to be clumsy, to learn in spurts, to perseverate, to have a short attention span, etc. Such understanding will eliminate undue criticism and will enable the parents to avoid situations that would cause a feeling of inadequacy on part of child.

12. Parents should receive training in a variety of simple behavior modification approaches useful at home with the child. They will continue to require access to the psychologist or consulting therapist to work out details as they arise and to receive encouragement for their continued efforts.

Chapter XII

LOW AVERAGE INTELLIGENCE

O F SPECIAL CONCERN to many educators and parents are the children who are too intelligent to be classified as retarded, but are also too dull to cope adequately with the demands of traditional academic work. In a surburban school district with a mean of 115 IQ, the low average children are perhaps 30 IQ points below the average child and are disadvantaged scholastically. They are handicapped to the approximate extent that average children would be in competing with very superior students in the same class. The markedly exceptional children, both the gifted and the deficient, are more likely to be specially educated while the slow learners struggle to maintain a pace for which they are ill-equipped. Not insignificant in numbers, they comprise about 15 percent of the normal population and a far greater proportion in urban schools (Johnson, 1963). Depending upon definition of "low average," the IQ range identifying these children encompasses between 75 or 80 IQ up to about 90 IQ.

Many of the low average children are apparently those who simply have less hereditary potential for scholastic ability than their classmates. Others may have the latent potential for average ability, but are disabled to some degree by virtue of single or cumulative problems. They may manifest specific learning disabilities, impaired health and sensory deficits, emotional difficulties, and suffer from inadequate educational experiences and minor neurological deficiencies (Baker, 1959). From this heterogeneous population often come problems in underachievement, motivation, and personality. As Dyer (1960) indicated, the group's problems may stem from the great numbers of un-measured variables which have contributed perhaps more to their achievement and adjustment than have their limited mental abilities. School systems rarely account comprehensively for such children at the elementary level and not surprisingly use retention in grade and ability grouping to accommodate for such slowness in learning. Even then, such children obtain fewer positive reinforcements from their teachers, and perhaps parents, than their "normal" classmates, as there is often little to reinforce if only achievement is considered as rewardable. Realizing that they cannot compete, their common behavior is to compensate with some variety of disruptive aggression or to dissociate from education at the earliest permissible moment. Thus, for those who require maximum education, they actually receive some of the least; the retardates are sometimes educated until twenty-one years of age, while the low average children may exit school at sixteen years of age.

A generally neglected group in the research (Blanco, 1964), they are often ignored for special consideration until serious problems occur. They detract from the educational program sometimes by not learning and by being too aggressive or too withdrawn for normal interaction. On this point, it is often the dull child whom educators wish to transfer to the retarded classes, patently an error in judgment and placement if not also illegal according to state law.

The prescriptions listed in this chapter only touch upon the solutions needed for the group as a whole. While they may be helpful in individual cases or supply hypotheses for educational research, they fall short in total impact at all grade levels and are palliative rather than corrective. Nevertheless, they are reasonable starting places for intervention. Fortunate is the child whose parents and teachers accept his intellectual limitations, try to remediate his particular disabilities, and offer reinforcing experiences in a suitable curriculum. It falls to the school psychologist, diagnostic teacher, and others to learn of his strengths and limitations and to devise suitable programs for groups as well as individuals of slow learning ability.

1. Never place a dull-normal child in a class for mentally retarded children.

2. If the dull child is to repeat kindergarten, he should profit considerably more by attending both morning and afternoon classes with the same or different teacher to increase stimulation input and to enhance his training experiences.

3. Place the child in a nongraded program at the primary level so that he can develop as slowly or rapidly as he is capable. Many such children have pronounced learning disabilities.

4. Select a classroom for the child with a teacher who can accept a slower rate of growth from pupils. It is preferable, however, to develop services for a class of slow learners by, say, offering a differentiated curriculum, perceptual training, concrete materials, etc., although the children should be integrated with regular pupils during other times and activities.

5. Do not retain the children of low average ability after the primary grades, but previous to this time one retention might be reasonable. Provide them with individual tutoring in school if possible.

6. A part-time summer school program for dull-normal children who are underachieving is recommended.

7. On a new child transferring from another school district or when no school records or test scores are forwarded, the elementary teacher should do an informal evaluation immediately of his basic reading and arithmetic. Proper grouping may prevent the initial school experience from being a failure.

8. Regarding underachievement in a child of low average intelligence, the question of retention is frequently raised by teachers when he is not at grade level. Retention has not generally been found of value to the child, unless he concurs in the decision. This decision should be made in conference with parents, the teacher, the principal, and child, but the principal should try to allow the child not to be bullied by either teacher or parents to agree with their demands. When a child wants to repeat a grade and feels it is at least partly his decision, then he may profit from it; if he feels victimized, he will continue to resist learning.

9. Each teacher of the dull child might examine her own feelings and attitudes toward the child. How often does she praise

him? How much work does she give him which is simple enough to insure at least moderate success? Consider a simple formula: lack of positive reinforcement equals drop-out from school.

10. Expect this child to require three to five times as much repetition of content as that necessary for "average" pupils. Basic facts may be adequately covered in a regular classroom, but depth and breadth of content will not usually be absorbed unless the concept is made particularly outstanding in some way.

11. The teacher should ask for a reexamination of intelligence on at least a group test if the child manifests higher ability than that suggested by the dull-normal classification on a previous test. Enter the new score in the cumulative record and treat the child differently if the score is different.

12. For low average children who are also underachieving in a basic academic area, tutoring at school or privately at the initiative of the parents is recommended. The goal is certainly not to "get him to grade level," but to get him to approximate the achievement expectancies for his low average mental age.

13. It is perfectly reasonable and justified to give the slow child shorter class and homework assignments, just as it is reasonable to give gifted students more complicated tasks.

14. Strive to develop understanding within the child at a simple level rather than require rote memory of meaningless material.

15. Use demonstration and visual cues as much as possible. Do not distract with too much verbalization. Use multisensory approaches.

16. Do not force the slow learner to compete with children of higher intelligence. Try to organize less strenuous academic programs which will not cause negative attitudes and rebelliousness toward learning.

17. It is important that simple concepts be presented to children at the outset of any instructional unit so that the material will remain at the child's level of understanding and will assure success. Materials, language, directions, and statements should all be within the child's comprehension.

18. Instructional materials that are too simple or too difficult tend to produce inattention and disinterest. Short, dynamic

periods are often more successful than long periods of any one activity. Dramatization of the material, the intensity of presentation, and varying ways of display all aid attention and learning.

19. This child should not be expected to keep up with the rest of the class. He should be handled as an individual and be required to work to his ability level regardless of where the class is.

20. The child should be given the kind of assignments, particularly in social studies and science, that are highly structured and concrete. Large projects requiring organizational and conceptual ability should be eliminated, and the child's contribution should be in terms of his capabilities, i.e. drawing, building models, lettering and decorating, researching a specific number of facts in books which the child can read and use.

21. Children with low average ability should stress overlearning in their studies and be offered favored jobs in the classroom and school as incentive.

22. Do not assume that the group test results of scholastic aptitude are necessarily correct for low average children. Gear the instruction to the functioning level of the children.

23. Many dull-normal children, if evaluated carefully, are those who are potentially of average intelligence but have emotional or physical problems which detract from their intellectual functioning. Remediate for the specific academic, physical, or emotional problems detected to encourage full use of latent ability.

24. Provide many opportunities for the child to experiment and practice new concepts with concrete materials in real or simulated situations.

25. Provide below-grade-level subject matter and experiences that approximate the child's low average mental age. There should be diversified reading material, e.g. SRA Reading Lab at different grade levels from which to give assignments and instruction. Lecture and verbal orientations are generally valueless for this child who, if anything, deals more comfortably in the concrete, tangible, simpler world of things, not words.

26. Well-planned activities decrease unacceptable behavior. There is little time for misbehavior in a busy and interesting

classroom. To discourage tardiness or discipline problems in school, for example, the teacher should start the day's work with interesting activities.

27. At the beginning of any instructional unit the child should be presented with familiar material, since meaningful material is acquired more readily.

28. Some dull children respond well to the guidance of a friendly but more alert "Big Brother" or "Big Sister" in the class to remind them of page numbers, test dates, and homework assignments.

29. Develop programs which relate academic material to practical, daily uses. For example, use newspapers, periodicals, and everyday mail to teach reading. Compute paychecks, deposit slips, and interest charges so that the child can learn arithmetic. If practical, help them look for jobs and help them deposit money in the bank.

30. Simplify directions given to the child and be sure that directions are understood by having the child repeat the directions back.

31. Suggested problems (alphabetically arranged) for children of low average intelligence and depending on achievement level:

> a. Achieving Perceptual Motor Efficiency of Barsch.
> b. Detect: A Sensorimotor Approach to Visual Discrimination; Distar; Reading for Understanding; Words and Patterns; Lift Off to Reading by Science Research Associates.
> c. Behavioral Research Laboratories in all academic areas.
> d. Educational Developmental Laboratories Tachistoscopic Programs.
> e. Fitzhugh Plus Program: Perceptual Learning and Understanding Skills by Allied Education Council.
> f. Frostig Program for Visual Perceptual Training by Follett.
> g. Kinesthetic Alphabet by R.N. Stone.
> h. MacDonald-Franklin Dictionary by Educational Media.
> i. Merrill Phonics Skill Texts Program.

j. Open Highways Program by Scott, Foresman.

k. Peabody Language Development Kit; Peabody Rebus Reading Program by American Guidance Service.

l. Reading-Thinking Skills Program; Useful Language by Continental Press.

m. Sounds and Patterns of Language by Holt, Rinehart and Winston.

n. Skinner's Write and See Program.

o. Sound Identification Cards; Language Building Cards; Something to Say All Through the Day by Interstate.

p. Sullivan Associates Programmed Reading by Webster Division of McGraw-Hill.

q. Think, Listen and Say by Eye-Gate House.

32. Inform the parents when it is quite clear that their child is a genuinely low average child, especially if the parents are college graduates or put great emphasis on education as a step toward upward social mobility. Share test scores of intelligence (IQ ranges) and achievement. Encourage them to have a private psychological assessment done on their child if they so desire.

33. What if the professional and managerial level parents of a genuinely dull-normal child ask about how their child can survive in a suburban school (mean IQ 120) which makes no real provision for him? Tell them that they may have to change the environment around him and that any plan has negative features. They may (a) seek a private school that will accommodate him more comfortably, (b) expect occasional retention in his present school and assignments to lower achievement groups all through school, or (c) move to a more average community where most of the child's peers will be average and offer him less academic competition.

34. Each low-average child should have a complete vision and hearing evaluation by medical specialists to rule out or correct for organic problems. Include an evaluation by a developmental optometrist.

35. Keep the parents especially well informed about the achievement and social development of their dull-normal child. Those parents who are anxious will be relieved to know of steady progress even if it is slow.

36. The parents should permit enrollment into noncollege, secondary programs that approximate the child's mental age and achievement level. The should also hear the school personnel's optimism about the child's finishing high school in a vocational-technical program. Educators should disagree with the parents should the latter insist upon unrealistic aspirations for the child.

37. Discuss frankly with the parents their child's intellectual limitations for academic achievement in order to prevent their pressuring the youngster toward unreasonable goals. Emphasize the number of opportunities in the world of work available to persons with their child's capabilities. Consult the Dictionary of Occupational Titles.

38. Prior to termination or graduation from high school, the parents may take the child to a vocational guidance agency to consider reasonable vocations and to undergo aptitude and interest testing. There they may review job training programs and appropriate job replacements.

39. Counsel parents about the fallacies in the popular American Myth: "You can do anything you want to do if you just try hard enough."

Chapter XIII

SENSORY HANDICAPS AND BRAIN DAMAGE

A MINIMUM OF PRESCRIPTIONS were offered by contributors in school psychology in the special areas reflecting, perhaps, a lack of wide experience with such exceptional children, a desire to contribute in areas of greater expertise, or their uncertainty in prescribing for physical and sensory handicapped youngsters in general. Most often the children with such difficulties have multiple problems stemming not only from organic sources, but also from concomitant social problems: feelings of rejection, dependency, and isolation, and the resulting inferiority feelings. "Mainstreaming" may reduce or possibly exaggerate such reactions.

In a culture which demands so much from even fully equipped persons, the added handicap of being impaired in the visual or auditory area or being damaged in the central nervous system compounds the problems of personal adjustment and social effectiveness. Although such disabilities are often associated with problems of depression and dependency, other children with the same general handicaps survive to accomplish much, irrespective of those problems and the prevailing culture. Some so afflicted have testified that the disability made them more capable in other dimensions and other endeavors once they overcame the dependence almost forced upon them by well-intentioned people.

In all likelihood, it is a matter of constitutionality, personal support, training, and expectation, to name a few factors, which keeps one blind or deaf child defeated while another strides ahead. The concepts suggested here for those with sensory limitations are provocative at best and all too brief in number for any comprehensive grasp of the problems and their rami-

226

fications. They may stimulate the reader to search out more detailed information through wide professional reading and personal experience.

The behavioral and learning problems derived from brain injury, while rooted in recognized medical problems, are nonetheless within the domain of educators and parents once the medical profession has provided its optimum services. Here again, few psychoeducational prescriptions were given, but those noted contain some sensible ideas for helping such children in their school and home environments. Such concepts may also prove sufficiently provocative to move clinicians and educators to expand their knowledge about disorders of the central nervous system and the multitude of subsequent problems.

Clinicians will recognize that the precise problems in learning and emotional adjustment of children with brain damage are often considered in detail in the previous chapters. Hence, the ideas do not require repetition. In a sense, all chapter materials are open for consideration on all cases since referred children have multiple problems requiring a series of remedial strategies and supports.

SECTION A: BLIND AND PARTIALLY SIGHTED

1. Not all blind children can learn Braille, especially those who have tactile limitations due to cerebral palsy or other neurological dysfunctions. Each Braille candidate must have a certain minimum sensitivity to develop a discernible "touch" for the embossed symbols. Further, if the blind child is trainable or severely retarded, it is doubtful whether Braille training will be worth the effort since only early primary word discrimination may be developed after years of effort.

2. An opticon is a very useful device for normally alert blind children and adults in offering another method of learning from standard English (or foreign language) texts or books. Blind students will vary tremendously in their ability to "read" rapidly on the opticon. Yet this instrument is quite expensive and is in no way a substitute for excellent instruction in all academic skills. Obviously the individual must learn the concepts and meanings underlying the words that he "reads." Each opticon trainee is still

required to have a normal, high-quality education in learning and language since the opticon is not a substitute for concepts, nor is it useful in everyday activities. With "mainstreamed" students visited by itinerant teachers, the opticon's expense may be prohibitive, but its cost is far less per student in a residential school where it may be used very frequently.

3. Since most blind or visually impaired students will have to rely heavily upon the auditory areas for learning, the teaching staff and parents may expect to purchase cassette tape recorders, record players, musical instruments, choral lessons, etc., for learning and recreation.

4. Blind and visually handicapped adolescents require realistic vocational and educational counseling from a person knowledgeable not only about the world of work for handicapped people, but also attuned to the problems and aspirations of such clients. There is a delicate balance between offering clients reachable goals and not discouraging their ambitions and aspirations. It is true that blind people are much more capable occupationally than most nonhandicapped adults believe, but it is also true that there are often far fewer jobs in music, radio announcing, teaching, counseling, etc., then blind adolescents would like to believe. Many will resist more ordinary and less exotic occupational suggestions offered by employment counselors and personnel agencies. Yet they must hear this informaion from knowledgeable adults and then learn perhaps through trial and error on their own.

5. An interesting development in medical research is that about two-thirds to four-fifths of infants originally diagnosed as "totally blind" at birth or early infancy, later were discovered to have some usable residual vision. However, since this small amount of vision was not capitalized upon or stimulated so that the children learned to depend upon it, they developed nonfunctional visual acuity and visual perception skills, a great loss to their learning. The logical conclusion now is that, with the exception of enucleated conditions, infants should be stimulated with light all through childhood on the possibility that some vision may develop through learning. This is a debatable issue which must be discussed with vision specialists.

6. Most visually handicapped children need counseling about their personal concerns. Often, these are not focused upon vision problems, but rather upon self-concepts, acceptance by peers, boy-girl relationships, projections into the future about education, work, and family living. Such counseling or therapy should be offered for adolescents through school, agency, or private sources as an aid in personal adjustment and in preparation for more independent living.

7. It is especially important that psychologists, teachers, and itinerant teachers recognize that the low vision child not only has acuity problems, but also has *visual perception problems* which often need remediation in school. Since acuity is often weak or distorted, it is only logical to believe that visual perception is also weak and distorted. Practice in visual perception exercises is recommended through copying, tracing, identifying forms and letters in the hopes of refining good visual perception. A developmental optometrist may be an invaluable asset in knowing what to train and how to do it after the ophthalmologist has finished the examinations and remediations for pathology.

8. Visually impaired students with learning and behavior problems will respond to the same psychological approaches as nonhandicapped children: Group and individual counseling, sex education, behavior modification, peer support, vocational and educational guidance, etc. Some may require "time-out" procedures for their temper tantrums and impulsive behavior, while others will respond to rewards and incentives, personal challenges, or sensitive and warm relationships with people they like and respect.

9. A crucial issue is whether or not the child or adolescent is better off at a residential educational setting or at home while attending "mainstream classes" and receiving the aid of an itinerant vision specialist. It is best to review this decision at least every two or three years since most of the variables change drastically. Some children definitely need the intensive, comprehensive training and education in a high-quality residential school: Mobility training, peer acceptance, an entirely trained staff knowledgeable about vision problems and special education, independence training through occupational therapy and

group living, and a wide array of recreational pursuits (handicapped athletic events, musical groups) rarely available to the child living at home. The home can offer, perhaps, the emotional security of affectionate parents and siblings, a sense of family belonging, familiarity with "the home town," etc., but the home setting and school most often lacks handicapped peers, the broad array of educational and recreational services noted above, and a definite feeling in the local school that the child is different and perhaps inferior. Obviously, some children should stay at home and attend local schools while others definitely need residential schools all the year long, except for vacations, or at least some portion of their school years, say, high school for vocational training. Psychological appraisal, especially clinical interviewing, is mandatory as well as sensitive work with the parents and educational leaders in both the local and residential settings to firm up rational decisions. Do not decide the issue on the basis of money alone.

10. Yellow acetate paper (like thick cellophane) when placed over ordinary or large print often enables the low vision student to see better due to increased contrast.

11. There is a myth which says that the school work, reading, and homework wears out the remaining vision of the low vision student and should be avoided. On the contrary, using the eyes does not decrease effectiveness, it increases it as it would with any other sense.

12. Blind children do not necessarily have to be placed in full-day programs for the blind. They can, under special conditions, function in their local regular classes providing that itinerant teachers are available for periodic visits.

13. No two visually handicapped children will require the same type of itinerant services. Each program is to be modified to suit the child's age, ability, degree of vision, level of achievement, emotional maturity, etc. Braille training should begin early.

14. For children who require magnification of print, the itinerant vision consultant can obtain appropriate supplies for the visually handicapped child in regular classes.

15. Children who need magnification of visual materials at school will require similar help at home: specially lined paper,

special dark-leaded pencils, etc.

16. Special materials for the visually handicapped are: "Talking Books" (books on record or tape), "live" reading services by an adult or nonhandicapped child on homework, and taped recordings of lessons.

17. Volunteers, children or adults, may read to the blind or partially sighted child.

18. Physical education activities at home and at school will likely have to be curtailed for children with problems of detached retinas. Consult the child's ophthalmologist.

19. Occasionally, there should be a reduction of school requirements as to the quantity of work required by children with certain visual limitations.

20. Touch typing is recommended to children of average ability from the fourth grade up. This can become an invaluable tool for children with progressive eye disorders.

21. Guidance services for both the children and their parents should be offered at all levels of the child's education. Also, the Lion's Clubs and the State Department of Public Assistance can sometimes assist the family with proper eye care equipment and medical care in cases of special need.

22. The State Bureau of Vocational Rehabilitation or the Association of the Blind may offer additional services, depending on the case.

23. The regular teacher should treat the child as normally as possible and especially not overprotect or indulge the child because of sensory problems. The child may or may not have mobility problems, but no one should carry the child, lead him by the hand or clothing (except in a fire emergency). Supervise the other children not to "baby" the blind or partially seeing child.

24. Should a blind child have a temper tantrum, do not attempt to reason him out of it or find out its cause, as he is temporarily quite unreasonable. Instead, remove the child from the hearing of his classmates. Let him finish crying and stomping by himself, perhaps in the hall or another room. No one can persist in a tantrum without an audience. Tell him that when he is all finished, he can return quietly to tell about the problem that caused the outburst.

25. To reduce a "blindism" of body-rocking, establish a reinforcement schedule of candy or some material reward to give to the child, contingent upon, say, two minutes of no rocking. Give the reinforcement often and consistently for the child's efforts at self-control for two minutes. In a few days, raise the requirement of getting the candy to, say, five minutes of no rocking.

26. Encourage blind children to "look" directly toward persons with whom they are speaking and to use the words "see" and "look." Seeing adults and blind children can and should use the phrases, "Glad to see you" and "How do things look to you?"

27. Give extensive training to the blind children in the social skill of polite refusal of help since many kind but infantalizing offers will be extended to them. The more unnecessary help they accept, the more dependent they may become.

28. After the approximate levels of mental ability and achievement have been determined, the child should be considered for placement in a class for the blind or partially sighted in the local school district. The more reasonable effort is to integrate these same children into regular classes but be available for contacts with an itinerant teacher.

29. If workers from the Society for the Blind are not locally available and when discussing travel and mobility training with the parents, tell them and the blind child's siblings not to lead the child by holding his hand, arm or clothing. Rather, they should (a) offer an elbow for the child to hold, (b) walk normally asking the child to keep his head up, and (c) practice left and right directions until the child knows them perfectly for orientation.

30. Buy the child an embossed-numeral wristwatch and teach him to tell time. Most sighted children seem to grasp the entire concept of time by eight or nine years of age.

31. The parents may purchase magnification aids to enlarge print in reading supplementary books (other than clear type texts) as well as for arithmetic and miscellaneous readings.

SECTION B: DEAF AND HEARING IMPAIRED

1. As many adults and siblings as interested should learn to communicate effectively through sign language. This skill

should consist of more than a bare minimum of words, but be extended through training to include many ideas, concepts, objects, etc., that are appropriate to the child's mental age level so that the child can share his life and feelings with parents, siblings, and friends. If only the teacher communicates with the child, he will understandably attach himself to her and perhaps be isolated from his family.

2. There are some distinct advantages in "mainstreaming" hearing-impaired children: Exposure to an array of language styles of peers, wider social relationships with hearing class-mates, an expectation for intelligible speech and age-appropriate language, the "testing" of total communication skills in the world, and the expectation of normal and independent function-ing in a hearing world. The disadvantages relate to the general inability to compete academically due to language deficiencies, the rejection by some peers, the irritation or frustration of some teachers who resent being assigned handicapped children with-out their own prior training or acceptance, the lack of intensive language and total communication services in regular classes, the self-imposed isolation of the hearing-impaired child from hear-ing children, etc.

3. A mature and congenial student could be asked to be a "listening buddy" or "helper" to aid the handicapped child by turning to correct pages, repeating instructions, taking notes (perhaps offering a carbon copy). Naturally such a system should only be offered when essential so as not to foster dependence on the handicapped child.

4. In terms of hearing-aid maintenance:
   a. Replace a defective battery.
   b. Check for correct installation, usage, and defective parts.
   c. Keep equipment away from moisture, extremes of temperature, and shock.
   d. Turn off hearing aids prior to removal from the ear.
   e. Let an expert repair the equipment.

5. The speaker, be it a teacher or a lecturer, should stand within ten or fifteen feet of the hearing-impaired child, but not be having him looking up constantly.

6. The child should not have to look into the light where the speaker stands.

7. Vary the child's seating occasionally to give practice in viewing a speaker from different perspectives.

8. Arrange desks in a semi-circle in a small class or group so that the child may see the faces of each classmate and teacher.

9. For a lecture, place the student (with a "listening buddy") in front of the speaker but perhaps off to the side a bit.

10. The speaker should realize that turning her back on the child during a verbal presentation will terminate communication.

11. Oral examinations may be changed to written examinations for the hearing-impaired student.

12. Do not exaggerate gestures as this changes the configuration of the lips.

13. Inquire about the student's comprehension by asking him to repeat a concept, define a word, or explain the point being made. This may give feedback to the teacher about the child's grasp of her instruction.

14. Give multiple synonyms for new vocabulary words to aid the child whose language development is probably quite delayed. Elaborate upon the language by visual presentations, examples, a grasp, pictures, overhead projectors, etc.

15. Request the student to express himself in class and to depend upon language to satisfy his needs and answer his questions in the regular and the special class.

16. Inform the handicapped student if he is speaking too loudly or softly and be sure to praise special productions as well as good academic work, courtesies, art, etc.

17. Give academic instruction to the child prior to the time it will be regularly presented in class so that the child is already familiar with the new vocabulary, concepts, and generally what to expect about the topic in the regular class. He should be urged to read ahead if possible to minimize confusion in class and perhaps also receive an outline about the forthcoming material.

18. Have the speech and language specialists explain to the child at least every year or two how the hearing problems developed and why the special services are necessary and available to him.

19. Young children often believe that they are being punished for something they did earlier and remain confused and guilty for years. Children cannot often connect an ambiguous medical event with a handicap and tend to blame themselves for the limitation. Children may resist the knowledge that the defect is permanent and often fantasize about magical cures. The school psychologist may be extremely useful in anticipating such beliefs, reflecting the child's feelings, and opening up a discussion about the lives of hearing-impaired adults and the situation specifically about the child himself.

20. Resource-itinerant teachers are invaluable in aiding the regular teacher with a hearing-impaired child and, if consulted, frequently have many creative ideas for supporting such a child at home and at school, especially in the instructional area.

21. A large defect in the placement of a deaf child in regular class, even a child with "total communication skills," is that he rarely has other similarly affected boys and girls to talk with. Thus the child is always "different" and truly needs the relief and relaxation of communicating with other handicapped children who can deal with him at the same language level. Clearly in adolescence and adult life, his friends should include nonhearing as well as hearing friends. The unresolved issue about oral-aural compared to manual skills is fundamental here and is partially resolved by total communication approaches.

22. All teachers of the child should at least learn the manual alphabet and a minimum of manual signs to aid the child.

23. Encourage the hearing-impaired child to participate in a full range of physical, recreational, and artistic activities such as those found in an extensively equipped residential school for the deaf. These opportunities for peer-group and boy-girl interactions may be imperative during the adolescent years as self-concept and identifications are especially important then.

SECTION C: BRAIN DAMAGE

1. Motor coordination skills are often the most seriously impaired in the brain-injured child. Physical therapy is essential to develop to a maximal level what is neurologically intact. Once a semblance of motor control is developed, the teacher may wish

to start the child with large crayon movement having more finely differentiated movements as a long-term goal. Sand box work, large printing, alphabet letters to be moved into place, etc., are eventually effective in aiding motor coordination.

2. The particular impairments of the child should be specified via psychological and neurological assessment. Are there receptive, integrative, and expressive problems in both the visual and auditory modalities? Which deficiencies are more severe? In short, where are the problems: input, organization, or output? Train for specific deficiencies even though there are currently theoretical objections to fractionation in remediation. Capitalize upon the Hawthorne Effect if that will motivate the child.

3. The teacher may share her general assessment of the child's strengths and limitations with the parents. She will likely wish to individualize the curriculum for each child. Token or food reinforcements may assist in initiating motivation and rewarding accomplishment.

4. Many but not all brain-injured children require highly structured and well-planned classroom activity. It is usually not wise to offer a highly permissive classroom atmosphere to either "normal" or handicapped children. In general, vary the program every 10 or 20 minutes depending on the ages of the students involved.

5. Some lessons from school can be continued at home via a reel or cassette tape recorder. There are various tape-playback educational devices and for those children who need extra training or whose greatest strength is in the auditory modality. Adult volunteers could tape their own reading of children's books for new learning.

6. Reinforce a child whose attention wanders by giving small primary rewards for a set amount of attention, say, one minute or 30 seconds if necessary. Reward the child if he maintains the attention span set for him. Gradually increase the time expectancy but not the reward. Incidentally, if the reward is food, make sure that the child is hungry enough to respond by requesting the parents to provide only a small breakfast or lunch.

7. Often a trained teacher aide can be a great asset in helping

the children to learn or overlearn their lessons, skills, etc. Can a calm volunteer be found?

    8. Promote reading comprehension by doing the following:

       a. Use the controlled reader for maintenance of pursuit and tracking in reading. Some children need to hold speed down.

       b. Provide a series of questions on the material before it is read. On lengthier projects provide a highly structured outline of the material and list specific questions to focus comprehension.

       c. Keep reading selections short and make provisions for immediate response to the material, i.e. tests, verbal discussion, etc. The lengthier the selection (and consequently the greater the delay between reading and responding), the less the recall, suggesting that some of a comprehension problem is a problem of visual retention and recall. The demand for immediate feedback may assist retentive ability.

       d. Employ oral responses as much as possible. Use of the tape recorder for this purpose benefits in several ways: it hastens the response (compared to writing) thus reducing memory loss, permits replay for self-monitoring and reinforcement and aids in the development of organized vocal expression.

    9. The teacher of teenage handicapped girls might develop a core course relative to essential life-adjustment skills and home economics, around which all other subject matter could revolve. Math would be centered around money management and such concerns as household weights and measures, while both math and reading would have carryover to home activities and potential employment.

    10. Train children to use a typewriter, with no pressure to use more than one finger. Some will develop more dexterity with practice but many will probably never be able to use all fingers. The typewriter will aid in visual recall and spelling, and it may serve to minimize the tension build-up that accompanies written work.

    11. Parents should seek medical and neurological evalua-

tion for the child first. Physicians may consider medication knowing that there is wide variance in the specific effectiveness of drugs, especially since placebos are also effective in certain cases to reduce parent or teacher anxiety. Some impulsive children behave poorly as a result of overprotective practices and not being required to develop better self-conrol.

12. The parents should be informed not only of the medical, biological, and neurological aspects of their physically handicapped child, but should also learn gradually about the educational, psychological, and social aspects of these problems. These latter dimensions will loom even larger as the child grows older and may require selective educational placement and social training.

13. Prior to educational placement in a special class, residential school, or institution, the parents should visit the setting to obtain a realistic first impression. They should discuss their reactions with an experienced staff member and also evaluate the advantages and disadvantages of such a placement. No plan is without flaw.

14. A brain-damaged youngster can perform only within the limits of his physical structure. Point out the merit of developing those skills which the youngster is physically and intellectually equipped to achieve and also discourage the practice of upgrading obviously permanent deficiencies. Avoid being too optimistic regarding ultimate proficiency—better to predict conservative progress. Stress the importance of not pressuring the child hard, illustrating that a bad situation can be made worse with added emotional strain. Suggest some professional books written for parent consumption on how to deal with the neurologically handicapped in the home. Such lists are found at cerebral palsy centers.

15. The parents might consider an affiliation with a local organization for parents with brain-injured children.

16. Some severely damaged children will need constant supervision. There may come a time when the parents will become unable to provide adequate care and supervision. Indeed, when such a child reaches young adolescence, he may become very difficult to handle in his own home. At such a time, both for

the child's sake and his parents', they may need to consider placement in an institutional setting where his behavior can be more easily controlled. There he can continue to develop under proper supervision and training.

17. For specific prescriptive strategies for young or preschool physically handicapped children in school, see Chapter III.

BIBLIOGRAPHY

Baker, Harry J. *Exceptional Children,* Third ed. New York: MacMillan, 1959.

Barclay, James R. Descriptive, theoretical, and behavioral characteristics of sub-doctoral school psychologists. *American Psychologist.* 1971, *26* (3), 257-280.

Bardon, Jack I., and Bennett, Virginia C. *School Psychology.* Englewood Cliffs, N.J.: Prentice-Hall, 1974.

Baumeister, Alfred A. (Ed.). *Mental Retardation: Appraisal, Education, and Rehabilitation.* Chicago: Aldine Publ., 1971.

Bayley, Nancy. *Bayley Scales of Infant Development.* New York: The Psychological Corporation, 1969.

Blanco, R.F.: Behavioral differences of children of low average intelligence. Unpublished doctoral dissertation, Case Western Reserve University, 1964.

Blanco, Ralph R. Fifty recommendations to aid exceptional children. *Psychology in the Schools,* 1970, 7(1), 29-37.

Blanco, Ralph F. *A Study of Treatment Plans from School Psychologists for Exceptional Children.* Final Report, Project No. 482192, Grant No. EG-0-70-0010(607), Bureau of Education for the Handicapped, Office of Education, H.E.W. (available in ERIC). Temple University, Jan., 1971, pp. 1-384.

Blanco, Ralph F. *Prescriptions for Children with Learning and Adjustment Problems.* Springfield, Ill.: Charles C Thomas, Publisher, 1972.

Blanco, R.F., Bardon, J.I., Nesvan, G., Farling, W., and Mann, L. The Pros and Cons of "Cookbook" Prescriptions. *Proceedings* of the Convention of the National Association of School Psychologists, New York: March 17, 1973.

Blanco, Ralph F., and Rosenfeld, Joseph G. *Case Studies in Clinical and School Psychology.* Springfield, Ill.: Charles C Thomas, Publisher, 1978.

Blanco, R.F. Family patterns in chronic underachievement: Types I, II, III, IV. Workshop for the Department of Psychological Services, Norfolk Public Schools, October, 1979 (unpublished manuscript).

Brutton, M., Richardson, S., and Manuel C. *Something's Wrong With My Child.* New York: Harcourt Brace Jovanovich, 1973.

Buktenica, N.A. Interpretation of clinical data by the school psychologist. *Psychology in the Schools*, 1964, *1*(3), 267-272.

Catterall, Calvin, and Gazda, George. *Strategies for Helping Students.* Springfield, Ill.: Charles C Thomas, Publisher, 1978.

Clements, S. *Minimal Brain Dysfunction in Children.* NINDB Monograph #3 (USPHS Publication #1415). Washington, D.C.: U.S. Department of Health, Education, and Welfare, 1966.

Comtois, Richard J. Book Review. *Psychology in the Schools*, Vol. XI, No. 1, pp. 108-113, January, 1974.

Conn, H. F. (Ed.). *Current Therapy: Approved Methods of Treatment* for the Practising Physician, 17th rev., Philadelphia: Saunders, 1965.

De re medica, 14th rev. Indianapolis: Eli Lilly, 1951.

Doll, E. The essentials of an inclusive concept of mental deficiency. *Amer. Jr. of Ment. Deficiency*, 1941, XLVI, 2-4-219.

Dyer, H.S. A psychometrician views human ability. *Teachers College Record*, 1960, *61*, 394-403.

Federal Register. Education of Handicapped Children. Regulations implementing Education for All Handicapped Children Act of 1975. August 23, 1977. Pp. 42474-42518.

Forness, S.R. Educational prescription for the school psychologist. *Journal of School Psychology*, 1970, *8*(2), 96-98.

Franks, Cyril M. Book Review. *Behavior Therapy*. Vol. 4, No. 2, March, 1973.

French Pictorial Test of Intelligence. Boston: Houghton-Mifflin, 1964.

Gardon, R. Planning a diagnosis. *Psychology in the Schools*, 1965, *2*, 81-85.

Garrison, M., and Hammill, D.D. Who are the retarded? *Except. Child.*, 1971, *38*, 13-20.

Gearheart, Bill, R., and Weishahn, Mel W. *The Handicapped Child in the Regular Classroom*, Second edition. Saint Louis: C.V. Mosby, 1980.

Grossman, H. *Manual on Terminology and Classification in Mental Retardation.* Baltimore: Garamond/Pridemark Press (American Association on Mental Retardation), 1977.

Group for the Advancement of Psychiatry. *Psychopathological Disorders in Childhood: Theoretical Considerations and a Proposed Classification.* New York: Group for the Advancement of Psychiatry, 6, Report No. 62, June, 1966.

Gustafson, S.R., and Coursin, D.B. *The Pediatric Patient.* Philadelphia: Lippincott, 1964.

Hammill, D.D., and Bartel, N.R. (Eds.). *Teaching Children with Learning and Behavior Disorders*, Boston: Allyn and Bacon, Inc., 1978.

Hare, Betty A., and Hare, James M. *Teaching Young Handicapped Children: A Guide to Pre-school and Primary Grades.* New York: Grune and Stratton, 1977.

Hartlage, Lawrence C., and Lucas, David G. *Mental Development Evaluation.* Springfield, Ill.: Charles C Thomas, Publisher, 1973.

Johnson, G. Orville. *Education for the Slow Learner.* Englewood Cliffs, New Jersey: Prentice-Hall, 1963.

Johnson, Stanley W., and Morasky, Robert L. *Learning Disabilities,* Second Edition, Boston: Allyn and Bacon, 1980.

Karnes, Merle B. *Learning Language at Home, No. 2.* The Council for Exceptional Children, 1920 Association Drive, Reston, Virginia 22091 (1978).

Kessler, Jane. *Psychopathology of Childhood.* Englewood Cliffs, New Jersey: Prentice-Hall, 1966.

Lerner, J.W. *Children with Learning Disabilities,* Boston: Houghton-Mifflin Co., 1976.

Lesiak, Walter J. Book Review. *Psychology in the Schools.* Vol. XI, No. 1, pp. 102-108, January, 1974.

Mann, Philip H., Suiter, Patricia A., and McClung, Rose Marie. *Handbook in Diagnostic-Prescriptive Teaching,* Abridged second edition, Boston: Allyn and Bacon, 1979.

Mercer, Jane R., and Lewis, June F. *The System of Multicultural Pluralistic Assessment (SOMPA).* New York: The Psychological Corporation, 1978.

Merck Manual of Diagnosis and Therapy, 13th, ed. Merck, Sharp, and Dohme, Research Laboratories, 1977.

Meyers, Joel, Martin, Roy, and Hyman, Irwin A. (Eds.). *School Consultation.* Springfield, Ill.: Charles C Thomas, Publisher, 1977.

Meyers, Joel, Parson, Richard, and Martin, Roy. *Mental Health Consultation in the Schools.* San Francisco: Jossey-Bass, 1979.

Mussman, M. Teacher's evaluation of psychological reports. *Journal of School Psychology,* 1964, *1,* 35-37.

Myers, P.I., and Hammill, D.D. *Methods for Learning Disabled,* Second edition. New York, Wiley, 1976.

Palmer, J.O. *The Psychological Assessment of Children.* New York: Wiley, 1970.

Phye, Gary, and Reschly, Daniel. *School Psychology: Perspectives and Issues.* New York: Academic Press, 1979.

Psychology in the Schools. Vol. XVII, No. 1, 1980.

Public Law 94-142, *Education for All Handicapped Children Act.* November 29, 1975.

Reger, Roger. Book Review. *Journal of School Psychology.* 1975, Vol. 13, No. 1.

Rosenfeld, Joseph G., and Blanco, Ralph F. Incompetence in School Psychology: The Case of "Dr. Gestalt." *Psychology in the Schools,* Vol. XI, No. 3, 263-269, July, 1974.

Ross, A. *Psychological Aspects of Learning Disorders.* New York: McGraw-Hill, 1976.

Rubin, Harold. Counseling the Mentally Retarded. In *Counseling Exceptional People,* Benjamin, Libby, and Walz, Garry R. (Eds.). Eric Counseling and Personnel Services Clearinghouse, ERIC/CAPS, The University of Michigan, 1980.

Sapir, Selma, and Wilson, Bernice. *A Professional's Guide to Working with the Learning Disabled Child.* New York: Brunner/Mazel, 1978.

Sarason, S.B. *Psychological Problems of Mental Deficiency.* New York: Harper & Row, 1969.

Schaefer, Charles E., and Millman, Howard L. *Therapies for Children.* San Francisco: Jossey-Bass, Publ., 1977.

Schaefer, Charles E., Millman, Howard L., and Levine, Gary T. *Therapies for Psychosomatic Disorders in Children.* San Francisco: Jossey-Bass, Publ., 1979.

Seiderman, Arthur S.: Book review. *J Optom Vision Ther, 4(2):* 1973.

Seiderman, Arthur S. Chapter 5: Visual Function Assessment. In Adamson, William C., and Adamson, Katherine, K. (Eds.). *A Handbook for Specific Learning Disabilities.* New York: Gardner Press, 1979.

Seiderman, A.S. An optometric approach to the diagnosis of visually based problems in learning. In G. Leisman (Ed.), *Basic Visual Processes and Learning Disability.* Springfield, Ill.: Charles C Thomas, Publisher, 1976.

Simmons, J.E. *Psychiatric Examination of Children.* Philadelphia: Lea and Febiger, 1969.

Tallent, N. *Clinical Psychological Consultation.* Englewood Cliffs, New Jersey: Prentice-Hall, 1963.

Todd, G. Book Review. *British Journal of Psychology.* Vol. 64, No. 4. November, 1973.

Ullmann, Leonard P., and Krasner, Leonard. *Case Studies in Behavior Modification.* New York: Holt, Rinehart, and Winston, 1965

White, M.A. Will school psychology exist? *Journal of School Psychology,* 1969, 7(2), 53-57.

INDEX

Animals
  cruelty to, 60-61
  imitation of, 34
Antagonisms to peers, parents, authority
    and siblings, 58-60
Anticipating child's needs, 32
Anticonvulsive medication, 164
Antisocial behavior, 74-82
  areas of potential confrontation, 74
  causes, 74
  characteristics of, 74
  cheating in school and games, 76-77
  firesetting, 77
  forging parent's name on checks, reports
      and letters, 77-78
  lying to authority and parents, 78-79
  stealing beyond expectations of subcul-
      tural group, 79-80
  truancy from school, 80-81
  vandalism, 81-82
Anxiety, 80, 102-103, 110, 115, 128, 158,
    163, 174
  about tests, schools, and failure, 116, 121-
      123
Aphasic-like symptoms, 32-33
Approval of desirable acts, 59
Arithmetic table games, 152
Arithmetic underachievement, 150-152
  material for remedial instruction, 150-
      151
Art therapy, 41
Articulation problems, 32, 201-202
Ask child for explanations of noises, sights,
    etc., 27
Assertive training, 124
Assignment of child to leadership posi-
    tions, 105
Attention, 60, 106, 182
Attention-seeking children, 105-106
Audio-calculator, 151
Audiologist, 32, 38
Auditory clues, 154
Auditory discrimination, 199-200
  consonants, 203-204
  vowels, 204
Auditory hallucinations, 164
Auditory media, 149-150
Auditory memory, 202-203
  games for, 202
Auditory modality, 176

Auditory modality problems   (*See also*
    specific topics)
  articulation, 201-202
  auditory discrimination, 199-200
    consonants, 203-204
    vowels, 204
  auditory memory, 202-203
  auditory perception, 198-199
  auditory reception, 200
  auditory vocal association, 204
  grammatic closure, 200-201
Auditory perception, 141, 149, 198-199
  preschool handicapped children, 25, 38-
      40
Auditory readiness, 175
Auditory reception, 200
Auditory sound blending, 200-201
Auditory stimulation, 26-27
Auditory-vocal associations, 141, 204
Authority problems, 88
  antagonisms, 58-60
  disobedience, 83-85
  lying, 78-79
Autism, 95-97
Autistic children, 50
Awareness, 156
  of need to be test-wise, 123

B

Backlash effect of retaliatory measures, 47
Badge earned for excellent behavior in
    cooperation, 56
"Bag of tokens" as reward, 145
Baker, Harry J., 218
Balance beam, 45
Balancing, 205-207
Ball kicking, 46
Ball rolling and throwing, 30
Barclay, James R., 8
Bardon, Jack I., xii, 4
Bartel, N.R., 192
Battle for independence, 144
Baumeister, Alfred A., 168
Bayley Scales of Infant Development, 168
Bed-rocking behavior, 70-71
Behavior modification, 28-29
  aggressive children, 52
  autistic child, 96
  emotionally disturbed children, 134

Obstacle course, 45
Occupational therapists, 44
  evaluation by, 40
Old Maid, 152
Ombudsman of child, 63
One-to-one therapeutic basis, 131
One Word Wrong Game, 210
Operant conditioning program for masochistic behavior, 71
Operational age
  chronological age versus, 27
  problems appropriate to, 27
Ophthalmological examination, 215
Ophthalmologist, evaluation by, 36
Opportunity to be "only child," 108
Oppositional behavior, 74-76, 82-91
  carelessness on tests and homework, 85-86
  causes, 74
  characteristics, 74
  disobedience to teachers, parents or au-
    thority, 83-85
  habitual, 83
  hostile behavior, 91
  negativism, 87
  passive-aggressiveness, 87-88
  provocation to teachers and peers, 88-89
  resistance, 87-88
  runaway behavior, 89-90
  teasing, 91
Opticon, 227-228
Optometric examination, 215
Oral examinations, 139
Organic damage, 48
Organization of games, 45
Original classroom work, 106-107
Otological examination, 215
Otologist, 38
Out-of-control behavior, 65
Overachievement associated with tension,
  156-157
Overambitious parents, 123
Over-ascetic child, 102-103
Overcompensation for perceived inade-
  quacies, 163
Overlearning to be stressed, 222
Overly conforming children, 106-107
Overprotective behaviors, 119

P

Padded wheelchairs, 69-70

"Paint-in," 81
Painting activities, 36
Pairing of anxiety-provoking mental im-
  ages, 103
Pairing of relaxation and recall of anxiety-
  provoking circumstances, 163
Palmer, J. O., 20
Panic, 119
Paper-and-pencil tracking exercises, 197
Parallel play, 31
Paranoid-like behavior, 103-104
Parent-child problem, 109-111
Parental pressures, 125
Parental rejection, 75-76, 88-89
Parents of handicapped children
  antagonisms to, 58-60
  antisocial behavior exhibited by, 75
  anxiety about school, 110
  anxious child, 122
  assistance to, xv
  awareness of child's aggressive behavior,
    58
  awareness of own aggressive behavior, 60
  behavior modification training to, 217
  compulsive behavior of child, 162
  conferences with, 93, 95, 105, 118, 143
  considerations in dealing with aggres-
    sive children, 56-58
  counseling with, 126
  disobedience to, 83-85
  excessive expectations of, 78
  excessive fighting of child disapproved
    by, 64
  fighting against expectations of, 144
  forging name on checks, reports and
    letters, 77-78
  girl's fighting, reasons for, 65
  increased pressure toward achievement,
    142-143
  indulgent behavior of, 48
  instruction of underachiever at home,
    146
  interview with, 18
  learning disabled children, 215-217
  low average intelligence of child, 224-
    225
  lying to, 78-79
  meeting with, 20, 104
  mild mental retardation of child
    help for, 183-187
    home activities for, 187-188